D1554973

Two Counties in Crisis

Measuring Political Change in Reconstruction Texas

Robert J. Dillard

Number 8 in the Texas Local Series

University of North Texas Press
Denton, Texas

Permissions:
University of North Texas Press
1155 Union Circle #311336
Denton, TX 76203-5017

The paper used in this book meets the minimum requirements of the
American National Standard for Permanence of Paper for Printed Library
Materials, z39.48.1984. Binding materials have been chosen for durability.

Library of Congress Cataloging-in-Publication Data

Dillard, Robert J., 1977- author.
  Two counties in crisis : measuring political change in Reconstruction Texas /
  Robert J. Dillard
      Pages cm
  Includes bibliographical references and index.
  ISBN-13 978-1-57441-907-8 (cloth)
  ISBN-13 978-1-57441-919-1 (ebook)
  1. LCSH: Reconstruction (U.S. history, 1865–1877)—Texas.
2. Reconstruction (U.S. history, 1865–1877)—Texas—Harrison County.
3. Reconstruction (U.S. history, 1865–1877)—Texas—Collin County.
4. Texas—Politics and government—1865–1950. 5. Harrison County
(Tex.)—Politics and government—19th century. 6. Collin County (Tex.)—
Politics and government—19th century.

  F391 .D56 2023
  976.4/061–dc23/eng/20230419
                        2023017177

Two Counties in Crisis is Number 8 in the Texas Local Series.

The electronic edition of this book was made possible by the support of
the Vick Family Foundation.

Typeset by vPrompt eServices.

For Robert Aditya Dillard,
a native Texan

Contents

Acknowledgments

This book would not have happened if not for the steady mentorship of Dr. Robert Wooster, a great historian who stuck with me
well into his own retirement because he believed that I had something important to say. It is not an exaggeration to say that he guided
me through every step, from the initial idea to the final revisions.
I can never repay him for the support he has given me. On the political science side, Dr. Isla Schuchs Carr and her intrepid assistant
Marion Carr went above and beyond. From structural suggestions to
orienting me toward the right political culture literature, I am forever
in their debt.

In addition to being the most cited scholar in this book by far,
Dr. Carl Moneyhon provided invaluable recommendations that
helped to dramatically strengthen my argument. Dr. Michael Johnston
provided recommendations that helped broaden the scope of the book,
making it truly interdisciplinary.

Thank you to Ron Chrisman and the editorial board at University of North Texas Press for taking a chance on something a little
bit different. Dr. Peter Moore and Dr. David Blanke at Texas A&M
University–Corpus Christi provided mentorship and strong votes of
confidence during the earlier phase of writing. Thank you to my (now
former) department chair, Dr. Dan Jorgensen. See Dan? I told you
I was working on something! Thank you to Mr. Joseph Woods for help
early on, and Mr. John C. Tatum for help toward the end.

And most importantly, thanks to God above for strength, my
always-supportive parental units, and my dear wife Sudeshna,
who kept things together during some difficult times.

Introduction

Perhaps the greatest myth of the American Civil War and Reconstruction in Texas is the notion of a state unified in its opposition to Northern aggression both before and after Appomattox. It isn't difficult to see why histories have often pigeonholed Texas alongside the rest of the South. Texas had seceded and joined the Confederacy, albeit after every other state in the Deep South. The protection of slavery was listed prominently in the Texas Ordinance of Secession in 1861, although the South's peculiar institution was concentrated primarily in traditionalistic East Texas. Texas participation in the war was significant, although the state did not suffer material losses on a level comparable to the more contested regions in Virginia, Tennessee, Mississippi, Louisiana, Georgia, and South Carolina. The Reconstruction era brought a renewed sense of resistance, and Texas was enveloped in a wave of violence against freed people and Republicans perpetrated by clandestine paramilitary groups and disorderly mobs. Life after Reconstruction in Texas saw segregation, a weak tax base, a deficient educational system, and an intractable constitution that Texas has managed to prosper in spite of. Yet compartmentalizing Texas alongside the remainder of the Confederacy risks ignoring the geographic, economic, and ultimately cultural complexities that make the state exceptional.

The story of Texas Reconstruction warrants retelling in its own right. Too many Texans are oblivious to their state constitution's many faults and the intriguing history that wrought such a document. Too many students of history and political science gloss over names like Davis, Pease, Hamilton, and Throckmorton, and the myth of Reconstruction as a Radical Republican conspiracy has left an unfortunate legacy that persists to the present day. But rather than simply recalling the events and the personalities, the current work is a synthesis of history and political science meant to illuminate the character of a place defined by its vastness and contrasts. For it is in the very essence of what it means to be Texan that we will find answers to why Reconstruction failed and progress in Texas was stifled for generations.

Political science research hinges upon modeling and typically utilizes case study analysis to satisfy predetermined theoretical conclusions that are otherwise impossible to quantify through measurable variables. The advantage to this approach is in the discipline's ability to draw comparative lessons, pushing the field ever closer to a unifying theory. Historians, on the other hand, focus the bulk of their work on primary sources, employing theory as a useful but not indispensable tool. Understanding the unusual course of events from 1865 to 1876, which saw the short-lived political rule of the Republicans followed by a statewide backlash resulting in the abysmal constitution of 1876 and a century's worth of Democratic dominance, can best be achieved through a blending of political science and history.

This work seeks to investigate social and political change by integrating elements of the political culture genre into a narrative of Reconstruction focused on a case study analysis of two dramatically different Texas counties, Collin and Harrison. The cultural evolution of these two counties illustrates how political cultures consolidate themselves, and how the process of achieving unity hinges not upon cultural commonalities between citizens but upon fear, distrust, and hatred of the oppositional culture that seeks to do them harm. This work also demonstrates the worst-case scenario of cultural opposition, wherein a consolidated culture can enact suboptimal policy that works to their own detriment in the name of continued resistance to said opposition.

Of the People, By the People, For the People

The current work is predicated on the idea that the constrictive and regressive Texas Constitution of 1876 was the culmination of a self-reinforcing cultural process, as it was overwhelmingly ratified by a popular vote, not implemented by elite consensus. If all constitutions are products of history and the political cultures in which they were written, then the Texas Constitution of 1876 was designed to restrain state government at every possible front in response to the policies of Reconstruction, which had attempted to do the opposite. This legacy of Texas's contentious Reconstruction era has, as a result, created a constitutional black hole of contradictions, amendment chaining, and ultimately inaccessibility for the citizens of the state.

The dominant paradigm of postrevisionist historians of Texas Reconstruction is that the legislative quagmire created by the constitution of 1876 was spawned through the machinations of either an elite planter class or the strongly unified protopopulist Patrons of Husbandry (the Grange) at the time of the 1875 Constitutional Convention.[1] In other words, the post-Reconstruction constitution is seen as an elite/agrarian conspiracy carried out to the detriment of the people of the state. However, through the integration of political culture literature, the current work argues that the renunciation of Reconstruction and the consequent ratification of a regressive constitution were the products of a widespread cultural backlash that extended well beyond the influence of any particular moneyed interest.

At the same time, while the popularity of the Grange was certainly an expression of popular will, its consolidated power did not represent the totality of the forces leading Texas toward its restrictive supreme law. The National Grange of the Order of the Patrons of Husbandry was (and still is) a Gilded Age advocacy group founded in 1867 on behalf of farmers' interests. The Gilded Age growth of fraternal organizations combined with the demographics of the state ensured that Texas wholeheartedly embraced the Grange, and membership in Texas chapters swelled in the latter years of Reconstruction. The National Grange's founders ensured its nonpartisan nature when writing the organization's bylaws to ensure maximum inclusiveness at a time when the nation was still healing from the trauma of war. But as historian Charles Postel notes, "The rules of Grange meetings prohibited discussion of partisan politics, yet the Grange was profoundly political."[2] And while the Grange's political influence in Texas was significant during Reconstruction, the current work will demonstrate that it was by no means the full embodiment of the political culture.

What follows is not a dismissal of the work of venerable historians like Carl Moneyhon, for the heavy hand of political and economic elites in guiding the state toward 1876 is irrefutable. However, by utilizing an interdisciplinary approach that blends political science theory and the traditional primary-source evidence so valued by historians, this book will offer a broader perspective on the persistent questions of Reconstruction's failure. Chapter 1 describes the political, economic, and social conditions in Texas at the end of the Civil War and introduces the significant political actors of Reconstruction. Chapter 2 demonstrates political change through the side-by-side case studies of traditionalistic Harrison County and individualistic Collin County. Chapter 3 discusses the tragedy of Reconstruction, and how national events shaped local events and political culture. Chapter 4 focuses on the final Reconstruction governor, Edmund Jackson Davis, a man who, despite the best intentions, became synonymous with carpetbaggery, corruption, and Radical excess to such a degree that his fall from political grace effectively ended Republicanism in Texas for a century. Chapter 5 is an analysis of the restrictive and reactionary constitution of 1876, which, through its exhaustive minutiae, continues to defy the basic best practices of good government prescribed by any constitutional law scholar. Chapter 6 analyzes political change through cultural theory and describes the legacy of the cultural backlash against Reconstruction in Texas. The failure of Reconstruction not only impacted the lives of Black Texans for generations but it also established a political culture defined by contrarianism that can still be felt today. While Texas has prospered and will likely continue to do so, its regressive supreme law reflects a moment in history when resistance to the demonized opposition was valued more than the common good of the people.

Chapter 1

1865

History, Political Science, and Culture

True scientific analysis of the amorphous concept of political culture remained elusive prior to Gabriel Almond and Sidney Verba's 1963 classic, *The Civic Culture*. Until their application of the necessary scientific rigor, the entire idea of political culture was premised on vague speculation. Historians and political theorists had always maintained a sense of what national or regional "character" meant, but it defied tangibility and remained absent as a usable variable in any sort of scientific modeling. Scholars and laypeople alike could appreciate Alexis de Tocqueville's ruminations on the American experience up to that point, but a society's character remained a persistently indefinable entity. Almond and Verba defined political culture as an aggregate of not only political attitudes toward the system of government (ideologies) but also attitudes about the position of the individual self in the system.[1] Like Tocqueville's conception of character, Almond and Verba's political culture was something thoroughly internalized in thought and feeling. And as much as Almond and Verba's breakthrough work legitimized the study of culture as empirical and quantifiable, it quickly came under fire from the more dismal sciences and was quickly supplanted by rational choice modeling in subsequent years.[2] Fortunately, significant works in the following decades would keep the genre alive until it experienced a true resurgence in the late 1980s and early 1990s.

Daniel Elazar's theory of political subcultures as laid out in *American Federalism: A View from the States* in 1966 has staying power that is exceptional in political science. Still a standard component of political theory taught at all levels of state and local politics today, it defines political culture as a "particular pattern of orientation to political action in which each political system is imbedded. Political culture, like all culture, is rooted in the cumulative historical experiences of particular groups of people."[3] The origin of political subcultures, for Elazar, lay in migration streams and the distribution of old-world ethnic, political, and religious values spreading across the United States based on an ever-changing geographic frontier. This definition is valuable because the present work is predicated on (1) The assumption that political culture matters and (2) the assumption that political systems are shaped by political cultures. For Elazar three key aspects of political culture exemplify this connection between culture and the structure of political systems: First, cultures embody a common perception of what a government is and is not responsible for. Second, there is a commonly accepted idea of what kind of people should be active in politics. And third, cultures establish the general manner in which government is practiced by all levels (citizens, politicians, and bureaucrats), given these perceptions.[4]

As a genre of political science, political culture did not truly come into its own until its revival in the late 1980s, hitting its apex in the 1990s with the "renaissance" of political culture, as Ronald Inglehart dubbed it.[5] Besides benefiting from the enormous advances in social science methodology that occurred in the decades after Almond and Verba and that had helped establish political science as a veritable scientific discipline, the resurgence of culture as an authentic field of study was at least partly attributable to the integration of elements from disciplines like social psychology and anthropology. Aaron Wildavsky, one of the leading political scientists in the rise of the genre in the late 1980s, posited that human interests both come from the maximization of self-interest and are products of our social relations.[6] This basic idea highlights something fundamental about human nature and decision making and extends the concept beyond pure economics. Decisions come from culture, and humans are hard-wired to be social animals. Taken a step further, cultures also shape governmental structures, while at the same time structures influence cultures—a point made by Gabriel Almond when the field was still in its infancy.[7] These points support the significance of culture as a shaping force in politics, but they pale in comparison to the importance of opposition as the defining feature of a political culture. Wildavsky clarified that no political culture is ever sustainable on its own; by necessity cultures need an opposing force. As Wildavsky explained, "It is only the presence in the world of people who are not like them that enables them to be the way they are."[8] This idea carries a great deal of explanatory power not only for understanding Reconstruction but also for understanding rivalry between political cultures in general.

Some of the more critical historians have argued that the field has not applied a similar level of scientific rigor to their conception of political culture, preferring a looser use of the term or disregarding it entirely.[9] Whether or not this is true, no theoretical perspective could be more apt for describing the state of Texas in the years following the American Civil War, a period characterized by successive state constitutions, violence, and political enmity on a catastrophic scale. If the political culture of Texas was a self-reinforcing entity driven not only by economic rationality and the socially binding effect of living through a losing war, but also by an in-group bias solidified against an opposing force, then the culture of Texas could find no greater bogeymen than the Radical Republicans. Edmund Jackson Davis, the last Reconstruction governor of Texas, was by no means the only symbol of Republican Radicalism. But as the current work uses primary evidence to argue, his reign represented the culmination of perceived Yankee aggression, leading to the consolidation of an oppositional culture that in many ways persists to the present day. It is also an oft-repeated process nationwide, and one that's plainly visible in American politics today. Barack Obama wasn't simply a man of progressive vision; he was also the antithesis of George W. Bush. Donald Trump was much more than a tell-it-like-it-is nonpolitician; he was also the anti-Obama. Joe Biden's election did not represent a new dawn in America. In fact for many, his assumption of the presidency was only significant because he replaced the highly controversial Trump. The Texas backlash against the efforts of Reconstruction was the product of Texas political culture, with Republicans like Davis as the focal point of conflict, thus giving Texas political culture its necessary legitimation.

Measuring Political Change

Potential measures of regional culture and change in the genre are virtually endless. Utilizing Elazar's conception of political subcultures based on migration patterns as a base, the neo-Tocquevillian political science scholars of the 1990s built the genre on a wide range of descriptive statistics. Ronald Inglehart's major contribution to the field is based on secular-rational values versus traditional values and well-being versus survival values.[10] Robert Putnam's work on both Italy and the United States, which would earn him widespread acclaim, is based on a study of associational life and its impact on civic culture.[11] Classifying Texas culture between 1850 and 1880 is notably problematic, beyond the obvious factor of the Civil War, due to the continuous stream of migrants into the state from the North, the South, and internationally. Additionally, geographic variations in climate, agriculture, and wealth created distinct regional subcultures within the state before, during, and after the war. Having achieved independence and statehood only one generation before secession, defining what made one a Texan at the time of the war and Reconstruction was as difficult then as it is now.

As enculturation and cultural consolidation are very often built on the effects of history and the simple contrarian nature of in-groups versus out-groups, the best means for analyzing the statewide backlash against political leadership being branded as Radical Republicans is to examine two sample counties—one individualistic and one traditionalistic, according to Elazar's typology. Elazar's classification scheme, as noted above, is based on migration streams and well suited for nineteenth-century Texas. Prior to the growth of major urban centers in Texas, which fostered political cultures more akin to the moralistic subcultures of New England, Texas was culturally split in two. East Texas was firmly built in the image of the Deep South and consolidated around a traditionalistic culture. North and West Texas were still defined by the frontier, and therefore classified as an individualistic culture. The comparison of counties from each of these political subcultures will illuminate the growing statewide consensus against Republicanism, the ultimate failure of Reconstruction, and the adoption of the constitution of 1876.

In his notable book *American Nations*, journalist Colin Woodard traces the early origins of the two cultures that would later define Texas in the nineteenth century, and his work emphasizes their political significance and their perpetual stability. Built upon an economic base of forced labor and owing to dramatic demographic disparities, Woodard attributes much of the Deep South's particularly harsh racial and social order to its origins in the late seventeenth-century British colony of Barbados.[12] The culture—essentially an importation of the Barbadian way of life established by their fathers and grandfathers into Charleston and then advanced westward throughout the Deep South during the colonial period—was defined by highly restrictive democracy, massive wealth and wealth disparity, and Black slavery. Woodard notes how extensive property requirements that were placed on the right to vote, deep ties between the wealthy and the Anglican Church back in London, and the continued importation of enslaved people helped to ensure the establishment of an elite political and economic class that was then propagated west, forming the region that would become the hotbed of secession more than a century later.[13]

By contrast, the culture that would eventually settle North and West Texas (including Collin County) originated, in Woodard's estimation, in a more bottom-up fashion. While the creation of the Deep South may have been driven by a wealthy elite importing plantation-style agriculture, what Woodard calls Greater Appalachia was formed by poor immigrants from northern England, lowland Scotland, and the northern part of Ireland on the run from war, natural disaster, and economic oppression at the hands of English landlords.[14] Happier living beyond the colonial control back east, the region of Greater Appalachia, starting in the mid-eighteenth century, began stretching from West Virginia to Kentucky, Tennessee, Arkansas, and finally into northern Texas.

The best historical analysis of traditionalistic East Texas in the second half of the nineteenth century, rapidly consolidating itself socially and economically as a Deep South plantation culture, is Randolph B. Campbell's *A Southern Community in Crisis: Harrison County, Texas 1850–1880*. Campbell's book is an astoundingly complete profile of traditionalistic Harrison County that serves as an ideal representation of East Texas. Through census, tax, military, and Freedmen's Bureau records, election results, personal correspondences, and media accounts, Campbell creates a portrait of a region in social flux that is unsurpassed in the genre. However, the complete story of Texas Reconstruction is one of cultural transformation along multiple fronts, for if the current work is meant to illustrate the course of Reconstruction through the lens of political culture, then it is essential that Harrison County be compared to a frontier Texas analog.

There are two methodological challenges worth mentioning here. Campbell himself notes a number of obvious statistical aberrations caused by underreporting in census and tax records at the time, particularly in the woefully inadequate 1870 US census.[15] If this problem was common in the more economically developed region of East Texas, then it should be presumed that such statistical anomalies would be amplified when analyzing any Texas county on the less developed frontier. Like Campbell's book, the current work fills in problematic statistical gaps by using prominent media publications, which serve as a proxy for public opinion. In the absence of public opinion data from 1850 to 1880, no more ideal example of Texas frontier culture exists than that of Collin County. Reconstruction governor James Throckmorton called Collin County home. And although the people of the time lived on the fringe, there is sufficient data to make a proper comparison with Harrison County.

While local media outlets serve as ideal sources for cross-county comparison, they simultaneously serve as the only viable sources for ascertaining generalities about political cultures in the absence of public opinion polls. While today most Americans in the era of "fake news" would agree that media bias is problematic and demands much of the consumer, brazen misstatement of facts and blending of commentary with hard journalism was the order of the day during Reconstruction. Modern observers agree that the internet provides readily accessible echo chambers that naturally amplify destructive confirmation biases, but the internet is merely a means for a human tendency that was readily on display in the nineteenth century. Yet the loose treatment of facts by local media outlets during Reconstruction is not a hindrance to the current work. In fact, the flagrant distortion of the truth seen in the newspapers of Harrison and Collin Counties serves to better illustrate the essences of two starkly different political cultures in a way that opinion polls probably could not. Respondents are seldom completely honest in public opinion polls. Response bias is attributable to a wide range of factors, but ultimately respondents will shape their answers around a common perception of what is socially acceptable. By contrast, how people choose their news media sources is completely private and free from social pressures. Newspaper circulation in the nineteenth century was the equivalent of clicks today, with the people placing their faith in individual editors as the filter through which they would process the events of the world. Therefore, if measuring political change in Reconstruction Texas is a matter of comparing Harrison and Collin Counties, then gauging public opinion in those two regions is a matter of comparing two newspaper editors, Robert Loughery of Harrison County and James Waller Thomas of Collin County. Indeed, historians have long used newspapers as a rough gauge of past public attitudes.

The Vox Populi

That slavery was the primary cause of Texas secession is indisputable. The Declaration of Causes written at the tail end of the Secession Convention in February of 1861 clearly declares both slavery and white supremacy part of the natural order. While the bulk of the declaration is devoted to this principle, the document also notes the federal government's failure to ensure frontier security and its infringement upon the principle of states' rights in violation of the Tenth Amendment to the US Constitution.[16] The implicit message from the convention delegates is an insistence upon local control, a guiding value that had carried Texas through its own revolution a quarter century prior. In fact, opposition to the centralization of power had been a guiding force in 1836 and would remain a powerful motivator after 1865.

To assess the aftermath of the Civil War in Texas, one could focus on lingering legal disputes over constitutional supremacy or social disputes over racial hierarchy—the same issues that defined the Reconstruction era throughout the greater South—and how white Southern resistance managed to ultimately thwart many of the Union's designs for a reconstructed America. But this would disregard many of the characteristics of political culture that make Texas unique among the seceding states. Carl Moneyhon, the preeminent scholar of Reconstruction in Texas, contends that the events that ultimately erased the progressive changes spearheaded by Radical Republicans during Reconstruction were manipulated primarily by the landed class in Texas, who rallied poor whites to the conservative cause by playing upon an impending sense of racial doom.[17] The threat of the loss of social position undoubtedly motivated poor whites, but to cast the landless white masses of Texas as sheep so easily led (or misled) might disregard the self-perpetuating nature of a regional political culture that had been reinforcing itself since before Texas independence. That the landed class had a significant influence on the conservative backlash against Reconstruction is undeniable. Facing the certain loss of the labor at the base of their enterprise, the landed elites were understandably motivated to continue resistance to perceived Northern tyranny, regardless of the outcome on the battle-fields. But to attribute the political forces driving Texas into seces-sion, war, and ultimately aversion to the efforts of Reconstruction as being identical to those in the rest of the Deep South would be a mischaracterization of a unique political culture that had been solidi-fying since the earliest American colonists came in the 1820s.

With independence from the Spanish Empire in 1821, the govern-ment of Mexico had been faced with the logistical challenge of project-ing power against a tide of Anglo-American settlers/squatters who were increasingly encroaching upon Mexican territory with impunity, thus necessitating the empresario system. Established under Mexico's Colonization Law of 1824, the empresarios sought to legally populate Mexican territory under the promise that the new settlers would abide by the law as loyal Mexican citizens, and in return the empresarios would be generously rewarded with sizable land grants of their own. Before the 1830s few empresarios succeeded at drawing in the number of new Mexican citizens the government sought for establishing legit-imacy over the territory known as Texas, with the most successful being Stephen F. Austin. When an 1829 presidential decree abolished slavery in Mexico, questions over Texas, with its Anglo enslavers, created friction between state governments and Mexico City, with state and local officials arguing that the legitimacy of Mexican rule in Texas was only as strong as the Texas economy, thereby necessitating the preservation of slavery.[18] This controversy, along with numerous other affronts to Anglo sensibilities, led to the Texas Revolution beginning in 1835. But prior to the outbreak of fighting, the Mexican govern-ment provided a dozen land grants to American settlers in the land that would become Harrison County after the war.[19] The new settlers in this far northeast section of Mexico found land, terrain, and soil that was immediately cultivatable and lent itself to the production of a cash crop. According to historian Randolph Campbell, "Thus, they were in an advantageous position to continue without serious modification the agricultural way of life they had known in the older South."[20] In this way Harrison County became an enslavers' community.

At the same time, the north central Texas land that included the future Collin County was part of Empresario John Cameron's territory, but no effort was made to settle it during the empresario period from 1821 to 1836. It was not until five years later, when the government of the Republic of Texas began providing generous land grants for the encouragement of immigration, that Collin County was populated. The establishment of Preston Road in 1841—connecting Dallas, Rockwall, and Collin Counties to the Texas Road that reached St. Louis—encouraged immigration from the north and northeast.[21] This would open the area for non–Native American colonization, and although the land was fertile, it was remote frontier and not readily profitable. As a result Collin County became a frontier community of individual family farms.

These two cultures, one plantation and the other frontier, developed relatively isolated from one another from the time of the revolution to the Civil War. The cultural variations that defined antebellum Texas do not permit easy categorization in a manner remotely comparable to the remainder of the Deep South. In fact, geographer Wilbur Zelinsky's cultural map of the United States, while splitting Texas between two major regions (the South and the West) labels the bulk of East and North Texas as uncertain in its status or affiliation.[22] Cultural geographer Terry Jordan, in the introduction to his 1966 book *German Seed in Texas Soil*, noted the statewide presence of not only Germans but also Czechs, Scandinavians, and Poles, each bringing "strands of Old World agricultural heritages to be woven into the rural fabric of Texas."[23]

While cotton may have become king in the Lone Star State, it was not the entirety of the Texas economy, nor did the interests of the planters in East Texas, with their proximity to the rest of the Deep South, coincide with those of settlers in dry frontier Texas. This point is particularly obvious in the current study, where Collin County's antebellum economy produced little cotton and had a significantly smaller enslaved population than that of East Texas's Harrison County. Similarly, Texas's position on the nation's borderlands brought a more heightened level of security concerns to the frontier while East Texas remained isolated. Texas was also characterized by a diverse demographic makeup that was distinctive among Southern states and shaped a more factionalized political culture. If migration streams are the predictors of Daniel Elazar's state political cultures, then Texas was the mutt of the South. An immigrant state comprised of Anglos, Mexicans, Germans, Bohemians, and others, the white population of Texas was politically and socially balkanized in a manner that set it apart from the other states that would make up the Confederacy.[24] How then can secession, the struggle of the war, and resistance to Reconstruction be explained by anything other than mass manipulation at the hands of political elites? The answer lies in the self-perpetuating nature of political cultures themselves.

Wilbur Zelinsky's theory of first effective settlement, as laid out in his original 1973 book on the heels of Elazar's work on political subcultures, tackles one of the most perplexing questions for historians, political scientists, and cultural geographers: How do we identify the culture of a nation defined by demographic and historical diversity? Searching for an intrinsic quality shared by early American colonists, Zelinsky found the diversity of cultural origins, socioeconomic statuses, education, and religion in the New World so varied as to render easy characterization impossible. Yet to conclude that American culture is a random pattern would be to deny the obvious common traits shared with British culture. From this Zelinsky established the doctrine of first effective settlement, which posited that when a migrating group occupied an unpopulated territory or removed an earlier population and established a sustainable society, the social and cultural imprint they left would be perpetually significant.[25] This is why the United States' greatest old-world influence is British, despite the presence of Indigenous, African, and other European influences in the earlier years, and the cultural imprint is remarkably stable over time despite continuous migration and mixing between different groups. Similarly, the initial Anglo colonists that found East and Central Texas inviting would subsequently define Texas culture as a whole despite the state's diversity, for the initial imprint they left would outweigh the influence of settlers from the upper South and other old-world origins. The strength and stability of this cultural influence would give slave-holding East and Central Texas a monopoly on state-level power that would drive Texas into secession.

Assuming the same coherent statewide zeitgeist that pushed secession is the same culture that repudiated Reconstruction, then the continued aversion to all things Union post-1865 was attributable as much to the populace as it was to the disproportionate influence of the landed elite or the pluralist power of the Grange. The Secession Convention of early 1861 that was so strongly opposed by the state's chief executive, Sam Houston, was suitably diverse in its makeup and represented a variety of interests beyond enslaving.[26] That Governor Houston opposed the secession convention is itself a notable exception among Southern states and indicates a lack of unity that must necessarily be tied to a broad diversity of interests. In his analysis of the delegates and the counties they represented in secession conventions across the South, Ralph Wooster (1962) took particular note of the Texas convention, which was made up of a "typical cross-section" of Texas society at the time, not an elite body of the state's largest enslavers. That Texas society wholeheartedly endorsed secession across demographic and socioeconomic lines is further affirmed by the overwhelming popular support for secession that followed in the popular election on February 23, 1861, with 46,153 voting for secession compared to a mere 14,747 voting against. Wooster notes that "the theory of a great planter 'conspiracy' for secession would certainly not seem valid in regard to the Texas Convention; of the 326 great planters with 50 slaves or more in the state, only twelve were in the Convention."[27] The current work, of course, is not about delineating the forces that spurred secession, but rather is about the culture of resistance that persevered throughout the war and Reconstruction and ultimately manifested itself in the constitution of 1876.

The political science literature notes that the United States is comprised of numerous regionally consolidated political subcultures, each characterized by their own cultural inertia. Daniel Elazar's conception of three major political subcultures contains a great deal of explanatory power for Texas, especially in Civil War / Reconstruction history. As both a Southern state *and* a borderlands state populated in the 1860s by new arrivals from a variety of other states and countries, Texas seems perfectly fit as a case study of the validity of Elazar's idea. The individualistic political culture that values government only insofar as it is an institution for the protection of individual economic interests dominates the western half of the state today, just as it did the frontier settlements of the 1860s.[28] Elazar assigns a businesslike conception to the practice of politics, wherein public officials are expected to deliver the best utilitarian results and there exists a strong impression of politics as a dirty game most laypeople choose to avoid.

The traditionalistic culture that assigns government a role in the protection of organically grown social hierarchies and maintains a special elite status for the political class suits East Texas today, just as it did in the 1860s as the region was progressively adopting patterns of social and economic life more akin to the geographically proximate Deep South.[29] Similar to the individualistic culture, there is an expectation of minimal citizen involvement, as politics is reserved for an elite class who often inherit their right to participate in the process of governance.[30] In fact, Elazar argues that traditionalistic subcultures are so inherently dedicated to the preservation of an elite class that they take on an anti-bureaucratic nature, because bureaucracy runs counter to the tradition that dictates government through interpersonal relationships among the political class.[31]

Elazar's third subculture type, moralistic, did not truly become viable in Texas until later in the twentieth century with the rise of major urban centers like Dallas, Houston, Austin, and San Antonio. But despite the dual nature of Texas political culture, the end result in the nineteenth century was an overwhelming and enthusiastic vote for secession, a popular devotion to the Confederate cause in wartime, and a unified repudiation of Reconstruction, all without the machinations of an elite planter class, if Wooster's conclusion is to be believed. Elazar's theory, therefore, can serve as a suitable background for understanding Texas culture, but a more in-depth look at political culture and social psychology is necessary for understanding 1860s Texas.

Despite the continued relevance of Elazar's theory in understanding the distribution of American political subcultures, it suffers from a basic flaw in the context of the current study: we don't have public opinion data from the 1860s and 1870s to confirm its veracity.[32] However, certain accepted patterns in human behavior help to establish the certainty of a self-perpetuating political culture in Texas that led to secession, war, ill-fated Reconstruction, and the constitution of 1876. Cultural theory tells us that similar personalities tend to migrate to the same location, even if it happens unconsciously. Biologically similar groups usually cluster together and typically stay in geographic proximity over generations.[33] And even outsiders who don't initially share in the collective behavior of a culture will typically adopt its general patterns of conduct and thought over time, a process called enculturation.[34] Zelinsky notes that individual migrants may carry with them a portion of their culture of origin, but the likelihood that they will change their new host culture is minuscule.[35] The result is the propagation of a collective personality over time, and political scientists have found that this corresponds with a region's core political characteristics, or political culture.[36]

One example that demonstrates these contentions in Texas Civil War history might be the German experience. Traditionally more supportive of the Union than Anglo Texans, it was long accepted that German Texans differed from the majority along two dimensions: their relative unanimity and their opposition to slavery.[37]

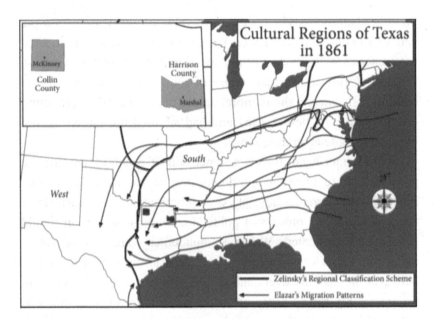

Located on the border of what Wilbur Zelinsky classified as the American West, the bulk of Collin County's non–Native American immigrants post-1841 came from Tennessee. Firmly ensconced in the Deep South, the bulk of Harrison County's immigrant population hailed from Alabama, Georgia, Mississippi, and Louisiana. According to Daniel Elazar's classification scheme for political subcultures based on migration patterns, Collin County represents an individualistic culture, while Harrison County is a traditionalistic culture. *Map by Charles David Grear.*

This popularly held belief stems from an 1854 convention of German intellectuals in San Antonio, wherein a resolution condemning the institution was passed.[38] However, Wooster's analysis notes that only five of the twenty counties in the state with populations that had German majorities voted *against* secession in the state-wide referendum.[39] Through the lens of cultural theory, there are a number of ways to interpret this. On the one hand, University of Texas geographer Terry Jordan notes that the idea of the German abolitionist in Texas was likely more myth than reality. Jordan contends that German settlers in East Texas wasted little time acquiring enslaved people as the region adapted more to the Deep

South's plantation-style agriculture.[40] This might demonstrate the validity of cultural theory's most basic assumption: that all individual preferences are the product of our social relations.[41] Perhaps German Texans, despite the insular nature of their community and initial cultural resistance to the immoral nature of slavery, were becoming enculturated long before 1861 and had adopted the slavery model because it made economic sense.

On the other hand, there's a dimension of enculturation that the political culture literature overlooks despite its particular significance for the current study: physical intimidation. As a variable in the self-reinforcing process of political cultures, intimidation should not be underestimated. Walter Kamphoefner's analysis of voting records indicates less than enthusiastic German support for secession. However, he also discovers substantial evidence that many German Texans simply stayed home when the referendum of secession was held.[42] This suggests that while German Texans may not have developed an affinity for slavery and secession, they were also hesitant to express dissenting views in the face of the Anglo majority, possibly out of fear.[43]

Although there were some instances of anti-Confederate resistance among German counties later in the war, their vote to secede (or choice to abstain) is evidence that public opinion influences public opinion, and political subcultures reinforce political subcultures.[44] This process may on occasion come about by force, but this does not necessarily diminish the impact of cultural theory for the current study, for it remains a clear example of a social force impacting individual preferences. German Texans brought no allegiances to particular political parties with them to Texas. And whether they were adapting to the culture they found themselves in for economic reasons or were silenced through fear of reprisal, they did not become a unanimous force for abolition, even if their European origin or the Texas rumor mill said they should. And while they may stand out as a cohesive group that is easily dissectible, it is reasonable to assume their story can help to inform us of the larger Texas story.

That there was factionalism in Texas over the secession question is beyond doubt. Walter Buenger suggests that one faction wanted secession before 1860, another wanted it when Abraham Lincoln was elected, others were opposed to it but hopped on the bandwagon after the fact, and another group never accepted leaving the Union at all.[45] How more recent European immigrant groups, such as the Germans, reacted to developing national events illustrates the natural progression of enculturation. Despite the absence of public opinion polls at the time, we can be fairly certain the number of Texans opposed to secession was, at a minimum, a viable and vocal faction in Texas politics. For it was this faction that elected Sam Houston as governor only a year before Lincoln's election. This group, despite their more deliberate approach to the secession question and its long-term impact on the state, would unfortunately be silenced by the more emotionally charged pro-secession factions.

When discussing the thought processes of extremely large groups of people, it is important to remember that in-group / out-group biases, the existence of which have been repeatedly reaffirmed by social psychologists, can be a powerful motivator. In fact, it can be a more powerful motivator than economic interest, a traditional go-to explanation in many academic fields. The seemingly irrational move of seceding from the Union despite the almost certainty of a war can only be understood as a form of group polarization run amok. After being removed from office in the wake of secession in March 1861, Sam Houston made a stop in Brenham on his way home. There he addressed an unruly crowd, amped up by the adrenaline of secession, and little concerned with his status as the hero of the Texas Revolution. The crowd's jeers did not stop Houston: "The Vox Populi is not always the voice of God, for when demagogues and selfish political leaders succeed in arousing public prejudice and stilling the voice of reason, then on every hand can be heard the popular cry of 'Crucify him, crucify him.' The Vox Populi then becomes the voice of the devil, and the hiss of mobs warns all patriots that peace and good government are in peril."[46] The same frenzied group irrationality present at Houston's speech would carry Texas through a costly war and was perhaps even amplified when that war was lost. The only difference between 1861 and 1865 is that the riotous energy of the mob once channeled onto the battlefield would now be focused mostly on the political arena during Reconstruction.

Secession had given the minority of loyal Texas Unionists a handful of unsavory options. Some chose to acquiesce to the new Confederate order, the path chosen by James Throckmorton, who would go on to serve in the Confederate Army and then reenter political life after the war. Some, particularly older political figures like Houston, chose retirement from public life to avoid being shamed as the rabid spirit of the Confederacy made life for Texas Unionists difficult. Andrew Jackson Hamilton, who would figure prominently in the postwar drama of Texas, chose to live in exile, fleeing to Mexico and then the Northern states, advocating emancipation and an invasion of Texas by Union forces. Elisha Pease, on the other hand, belonged to a steadfast and vocal group that braved the threats of Confederate harassment and remained in the state.[47] Edmund Jackson (E. J.) Davis fell into perhaps the smallest faction of all. Fleeing like Hamilton, Davis was part of the slim minority that went so far as to take up arms for the Union. His experiences during the war shaped a political attitude that was not overtly combative or vengeful, but focused and uncompromising to such a degree that his list of enemies would become long and distinguished throughout the course of Reconstruction.

Rebels, Unionists, and the War That Never Really Ended

If not for the turbulence of history or the overpowering noise of the vox populi, E. J. Davis, the last Reconstruction governor, might have gone down in the early written histories of Texas politics as a good man. Oran Roberts, the Texas rebel/governor/historian was, in more ways than one, the Bizarro Davis.[48] His 1898 *A Comprehensive History of Texas*, which set an ideological tone for Texas histories to come, is anything but kind to Davis. Suffice to say, words like *tyranny* get used often and with great intensity. A decade later the influential Dunning School historian Charles Ramsdell would throw gas on the fire of Davis's reputation, thus ruining him in the eyes of Texas for another seventy years or so. But Davis's experience was so typical of successful men in the early days of Texas statehood that it is hard to distinguish his background from that of the more rebellious sort that the early historians celebrated.

Originally hailing from St. Augustine, Florida, E. J. Davis (1827–1883) had moved with his family to the Galveston area at the time of the Mexican War. He subsequently left home to practice law in Corpus Christi and never found himself having to look very hard for work.[49] His time in Corpus Christi was short, however, as he soon left for Laredo and the promise of the full-time salary of a customs inspector. The stability of his federal position allowed him to continue working for clients, and his reputation in the legal community grew. In 1854, having impressed then-governor Elisha Pease, Davis received an appointment as temporary judge for the Twelfth District, a position that he would subsequently earn through election in 1855.[50] He was very young at the time and was making a significant name for himself in Democratic politics, as indicated by the governor's favor. But despite his status as a rising star, Davis's own ideological evolution was leading him astray from the Democratic Party by the latter half of the 1850s.

As the passions of secession were gathering steam in reaction to the perceived tyranny of the North and widespread fear that enslaved people would revolt, Davis was growing more and more disillusioned. He believed that the undue political influence of the planter class and the fervent rush to sever ties with the Union in the name of preserving slavery would inherently endanger other vital state interests—namely, frontier protection. This same concern fueled Sam Houston's gubernatorial campaign in 1859 and likely led to Davis to support him.[51] Still, Davis was by no means intent on becoming an avowed Unionist. In fact, it is ironic that the Texas media and the early

Civil War and Reconstruction histories would later characterize Davis as a carpetbagger, scalawag, Radical, and Black Republican all rolled into one devious ball. Davis was unquestionably a Southerner. A native of the Deep South, his family had enslaved people. He continued to endorse the basic Southern grievance as late as 1857 that an attack on the institution of slavery was a violation of the conditions of Texas statehood, but Davis could also see the invisible hand of the vox populi pushing the state closer and closer to the point of no return.[52] And it was the pressures of extreme group polarization that led Davis to the Union, for he rightfully feared the whirlwind that would be reaped in the event of war caused by secession. Knowing the risks to person and family associated with dissent in the Confederacy, Davis demonstrated considerable courage when he left the state in May 1862 and joined the Union ranks.

While Davis had succeeded in public life as an attorney, customs official, and judge, he had always been drawn to military life. He had attempted, and failed, to secure an appointment to West Point as a young man, but the fighting spirit never abandoned him. It is notable that of the two thousand or so Texans who served with the Union Army, only two achieved the rank of brigadier general. One was Andrew Jackson Hamilton, whose service was primarily in the realm of civil affairs. The other was Davis, who raised his own regiment, the 1st Texas Cavalry (USA), and saw action in Louisiana and along the border with Mexico.[53] Although Davis's role in the war effort might have been marginal in its strategic impact for the Union, his actions had a twofold impact on later events. On the one hand, they likely played a role in building his own personal sense of justice when he took on a prominent role in Reconstruction politics. On the other hand, his actions in the war unwittingly planted the seeds for a reputation as tyrannical, vindictive, and antiwhite. These attributes of his reputation, however exaggerated, would stick with him throughout his postwar political career.

For example, in an event that was either the beginning of negative public sentiment toward Davis or merely an ominous foreshadowing of things to come, rumors spread like wildfire throughout the city of Brownsville in October and November of 1863 that Davis was leading a force of "ten thousand drunken negro troops" to exact an especially cruel brand of vengeance upon the inhabitants.[54] In reality, Davis's wartime experience was characterized more by an endlessly frustrating search for more troops and more resources than by gallant battlefield victories or war crimes against civilians. His cavalry regiment never came close to achieving the level of battlefield viability he sought, and none of the troops were Black. He also rarely had usable horses, weapons, or ammunition.[55] Davis's later tenure as governor would also be plagued by limited resources and unfounded rumors that, for many of his critics, were affirmed by his Radical actions.

While Davis may have been on hand for the Union occupation of Brownsville, the far greater share of responsibility in its wake was awarded to Andrew Jackson Hamilton (1815–1875). To the people that knew him, he was Jack Hamilton, but in some corners he was "Colossal Jack" Hamilton.[56] By virtue of his time spent in the Texas House of Representatives and brief stint as attorney general, Hamilton was easily the more notable Texas Unionist throughout the war. He managed to draw the bulk of the partisan media's ire, owing to his longstanding reputation as a Democrat who vocally opposed not only slavery but also most of the major tenets of his own party. This, along with his mouth, earned him the "Colossal" moniker.[57] After burning innumerable political and personal bridges, Hamilton had fled to Matamoras, Mexico, in spring 1862 and subsequently gone north to wage a campaign of words against both the rebellious forces misguiding his own state and the divisive nature of the institution of slavery.[58] His departure from Matamoras was noted by the *Houston Tri-Weekly Telegraph*, which urged calm among its readers, as Hamilton was a "useless expenditure of ammunition" that was better left alone, wherein he could "blow his brains out with a brandy bottle" anyway.[59]

When Federal troops, including Davis and his 1st Texas Cavalry, seized the city of Brownsville in late 1863, it was Hamilton who set about reestablishing Federal control in his capacity as military governor. This was a position granted to him by President Lincoln, upon whom he had made a favorable impression with his bellicose talk of invading Texas, despite not being much of a military man himself.[60] Despite a political relationship characterized by contentiousness during Reconstruction, Hamilton and Davis found themselves very much allied as the most prominent faces of Texas Unionism during this phase of the war. With Davis pushing the fight against the rebels on the battlefield and Hamilton working in the sphere of civil affairs, both men were setting themselves up for prominence in the postwar political arena.

If the chain of events that constituted the meandering course of Reconstruction in Texas could have been predicted, Elisha Marshall Pease (1812–1883) might have left the state in 1861 and never come back. Pease had been in Texas longer than Davis or Hamilton, arriving just in time for the Texas Revolution and later serving as the fifth governor of the state. Respected before the war, he had joined Sam Houston in his vociferous but ill-fated opposition to secession. When his efforts failed, Pease chose to ride out the war in seclusion, without issuing political opinions, in hopes of avoiding Confederate harassment.[61] Living in solitude and isolation, it turned out, may have foreshadowed his experiences in Reconstruction, where he won few friends despite his best efforts to serve the interests of the state[62]—this despite the fact that he was personally popular, a quality that even Charles Ramsdell acknowledged in his early history of Texas Reconstruction.[63] Unfortunately, the unenviable position of appointed provisional governor, granted to Pease in 1867 by General Philip J. Sheridan in his capacity as military head of the Reconstruction government, could perhaps only be outdone by agent for the Freedmen's Bureau in its overall distastefulness in the eyes of white Texans, and Pease ultimately fell victim to the overwhelming tide of anti-Radical sentiment. That he was chosen to replace an elected governor as the state worked toward the reestablishment of civil authority only clarified in the minds of most Texans that federal authorities were veering toward authoritarianism.

Pease had replaced James Webb Throckmorton (1825–1894), the reluctant Confederate. A state legislator from North Texas prior to the war, he was one of eight dissenters at the Secession Convention of 1861. Unlike Sam Houston, a Unionist who never developed a particularly strong affinity for the Confederacy, Throckmorton would come to embrace a number of the Confederacy's central tenets. His biographer, Kenneth Wayne Howell, correctly identifies prewar Throckmorton as an "enigma" in Texas politics, as he upheld the social value of white supremacy while remaining wary of the disproportionate influence of an elite planter class.[64] His distrust of the cultural passions of secession and the behind-the-scenes engineering of the political elite were well-known prior to the secession convention, and his vote against splitting from the Union did not come as a surprise. However, unlike Davis and Hamilton, he did not leave and he did not remain a Unionist. And unlike Pease, he did not remain quiet.

Throckmorton's war experience would bring him more in line with the Confederacy, and while this was seemingly a suitable fit based on his ideological leanings, his affinity for the Southern cause really came about for practical reasons as he remained stubbornly devoted to the needs of his constituents in Collin County. As a traditional Whig, Throckmorton's Unionism was motivated primarily by what he wanted for the people of Collin County: railroad development, protection for small farmers, and security on the frontier.[65] He begrudgingly came over to the Confederate side to maintain a hand in state policy making but by the war's end would see military service for the state and Confederacy. His subsequent election as Reconstruction governor, his white supremacy, and his lenient attitude toward former rebels was typical in the Southern states, where few whites welcomed the forces of Republican Reconstruction. The postwar political success of men like Throckmorton would serve as justification for Congress to assume control over Reconstruction. As Carl Moneyhon puts it, "Throckmorton epitomized the attitude that demonstrated to Unionists the reluctance of ex-Confederates to accept the war's results."[66]

In many ways Howell's characterization of Throckmorton as enigmatic seems appropriate for the state as a whole. That the Unionists and the forces of secession seemingly played off of one another is an obvious conclusion in light of political culture literature. The two factions, strikingly similar in their zealousness, perpetuated one another toward extremes, which made conflict a certainty. Historian Walter Buenger dissects the conundrum of dualism that characterized pre-secession Texas even further by noting the way conflicting factions had compartmentalized their preferences to allow for self-assured (and somewhat delusional) ideological consistency. The most obvious example is slavery, which Texans supported while simultaneously electing Sam Houston as governor in 1859, thus suggesting they still favored preservation of the Union. The result is that prior to the rapid polarization brought on by events such as Harpers Ferry and Lincoln's election, Texas could easily have been characterized as moderate, supporting slavery locally while still maintaining nationalistic sentiment.[67] With the secession crisis and the onset of extreme group polarization, the key figures identified here in the story of Texas Reconstruction were left with little choice but to embrace the extremes of the political cultures in which they were now enmeshed. Most Texans followed suit. Cultural theory stresses that individual decisions are simultaneously choices of culture or based on social interactions.[68] This does much to explain the courses of action chosen by Hamilton, Davis, and Throckmorton, and makes the recusal from public life of Elisha Pease seem even more exceptional.

Hamilton, Throckmorton, Pease, and Davis would ultimately each get the opportunity to hold the reins of power during a time in Texas that was arguably just as significant as the Civil War itself. The immediate policy concerns facing a state wherein external (and often internal) authority had evaporated with the Confederate surrender would have been challenging for even the most skilled politician. First and foremost was the lack of civil authority and corresponding surge in violence statewide. Identifying the underlying causes of violence as a means of understanding Texas culture at the time is, however, problematic, and would carry political ramifications for Texas leadership. The historical interpretation of the violence, like so many other aspects of Reconstruction, has evolved with the historiography. Charles Ramsdell, the Dunning School historian who wrote the first history of Texas Reconstruction, argued that violence against Freedmen and Unionists was part of a larger sense of disorder in the state attributable to the general chaos left in the wake of the Confederacy's dissolution, rather than politically motivated.[69] Naturally, revisionist historians disagree with this assertion. Gregg Cantrell argues that the political motivations for violence in Texas were inherent. The simultaneous loss of the war, emancipation, and occupation by external military forces left white Texans without a political voice, and freed Blacks became a symbol of Northern aggression, and thus the perfect scapegoat.[70] Whatever the ideological underpinnings of the violence, and whatever points of argument politicians used to exaggerate or diminish the significance of that violence, there was a general consensus that reestablishing the legitimate authority of the state was paramount.

Chapter 2

Two Counties in Crisis

U sing Daniel Elazar's conception that political cultures are rooted in the cumulative historical experiences of the people, it isn't hard to see why a place like Collin County was among the dissenting voices at the time of secession. Economically, socially, and politically, Collin County was not East or Central Texas. It also becomes clear why such a significant ideological shift occurred, as the trauma of war left an indelible psychological scar. Reminiscing nearly a half century after his experience in the Civil War, J. L. Greer of Collin County said, "The space is too limited to begin to sketch out our experience of suffering from exposure, hunger and wounds. Our humiliation in defeat (not defeat, but failure) has caused more mental pain, and is harder to bear, than was all the exposure, hunger and wounds during the war. It rankles my heart still, and I am not reconstructed yet. I want this on my tombstone: 'Here lies a Confederate soldier.' "[1]

The fact that the experience was powerful enough to reshape the region's collective psyche provides a rare opportunity to analyze political change—a rare occurrence in the political culture literature.

Here lies the value of an interdisciplinary approach to measuring political culture, as historical research can fill in the gaps of political analysis.

The Throckmorton Enigma

James Webb Throckmorton's reluctance to support the Confederate cause was seemingly in line with the popular sentiment of Collin County. Despite Throckmorton's own ambivalence toward the perpetuation of slavery and his white supremacist leanings, his devotion to his constituents remained true and laudable. Kenneth Howell notes in his biography of Throckmorton that his overriding concerns regarding frontier defense, establishment of transportation infrastructure, and fear of the accumulation of wealth and assets in the hands of the established planter (enslaver) class were typical sentiments held by the early settlers of North Texas.[2] Yet neither Throckmorton nor his base of support in Collin County could form a significant enough bloc to prevent the break from the Union. The esteemed historian Walter Buenger said it best: "Perhaps no one better illustrates the complexity of Unionism and the reasons it failed to prevent secession than James Throckmorton."[3]

The post-Whig conservative Unionist message of Sam Houston was consistent with sentiment in Collin County when the question of secession became a pressing reality as the 1860 presidential election approached. Carl Moneyhon argues that despite Houston's relative success prior to 1860 in bringing together a broad coalition of Texans opposed to the more elite-focused Democratic party, the racial doom preached by men like Oran Roberts and other vociferous secessionists was simply too much for the state's poor whites to ignore.[4] But such Democratic scare tactics did not seem to have the same effect on the white frontier settlers of North Texas. James Waller Thomas, editor of Collin County's leading publication, *The McKinney Messenger*, openly advocated "a Union of Conservatives and the defeat of sectionalism" in September 1860. *Sectionalism* was the term used to described Lincoln and the emerging Republican Party.[5]

The implicit message here is one of cultural contrarianism built more on a distrust of Democratic leadership than on a love for slavery, along with a yearning for continued self-determination in the face of an ever-encroaching federal government. In the 1860 general election, the people of Collin County were appropriately dismayed by the lack of choices they had been given they had been given by the major political factions of the day, but ultimately chose Southern Democrat and Vice President John C. Breckinridge, the overwhelming winner in Texas.[6] The desire to maintain antebellum Southern cultural sensibilities without pledging loyalty to a Democratic Party that was out of touch with the needs of simple white frontier folk also drove James Throckmorton.

That Texas was the last Deep South state to secede illustrates not only that the interests of the frontier were still very pertinent but also that the conservative Unionist ideals of Sam Houston and the coalition he'd assembled still mattered greatly. Ralph Wooster notes that as part of the slim minority opposed to breaking ties with the Union at the secession convention, James Throckmorton was met by the most pronounced cacophony of hisses and boos during the convention's roll-call vote. "Mr. President [Oran Roberts], when the rabble hiss, well may patriots tremble," he replied to the mob after his vote against secession.[7] The people of Collin County needed internal improvement, equitable tax burdens for small farmers, and protection against Native American incursions, and secession provided none of these. In all, seven of the eight delegates casting votes against secession represented counties in North Texas, geographically demonstrating the state's cultural divide.[8]

In Throckmorton's eyes the urgent rush to leave the Union would only further accommodate the needs of the largest cotton growers of East Texas, and the accompanying withdrawal of United States Army garrisons would leave the Red River borderlands open to attacks from Native Americans. A week after the popular vote on the ordinance of secession in February 1861 (which the voters of Collin County opposed 948 to 405), the *McKinney Messenger* questioned

the very legality of the secession convention while darkly acknowledging the inevitability of conflict: "A deep gloom is settling over
our fair land, and soon, alas, how soon we know not, the tempest may
burst upon us with the terrific and desolating fury of the tornado."[9]
The war of disunion that Collin County didn't want would force
Throckmorton and his constituents to make a number of gut-wrenching
and pivotal decisions.

For the people of Harrison County, secession couldn't come
quickly enough. The East Texas cotton growing county boasted
the state's largest number of enslaved persons by 1860 and was
home to 145 planters who enslaved at least 20 people.[10] In terms
of wealth distribution, this made Harrison County the antithesis of
Collin County, which was based around smaller individual farms.
And when voting to break ties with the Union in February 1861,
Harrison County voted 866 to 44 in favor, signaling both the influence of the landed elites and the consolidating effects of a political
culture.[11] The political tone of Harrison County's main population
center, Marshall, was summarized in *The Texas Republican*, which
since 1851 had been under the control of editor Robert W. Loughery,
who regularly advocated secession, states' rights, and the protection
of slavery. In March 1856, as Free-Soilers and Border Ruffians were
bleeding Kansas dry in what would become an important precursor
to the Civil War, Loughery used the *Texas Republican* to express
the social and economic apprehensions growing in Harrison County:
"Texas is more directly interested in the question of slavery than
any of the other Southern States. She occupies, in the first place,
a frontier position, with an immense freesoil boundary, and is consequently more open to attack from the enemies of the institution than
any other. In the second place, she is the last of the cotton and cane
growing States. From the immense extent and extraordinary fertility
of her lands, she is destined to become the recipient of most of the
slave population of her sister States of the South."[12]

In an era when news media objectivity was rare, the people
of a geographic area signaled their values by the newspaper they

consumed, and Loughery's *Texas Republican* was the voice of Harrison County. At the same time, Loughery was fully aware of the influence of the news media, and the power that he wielded. In May 1849 the inaugural issue of the *Texas Republican* under Loughery's predecessor, Trenton A. Patillo, announced its unabashed commitment to Democratic ideology: "The character of a newspaper is more important, perhaps, than generally imagined. If conducted with ability, it will give tone to public sentiment, and concentration and direction to public opinion; inspire a love of intelligence; diffuse morality and virtue, and keep alive a spirit of patriotism, wherever it circulates."[13] Loughery assumed editorship of the Texas Republican only two months later, similarly committed to controlling public opinion.

The political culture of Harrison County had been shaped in the image of the Deep South. The soil and climate were suited to plantation agriculture, and the debate over slavery and states' rights held special relevance for the community's future. Political cultures like Harrison County were characterized, in Daniel Elazar's estimation, by an acceptance of government as an actor for the common good, but unlike moralistic political subcultures, traditionalistic cultures believed in limiting their government's role primarily to the maintenance of the traditional (enslaving) order.[14] For this reason many in Harrison County were as eagerly charged for a fight against the Union as their counterparts in South Carolina.

Walter L. Buenger's cultural classification of Texas counties identified Collin County as upper South, with an economy based on smaller farms that grew wheat and corn instead of cotton.[15] According to the 1860 census, while Harrison County produced 21,440 bales of cotton, Collin County grew a total of 16. By 1870 Collin County's cotton production had grown to 4,371 bales, but culturally speaking, it isn't difficult to delineate the differences between the two counties.[16]

Daniel Elazar's classification of political subcultures would characterize a borderlands county like Collin County as an individualistic political subculture. The characteristics that defined much of westward expansion and, in Elazar's estimation, defined the American Southwest were perfectly apt for Collin County. The old-world tradition of hard work and self-reliance along with American Protestantism—identified by Elazar as the basis of an individualistic political subculture—hinted at Weber's Protestant work ethic described over a half century earlier. The individualists of frontier counties like Collin cooperated with one another while generally disdaining collectivism propagated by the government.[17] The culture of the frontier had little concern for Southern conceptions of elitism evident in traditionalistic Harrison County and the Deep South. And while both Harrison and Collin Counties possessed their own strain of conservatism, their political cultures naturally dictated dramatically different expectations about the role of government. According to Elazar, "In this respect, plains conservatism is unlike that of the South whose conservatives are often willing to accept and even encourage considerable state activity."[18] The differences between Southern and Plains conservatism would take on special significance at the latter stage of Reconstruction and the writing of the Texas Constitution.

At the time of secession, of course, Collin County lacked the political clout to challenge the more dominant Deep South culture that had subsumed the state. James Waller Thomas, while unapologetic in his commentaries in the *Messenger*, understood the difficult situation Texas Unionists were faced with in the wake of secession: "We wish our Union friends to understand that we have no intention of resisting, *forcibly*, the new order of things which the secessionists may succeed in inaugurating. The only weapon we propose is to use the pen, and so long as freedom of opinion is tolerated, we shall boldly and fearlessly give expression to our honest convictions, however distasteful they me be to tyrants and usurpers."[19] That Texas was ruled by two distinct political subcultures is by no means unprecedented in Elazar's classification scheme, and the general submission of the frontier culture to the stronger Southern culture through the course of the Civil War and Reconstruction is similarly expected.[20]

By the time of secession, Harrison County was more developed than Collin County by most measures. In fact, with cotton as the economic foundation, East Texas as a region had developed into a formidable political bloc. Of Harrison County's 15,001 inhabitants in 1860, 8,748 were enslaved, making it a white minority-county and underscoring the reliance upon slavery and dependence upon cotton. The estimated cash value of farms in Harrison County was $2,668,809 in 1860, compared to $2,090,058 for Collin County, with Harrison County also commanding a vast advantage in acres of improved farmland.[21] Randolph Campbell persuasively argues that although these statistics can provide only the bones for imagining a community's social structure, successive census reports detailing population growth vis-à-vis agricultural indicators can be quite valuable for understanding life for a typical white Texas family.[22]

Economics aside, Collin County is easily discernible from East Texas demographically as well. Whereas the increasingly plantation-based Harrison County was predominantly African American in its makeup prior to the war, enslaved people made up only 11 percent of the population of Collin County.[23] This would have special political significance after the war and emancipation when they became voting freedmen and it was time to let the people speak on Reconstruction, Republicanism, and redemption. Prior to the war, far from being characterized as abolitionists, the people of Collin County simply had more pressing concerns than slavery. For the people of the borderlands, disdain for slavery sprung not from a common moral concern but rather from the idea that the institution was a means for wealth consolidation in the hands of the haves while they, the have-nots, sought nothing more than absolute independence and self-sufficiency in their economic and social lives.[24] Collin County was individualistic, through and through, and not particularly enthusiastic about struggling to preserve the wealth of plantation owners.

Like most of Texas, Collin County's white population was comprised in large part by people from other Southern states. The particular origins of these Southern immigrants left a clearly identifiable cultural pattern, with immigrants from the upper South perpetuating an individualistic culture and immigrants from the Deep South propagating a more traditionalistic one. The largest portion of Collin County's Southern immigrant population hailed from Tennessee, and the 1,932 Tennesseans represented nearly 14 percent of Collin County's population in the 1870 census.[25] Similar data is unavailable from the 1860 census, but this general characterization of Collin County remains valid based on the available agricultural data from both 1860 and 1870. The number of Collin County immigrants from Tennessee was greater than the population of immigrants from the Deep South powerhouses of Alabama, Georgia, Mississippi, and Louisiana combined.

Almost perfectly in line with the cultural typologies of Elazar and Woodard, Collin County was settled by immigrants from Greater Appalachia, while Harrison County's immigrant population was almost the opposite. In Harrison County Deep Southern states represented 26 percent of the population compared to a mere 726 individuals from Tennessee, or 5 percent of the population.[26] As political power consolidated in East and Central Texas was based on a traditionalistic culture akin to the lower South, the immigrant influence from the upper South on places like Collin County further divided the state and made the frontier region averse to slavery and secession.

Faced with an unstoppable tide of public emotion elsewhere in Texas, the people of the borderlands had little choice but to accept reality. James Throckmorton believed that only through pledging allegiance to the Confederacy could the counties of North Texas avoid becoming targets of the paranoia that infected Austin and the eastern half of the state. As a Unionist based in Central Texas closer to Austin, former governor Elisha Pease might have been able to ride out the war in relative anonymity in order to avoid mobs of Confederates seeking to stifle dissent, but an entire county's worth of military-aged men continuing to openly resist the Confederacy would have created an unwanted sectional conflict the people of Collin County would rather avoid. If James Throckmorton was a reluctant rebel, so too were his constituents, and the prospect of creating division within the state itself appealed to few. In time Throckmorton did develop an interest in protecting slavery, however indirectly. For with emancipation would come fears of a migration of freedmen seeking economic opportunity as they abandoned the East Texas sites of their previous enslavement. The white population of Collin County was already deeply entangled in the struggle against Native Americans, and the potential social upheaval brought by non-Anglos seeking land to work was too much to bear.[27]

It is worth noting that geographically, Collin County is immediately north of Dallas County, and the two were demographically similar. Like Collin County, Dallas County was characterized by fewer enslaved people, relative to plantation-based East Texas, and economically focused on subsistence farming. Yet Dallas County overwhelmingly voted for secession despite lacking any apparent economic motivation to do so.[28] The ideological impetus for Dallas's secession vote and subsequent heavy participation in the war demonstrates the power of public opinion in fostering cultural conformity, as well as the cogency of local media outlets as a suitable gauge for public opinion. A lengthy editorial in the *Dallas Herald* in mid-January 1866 enumerated the examples of grievances about so-called Northern aggression against the economy and the social fabric of the traditionalistic South: "For years a relentless social war has been waged against the most vital institution of the South, and now unmistakably threatens our very existence as a people."[29] While it isn't difficult to understand the desperate sense of economic doom conveyed by this editorial for the greater cotton-growing South, it is a bit perplexing that such a message would resonate in Dallas County, which was not built on a foundation of enslaved labor. Even more striking is the difference in how Dallas and Collin Counties would decide on secession, with Dallas supporting disunion by a 741 to 237 count, and Collin County voting almost exactly the opposite. Obviously, there was no statewide unanimity on secession.[30]

Measuring the perceived costs and benefits of secession in East Texas, where plantation culture had already become heavily ingrained in the public consciousness is, by comparison, significantly easier. If the primary policy concerns of the day for Collin County were the frontier and its security, then Harrison County was driven chiefly by economics and the destruction of the social hierarchy. The prospective loss of slavery meant much more for Harrison County than any community on the frontier. As the secession crisis in Texas was building toward its climax in February 1861, we get a rare glimpse of Texas's own internal sectionalism conveniently provided by Harrison County's *Texas Republican*. Referring to the people of Collin County as "submissionists," the *Texas Republican* criticized Collin County's hesitation to even elect delegates to the secession convention. Collin County's subsequent choice of Unionist delegates (of which Throckmorton was the most prominent) drew the ire of Robert Loughery, who seized the opportunity to go after Collin County, as well as the *McKinney Messenger*: "The following was the result, Disunion 215. Union 716. Majority for submission 501. The [McKinney] Messenger is jubilant. This result is attributable, doubtless, to the want of correct information of the people among whom it circulates. The editor seems to think the sun rises and sets in Collin. We would say to him, 'My dear fellow, Texas will be out of the Union before a large portion of your people are aware of the fact that there has been any political excitement in the country.'"[31]

However, when secession led to violence, the culturally consolidating effects of war on the people of Collin County immediately became visible. Despite misgivings about the Confederate experiment, a bonding sense of duty against an external threat quickly drew the community together. After an initial month-long foray into military service to secure the military outposts abandoned by fleeing Federal troops in May 1861, Throckmorton was called again to recruit additional cavalry in June for frontier protection against two enemies: Native Americans and the Union.[32] *The McKinney Messenger* recounts an exchange between a Miss Hazlewood, who represented the women of

Collin County, and Throckmorton upon presentation from the women to Throckmorton's company of a flag to carry in battle. The paper printed both Miss Hazlewood's letter and Throckmorton's letter of gratitude, which included a strong indication of how quickly he and his recruits were adopting the Confederate mindset.

> It is said that the chains of slavery have already been forged, that are to manacle the free born son and daughters of the South. . . . This flag, the representation of our nationality, the contribution of warm hearts devoted to the cause of our section, shall attest how well the men of Collin county acquit themselves in this momentous struggle. Fair lady, we thank you, and those whom you represent, more than language can express, for this beautiful banner—and we thank you a thousand times over for your sympathies so touchingly expressed in behalf of the endearments and sacred associations of home, sweet home, and the dear ones there. It is for these—for their protection, and in their defence, that we go forth to battle.[33]

This statement reveals an immense ideological transition for Throckmorton and exemplifies the rapidity of enculturation. The men of Collin County, who only six months prior had voted overwhelmingly against secession, were now indistinguishable in their mindset from the men of East Texas. Publishing in the *American Political Science Review* in 1988, Harry Eckstein compared the continuity of political culture to that of physical inertia, wherein there is a natural resistance to change. It is only through the imposition of exceptional forces (like war) that cultural change is brought about.[34] But to understand the attitudes of the men of Collin County, neither a deep understanding of political culture literature nor Newtonian physics as cultural metaphor is necessary. They were bound by the commonality of their experiences, and although secession and war were not actively sought by the majority of settlers in their region, once battle lines were drawn it was obvious which side they were going to support.

There is nothing particularly striking about Throckmorton's quick change of sentiment regarding the Confederacy. In fact, as the presentment of the banner demonstrates, most residents of Collin County would go on to embrace, if not Confederate nationalism, at least the bonding sense of togetherness as a community fostered by the common fear of Federal troops, Native American incursions, and even homegrown insurgency. Despite opposing secession, the people of Collin County were accustomed to frontier life and knew its hazards and likely acquiesced to the Confederacy rather than disturb local peace in the name of continued resistance.

Lingering elements of Unionism nonetheless disrupted the peace of Collin County. In a perfect example of fear begetting fear, the perceived threat of conspiring Union sympathizers in North Texas inspired enough hysteria to provoke a violent extralegal counterinsurgency. Despite his previous anti-secession leanings, the threat to security from underground dissenters proved too great for Throckmorton and most of his Collin County constituents.[35] Already less than pleased with having secession foisted upon them, Collin County citizens might have been able to maintain a less committed stance toward the Confederacy and the war if not for the Conscription Act of 1862 and its aftermath. The act, which made most white males aged 18–35 liable for military service, provided the necessary fodder for what became known as the Conspiracy of the Peace Party in October of that year, when dissenters from Grayson, Denton, Collin, Cooke, and Wise Counties made plans for an uprising.[36] Resistance to the draft and the establishment of a spy network for the Union Army were the Peace Party's objectives, although the actual seriousness of the threat they posed to civil order is debatable.[37] What is certain is the mass hysteria that followed, for the very possibility of a semisecret Union cabal operating in North Texas confirmed the suspicions of the more ardent rebels who sought to quash all forms of dissent.

The informal reaction to the Peace Party that became known as the Great Hanging of Gainesville left forty-one suspected Unionist conspirators dead in October 1862, some of whom were known to Throckmorton personally. The discovery of the Peace Party plot stirred a hornets' nest of Confederate vitriol and might have resulted in more dead if not for Throckmorton's personal intervention. Knowing that a number of the condemned were Unionists of otherwise upstanding character, Throckmorton initially objected to the mob violence, especially in light of the fact that he agreed with their position on the Conscription Act.[38] Ultimately, however, he later expressed at least partial support for the mob's actions, as he could not stomach the potential threat to the local community that a secret Unionist society might pose.[39]

By confirming fears of Unionist subversion, the Peace Party plot propelled the process of cultural change already underway in North Texas. Devotion to Texas had already supplanted loyalty to the United States, and the threat of local violence further encouraged a cultural transition. Richard McCaslin notes that additional threats to Collin County cultural sensibilities would accumulate over the course of the war as the African American population increased 70.7 percent by 1864 and the county was inundated with refugees and deserters.[40] While economic and security concerns may have produced the initial hesitancy in Collin County to embrace secession and the Confederacy, this multifold attack on the culture of North Texas, particularly the perceived threat to life and limb, was enough to turn them into committed rebels.

For better or worse, the men and women of Collin County did their duty in the war, even if doing so took a certain amount of prodding from the Confederate government. Approximately 1,500 men from Collin County enlisted in the Confederate Army, which, from a population of 9,264, likely represented the bulk of eligible male residents of military age.[41] Inspired by more than just the example set by Throckmorton himself, some Collin County residents felt the call of burgeoning Confederate nationalism once secession became war, but more immediate concerns drove many of their actions. Native Americans, deserters, draft dodgers, and jayhawkers all represented a perceived threat to community order, no matter what nation they pledged loyalty to. The combative nature of Pendleton Murrah, who took office as governor of Texas in 1863, would ultimately be instrumental in protecting the citizens of Northwest Texas. Although in many ways Murrah exemplified the Confederate spirit of death-before-dishonor and he fled to Mexico at the war's end, his devotion to the needs of his constituents would keep the borderlands safer than it might have been in the hands of a governor who was more willing to cooperate with the Confederate government. With the end of the war and the dissolution of the Confederacy, frontier defense entered its darkest period. As David Paul Smith described it, "The Texas frontier suffered as never before in the years immediately following the Civil War, particularly from 1865 to 1869."[42] As the volunteer army that had won the war was rapidly demobilized, the remaining US regulars were simply overwhelmed by competing demands for their services in the immediate aftermath of the war. While the US government was not blind to the threats of the frontier, stationing troops there was no small task, and the delay likely contributed to the deaths of 160 Texans at the hands of Native Americans between 1865 and 1867.[43] The resulting cultural impact further contributed to the growing animosity between the people of Collin County and the federal forces determined to Reconstruct them.

Neither Collin nor Harrison County suffered the catastrophic losses that befell much of the Deep South. The geographic advantage that Texas enjoyed largely prevented invasion from US troops, and while Texas soldiers fought and died bravely, their home state escaped relatively unscathed. However, the emotional toll, as it was throughout the Confederacy, was palpable. In fact, such despondency had not been felt on the home front since the onset of the war itself. Robert Loughery's reaction to Lee's surrender at Appomattox and the effective end of the war was a mixture of disbelief, anger, and sadness, even while he maintained a sliver of hope for continued resistance; as editors of the *Texas Republican* put it, "These odious results are connected with submission, an event that will never take place unless our people are willing to basely surrender their birthright of freedom. We should never lose confidence in our cause or in the fidelity of the government."[44]

Andrew Jackson Hamilton had already made a name for himself in Texas politics before secession. Giving speeches throughout the North during the war, he was easily the most recognizable Texas Unionist and the obvious choice to lead the state when the Confederate government dissolved.
From the Lawrence T. Jones III Texas Photographs Collection, DeGolyer Library, Southern Methodist University.

White Texans lived up to Loughery's call for continued resistance as the last battle of the war, the skirmish at Palmito Ranch near Brownsville, happened over a month after Appomattox. In the same publication, Loughery expressed a vindictive farewell to the "monster that disgraced the form of humanity," the late Abraham Lincoln, while offering an exaggerated appraisal of how his successor, Andrew Johnson, would handle duties as president. "We have reason to believe that he [Andrew Johnson] hates the South with a malignity that is boundless," proclaimed Loughery. "His powers of mischief, however, cannot be greater than his predecessor."[45] While flush with hyperbole regarding Lincoln's successor, Loughery's assessment captures public opinion in Texas, even among counties that had been hesitant to join the failed Confederate experiment.

Isolated as they were from the physical dangers of war and relatively free from the Federal presence that characterized much of the Deep South, it is understandable how the exaggerations of prominent media voices became the reality. The same expressions of doom that accompanied E. J. Davis's arrival in Brownsville two years earlier were on display as Texas entered Reconstruction. Either left alone in the borderlands or faced with a shocking new cultural/racial order, the white citizens of Collin and Harrison Counties let their imaginations run wild, fueling group polarization that led them to the extremes of the political spectrum, making the prospect of Reconstruction almost doomed to failure before it even began.

Chapter 3

Rebuilding Texas Government

The first priority for federal authorities after the dissolution of the Confederacy was the reestablishment of law and order and the restoration of civil authority. If the heedless rush to secession was the result of a self-propagating culture whose epicenter was the agrarian class of East and Central Texas, then President Andrew Johnson likely could have made no better selection for provisional governor in the wake of the Confederacy's demise than Andrew Jackson Hamilton. Already known throughout the state for his years as Texas attorney general and House representative for Travis County, Hamilton had spent the war giving speeches throughout the North, and in the process had made a favorable impression on Abraham Lincoln. This reputation earned him the trust of Andrew Johnson, and Hamilton arrived in Galveston on June 22, 1865, as the appointed provisional governor of Texas, responsible for restoring civil government and leading Texas toward a new constitution.

Provisional Governor
Andrew Jackson Hamilton

Hamilton was a very reasonable choice for Johnson. Having established himself as the preeminent voice of Southern Unionism before and during the war, there was little reason to suspect he might work toward the restoration of civil government in Texas without putting Union loyalty first in his appointments of state officials. Carl Moneyhon notes, however, that the prospects for successful Reconstruction were dim even before it began, owing to a lack of coherence among Unionists.[1] It was immediately clear that Radical Republicans in the North would demand much from the provisional governors. Hamilton, having served in the Union Army, was a satisfactory choice in the more radical circles. At the same time, conservative Unionists like Throckmorton who were willing to accept that slavery was dead nonetheless remained steadfast in their disapproval of civil rights. Throckmorton also expressed to Hamilton his desire to see the basic governmental infrastructure of county and local officials in place at the time maintained until a new state constitution was in place.[2] Edward Hopkins Cushing, a Democrat and editor of the *Houston Tri-Weekly Telegraph* who was notable among Texas publishers for an exceptional sense of Confederate nationalism, joined Throckmorton in advising patience. A strong advocate before the war for Southern independence and self-sufficiency, with slavery as a fundamental cornerstone, Cushing urged open-mindedness toward the newly appointed provisional governor.[3]

> It will be for the interest of all parties, and for the good of the State and the Union, that there should be as much good feeling and harmony between Gov. Hamilton and the people whom he is to govern, as the nature of the case will admit. We have no doubt, from our knowledge of him, from our knowledge of the purpose of the President in making these provisional appointments, and from the fact that he has been entrusted with the important duty of carrying these purposes into execution, that he will devote himself, his energies, and his great talents to the accomplishment

of those ends which are necessary to the restoration of the State, as soon as possible, to harmonious relations with the Government of the United States.[4]

While this is a far more charitable assessment of Hamilton's character than what Cushing published three years prior, the tone of reconciliation expressed is indicative of a political culture that was both resigned to its reality as a conquered foe while also just plain tired of war.

Initial reactions were hopeful, as most white Texans by June 1865 were coming to terms with the idea that war, slavery, and countless other elements of their previous life were now finished. *The Texas Republican* was cautious but open to giving Hamilton the benefit of the doubt. Of Hamilton it said, "No man better understands public sentiment in Texas; no man is better acquainted with the feelings of the great body of the people."[5] Despite the fears of many former rebels, Hamilton's immediate goals for the restoration of civil government in Texas, as well as the new state constitution, were not based in a sense of retribution against the rebels who had forced him out of Texas during the war. In fact, early Texas Reconstruction historian Charles Ramsdell, despite the lost cause nature of his famous book, acknowledges Hamilton as realistic.[6] With a tone of reconciliation as he approached the office and the imminent creation of a new state constitution, Hamilton knew a firm rejection of both slavery and secession were necessary for readmittance to the Union. However, his (and E. J. Davis's) acceptance of basic civil rights for formerly enslaved people was enough to raise the hackles of the most ardent rebels and soon earn him the reputation as "radical."[7] Politically, his greatest challenge was the reunification of the hodgepodge of Unionists that Houston had represented before the war, something neither he nor Davis would accomplish.

Despite the optimism for how Hamilton would execute his duty administering presidential Reconstruction, the elephant in the room remained race. While emancipation and basic civil rights threatened a complete upheaval of the social framework that had shaped most of Texas life, the frontier included, the more immediate outcry over the changing status of African Americans was economic. Modern naysayers seeking to divert Texas's culpability in the preservation of the South's peculiar institution needn't look any further than the Declaration of Secession to find slavery's preeminence.[8] Despite any expressed optimism for life under federal rule and the governorship of A. J. Hamilton, emancipation represented a huge challenge for a society built upon enslaved labor.

Editor Robert Loughery initially framed his writing around an economic concern with ramifications for the South and the North. Loughery's faint hope for the preservation of slavery is obvious: "The legislation which destroys or inflicts major injury upon our prosperity will have a corresponding influence upon that of the North; and we think the time will come, when the people of that section will be glad to witness a return to a system attended with more philanthropy and happiness to the black race than the one which they seem determined at present to establish; for they will find that compulsory labor affords larger crops and a richer market for Yankee manufacturers."[9] Here there is also a suggestion on Loughery's part of the necessity of a paternalistic relationship between enslaved and enslavers that would subsequently become a major talking point for Texas Democrats, particularly when Reconstruction became Radicalized.

For many conservative Texans in Reconstruction, freed people would now constitute a protected class, reliant on the white power structure to give them the basic means of survival in exchange for a promise of labor, which could no longer be guaranteed through the institution of slavery. Loughery expressed his continuing concerns over what he saw as the shattered natural order a month later:

> If some compulsory means cannot be devised to make the negro work, his destiny is accomplished and he must soon cease to exist. He will be elbowed and driven out of competition by the superior intelligence and energy of the white laboring classes. Irish and German draymen laborers will rapidly usurp the places

formerly occupied by the male negro—and their uncertainty and irresponsibility will prevent the female negroes from being employed. If they do not work to good advantage on plantations, the proprietors will drive them forth and cease to feed them. They become vagabonds without homes, picking up a precarious subsistence by stealing, and by certain and rapid degrees dying off by disease, starvation, and exposure. They cannot live in such a community as ours—a community impelled and vitalized by the restless energy of the Anglo Saxon and the healthy flood of immigration that sets towards our shores—without working and working well.[10]

On the one hand, this captures the sense of loss felt in Harrison County over the disappearance of their economic base. But on the other, it is quite illustrative of claims that Texas Democrats would spout throughout the Reconstruction era. Steering their argument away from white supremacy, the Democrats would instead try to establish former enslaved people as a protected class in need of their help. This effort to reframe their relationship as paternal rather than domineering was primarily meant as a means to enlist Black support away from Radical Republicans and to appeal to Northern conservatives, and it would last through Reconstruction and beyond, especially in Harrison County.

The Freedmen's Bureau

The acrimonious relationship between white Texans and the newly created Freedmen's Bureau did much to encourage the steady consolidation of the state into a single conservative culture. Historian Barry Crouch was careful to identify an unusual set of circumstances surrounding the Freedmen's Bureau in Texas that made its existence exceptional among the Southern states. As with so many other aspects of Reconstruction, the insulation from war that Texas enjoyed manifested itself in a unique form of vitriol directed toward the bureau. For many white Texans, the mere existence of a free Black man represented a humiliating act of social aggression from the North. The Freedmen's Bureau, then, was to blame for facilitating their equitable treatment and became a symbol of not only racial humiliation but also continued infringement upon state and local authority.

Initially established under military control in March 1865, the Bureau of Refugees, Freedmen, and Abandoned Lands, or simply the Freedmen's Bureau, was established in the South to assist African Americans in the transition from enslaved to free labor. This general mission expanded to include regulation of all aspects of the Black labor force, including legal advocacy and physical protection for freed people until the bureau's withdrawal, at which point the sharecropping model took hold.[11] The bureau's short existence (1865–1868) was controversial from the beginning, as it was perpetually plagued by want of resources and endlessly compromised in its very structure. Historian William Richter pointed out that beneath a seemingly benevolent motivation on behalf of free African Americans, the bureau might not have come to fruition at all if not for the other elements of its title: refugees and abandoned lands, both of which involved primarily white interests. At an even deeper level, Richter noted the bureau's unspoken mission of guaranteeing a predictable level of economic stability in the South, as making free labor palatable for freed people in the South would prevent them from migrating to the North in too great a number.[12]

Establishing a bureau in Texas was initially impossible due to remoteness, and it was not until September of 1865 that Edgar Gregory assumed control as bureau chief for Texas.[13] The preceding period from June 19, 1865 (now celebrated as Juneteenth), to September was characterized by a plea from Hamilton to both formerly enslaved people and former enslavers to continue working for the sake of the community and to provide adequate compensation, respectively. His hopes were summarized in his July 25, 1865, proclamation issued from Galveston:

> The negros are not only free, but I beg to assure my fellow-citizens that the Government will protect them in their freedom. For the time being, the freedmen are recommended to engage

with their former masters for reasonable compensation, to labor at least till the close of the season from gathering their present crop. For them, generally, to do otherwise, would be greatly to the injury of themselves and the community at large. But let it be understood that combinations among those interested in securing their labor, to prevent them from hiring to persons who will pay the best price for such labor, and to ostracise [*sic*] in society those who oppose such combinations, will meet with no favor at the hands of the people, or Government of the United States.[14]

The best assessment of affairs during this period comes from reports out of Louisiana, where the bureau was assisting East Texas counties as best it could. The Louisiana Bureau was able to report 6,461 laborers under contract in Marion and Harrison Counties in July 1865, which Crouch acknowledged as a "remarkable feat" given the lack of tangible protection provided by Union troops in Texas. Unfortunately, the bulk of reports indicate chaos in the wake of emancipation, with widespread acts of violence and the continuation of slavery in the absence of the bureau.[15]

Naturally, the editorializing in the *Texas Republican* extended well beyond Loughery himself and is indicative of Harrison County's general level of trepidation regarding the impending upheaval of the racial order. An anonymous open letter to Louisiana governor James M. Wells on July 21, 1865, printed in the *Republican* encapsulates the hesitations of East Texas whites:

> The fatal blow has been struck at the African in this country, and it is almost as great a disaster to the white man. Home is a term he will never know again as long as the white man predominates, and he undoubtedly will. No man now, white or black, has anything to hope for under the present condition of things. Every one is for winding up his affairs and getting away. It would be intolerable to live in the country associated with free negros. Neither rich nor poor can stand it. Mexico, with its mixture of races, and the Southern American States, with their mongrel populations, could not be worse than this country is to be, the negroes remaining in it free.[16]

So heavily inculcated with a sense of racial hierarchy were Texas's poor whites that hatred for the bureau would, in time, transcend class difference and economic concern.

The first two assistant commissioners for the Freedmen's Bureau in Texas, Edgar Gregory and Joseph Kiddoo, served from September 1865 to January 1867, at which point control over Reconstruction policy began transitioning to Congress.[17] Crouch is charitable in his appraisals of Gregory and Kiddoo, recognizing their efforts to stabilize the labor system, foster civil rights, and establish a basic system of education. Both were crippled in their duties by a lack of resources and authority, and their repeated pleas for assistance in response to widespread racial violence received little notice from the Johnson administration.[18] Regarding these pleas, conservative Texas media outlets were simultaneously defensive and reactionary, seizing the opportunity to reframe the issue of violence toward freed people as one of state affairs:

> Granting more troops to General Kiddoo, as he desires, will not remedy the evils of which he complains, but make matters worse, and get up bad feeling between the races, which now has no existence. The remedy is to be found in the withdrawal of the troops and the Bureau, and leaving the freedmen to the friendly protection of the State authorities. Why should we be distrusted? Why should our good faith be questioned? Let us alone and give us a fair chance, and you will see that we can be true to our word and do justice to both black and white.[19]

This statement from Austin's *Tri-Weekly State Gazette* is a retort to Kiddoo's widely publicized August 1866 report, which proclaimed evidence of widespread violence and murder of freedmen in the Texas interior. Violence and a lack of federal response to it would characterize the environment under which Texas transitioned from Confederate to Radical to redeemed. It plagued the existence of the Freedmen's Bureau and impacted national policy as Congress grew less and less patient with President Andrew Johnson's handling of affairs in the South.

Presidential Reconstruction

For classification purposes, the phase of Reconstruction from June 1865 to March 1867 is commonly known as Presidential Reconstruction, with Johnson controlling the process of readmission for the Southern states. Almost immediately the disconnect between Johnson and the more Radical Congress began to stir up further animosity in the South, as the president sought a more lenient approach while Congress was more determined to protect the rights of freedmen and Unionists. From the Union perspective, Texas represented one of the great unknowns as Reconstruction began. Not only was Texas never fully occupied by Federal troops, but the same information gap that kept many Texans in the dark throughout the war had similarly kept Union authorities ignorant of the challenges they faced there. Like any other Southern state, the conquered white population of Texas was naturally resistant to any effort to remold them in the image of the North. The first order of business under Johnson's Reconstruction was for the appointed provisional governors to call state constitutional conventions. Only delegates officially pardoned or who had taken a loyalty oath would be allowed to participate, and the new state constitution would be required to recognize Union victory in the war.[20] Based on his long history of service, unflinching loyalty to the Union, and national reputation, Andrew Jackson Hamilton was a natural choice as provisional governor.

Texas newspapers of the time reveal how national events were shaping the consolidation of the postwar culture in Texas. The ideological schism over the course of Reconstruction that would divide the Republicans nationally became manifest with the Fortieth Congress meeting in March 1867, made up of the largest majority in both chambers ever held by the Republican Party. This represented the shift to more Radical Reconstruction, but its inevitability was felt in Texas well in advance. The noted abolitionist, Congressman Thaddeus Stevens of Pennsylvania, in his role as chairman of the House Appropriations Committee, had already become one of the more prominent faces of Radical Republicanism, as well as public enemy number one among conservatives in Texas. Perhaps sensing the split between moderate and Radical Republicans (which many white Texans hoped might enable them to retain their political dominance), Robert Loughery said, "It is stated, that the President will not budge a hair's breadth from his position, and, as this is now pretty well known, no bill Mr. Stevens or his friends can frame, contemplating treating the South as a nation of subjugated foreigners, can pass either house of Congress. There is said to be evidence of a split in the Republican camp. We hope it may prove true."[21]

President Johnson was already no friend to the Republicans in Congress and was quickly losing support among Southern Unionists as well. A. J. Hamilton's vision for the reestablishment of a loyal civil government in Texas was under pressure from Johnson throughout the fall and winter of 1865. Johnson valued quick readmission to the Union above all, which was at odds with Hamilton's primary motivation to build a government of officials loyal to the Union.[22] The divide over the goals of Reconstruction at the national level were very tangible at the state and local level in Texas as well, as noted in the *Texas Republican*: "We have believed from the beginning, that if President Johnson had planted himself firmly and squarely upon the constitution, and had recognized the great political, practical, and logical deductions from his own theory of the government, he would have stood in a much better attitude to have defended himself against the assaults of the radicals. But he thought otherwise, and the Southern people had no alternative but to follow him."[23]

It is also interesting to see that the retrospective myth making that would ultimately take root in scholarly circles as the lost cause was already taking root among Texas conservatives. Disregarding Texas's own obstinate desire to maintain slavery in everything but name through the infamous Black Codes, Robert Loughery was already shifting the focus of the war itself toward perceived Northern aggression. "The truth is, a desire for sectional domination is answerable for the war and every drop of blood that was spilt in it," wrote Loughery. "And, as a proof of it, now that slavery is dead, the same fell spirit, like a vast conflagration, is more powerful and rampant than ever."[24] A true sense of the political culture of East and Central Texas is reflected in this quote, as few things create a consolidated and unified cultural front more than the perceived threat of oppression from an outside foe.

Regardless of cultural change, A. J. Hamilton faced a mountain of work. His first order of business was getting the proper county officials in place, allowing the basic day-to-day operations of state government to continue under the control of loyal Unionists. James Throckmorton visited Hamilton in July 1866 to discuss this matter, and while warmly welcomed by the provisional governor, he was ultimately rebuffed in his suggestions. Throckmorton advocated for the preservation of county and local officials, likely out of a sense of pragmatism for quick readmission combined with his own white supremacist leanings, which put him squarely in line with Presidential Reconstruction.[25] That Hamilton would differ on this should have come as no surprise to Throckmorton, for he had not built his reputation on moderation. Three years earlier, while establishing himself as the face of Southern Unionism in the North, a letter from Hamilton to Abraham Lincoln looking ahead to the question of Southern readmittance to the Union was published in William Lloyd Garrison's *The Liberator*. Under the capitalized headline, "NO COMPROMISE," *The Liberator* noted Hamilton's emphatic belief that anything less than absolute submission to the Union would sink the prospects of Reconstruction: "Gen. A. J. Hamilton, of Texas, has written President Lincoln a very forcible letter on the importance of refusing all compromise with returning rebel States. He says that the [emancipation] proclamation is irrevocable; that discretion and power ceased with the act which, in the exercise of constitutional power, proclaimed freedom to the slaves in the States it embraced. He entreats the President not to listen to the advice of the friends of slavery, and so rob himself of the gratitude and admiration of mankind."[26] Such a position on emancipation naturally put Hamilton and Throckmorton at odds. That there would be political pressure to compromise on the status and labor of freedmen, the legal status of former Confederates, and a host of other issues was understood.

Hamilton's next order of business was calling a constitutional convention. On November 15, 1865, elections for delegates were set for January 8, 1866. Eligibility for voting among former Confederates was determined by President Johnson's general amnesty proclamation and presidential pardons. As Kenneth Howell notes, this, combined with general voter apathy, produced a modest turnout.[27] *The McKinney Messenger*, in a fashion not completely dissimilar from its stance in 1861, questioned the very legitimacy of the constitutional convention with a lengthy dissection of its very existence. The *Messenger* strongly advocated a purely advisory role, with the amendments to the state constitution necessary for readmission being produced through the legislature: "That the declaration of 1861 known as the 'ordinance of secession,' is and was from the beginning NULL And VOID. That slavery has ceased to exist within the State of Texas, and consequently that all laws and parts of the constitution having references to slaves or slavery are objectless and therefore without force or effect. In addition, let the convention advise the calling of the legislature and the enactment of such laws as may be necessary for the protection of the freedman in his newly acquired rights."[28] While not addressing every issue at stake in the debate over readmission and Reconstruction, the *Messenger* revealed the cultural disposition of Collin County on the three crucial issues at stake in the postwar climate: secession, slavery, and basic civil rights. Whether the culture of Collin County was in line with editor Thomas's progressive views on race is debatable, but an acceptance of the reality of Union victory is apparent, while the independent streak that defined the character of the frontier is still visible in this plea for Texas legislative control in lieu of submission to a convention foisted upon the state by federal authority.

The constitutional convention called by Hamilton received a much less generous appraisal by the *Texas Republican* and whites in Harrison County. While accepting the end of slavery, one letter to the editor drew a firm line in the sand regarding civil rights, suffrage, and war debt:

> To acknowledge that all slave property has been wrested from its owners and that there is now no such property, would be only a candid avowal of facts. But to declare Texas a willing party to the transaction; to declare the African the equal of the Anglo-Saxon; to legislate him into equality in any respect, either by any franchise additional to what he now enjoys, or otherwise; to repudiate a just and legitimate debt; and to fail to meet the demand of the General Government for any and all of these, by a firm and earnest protest, would be falsehood, robbery, and a betrayal of the rights and interests of the people.[29]

A plea for continued resistance through political means saturates this letter to the editor, and there is little indication that Harrison County was ready to submit on many fronts at all.[30] With African Americans still largely unable to participate, the voters chose Colonel John Burke as representative to the constitutional convention, which is both telling of the county's cultural disposition and foretelling of the failure of Presidential Reconstruction and the constitution of 1866. A notable criminal defense attorney in Marshall prior to the war, Burke served with distinction in the Confederate Army, first in Hood's Texas Brigade and later as a scout and spy before becoming Texas adjutant general under Pendleton Murrah.[31] With the collapse of the Confederacy, Burke joined Murrah when he fled to Mexico, only returning home to Marshall after Murrah's death.

Even before the Eleventh Texas Legislature, created under the constitution of 1866, signed its own death warrant in federal eyes by selecting leading secessionist Oran M. Roberts as a US senator, Burke's presence at the constitutional convention served as a strong indication of Harrison County's cultural disposition toward Reconstruction. In a circular printed in the *Texas Republican* on December 29, 1865, announcing his candidacy as a delegate to the convention, Burke towed the (Democratic) party line on questions of war debt, the Thirteenth Amendment (which he opposed), consolidated power of the governor (which he opposed), and civil rights: "Fellow Citizens, it is impossible for me to vote for any measure which makes the negro the equal of the white man."[32] Burke was not alone in his sentiments, which were revealing of white public opinion in Harrison County.

The Constitutional Convention of 1866

The Texas State Convention convened on February 7, 1866, with a sense of optimism for progressive change among some delegates that was easily overshadowed by the majority desire to make the bare minimum of changes necessary for readmission. Throckmorton was present on day one as representative for Collin County, while E. J. Davis represented Webb, Nueces, Duval, and Encinal Counties. John Burke would not arrive to represent Harrison County until February 14.[33] James Throckmorton was elected president of the convention the next day, a safe choice that was satisfactory to both conservative Unionists and moderate secessionists. Addressing the convention after his election, Throckmorton expressed a common devotion to the federal Union and a spirit of reconciliation: "Let us bury, upon the altar of our common country, all the recent past, with all its painful associations and recollections; and, upon that altar, hallowed by the clustering reminiscences of three quarters of a century, renew our devotions to the Government of our Fathers—a government reared by sufferings, and consecrated by their blood, and in the glories of which we have an inheritance."[34] While such sentiments were in keeping with Throckmorton's own ideological leanings as a reluctant Confederate, he and others were also fully aware that they were being watched and every move they made being judged as they worked toward readmission.

Not only was the convention under the watchful eye of Northern critics, but it was also being closely scrutinized by Texas Unionists who had ample reason to suspect the motivations and loyalties of many delegates. The February 10 message from Hamilton to the convention was an expression of optimism, a plea for submission to the Union, and a call for fundamental civil rights for formerly enslaved people. At the same time, Hamilton recognized that his position was far more

Republican than the convention would be willing to accept: "I cannot assume to know the individual views of the gentlemen who compose this body; but I have reason to apprehend, from what has met my eye, in the form of published circulars to the people, before whom many of you were candidates, and leading articles in many of the most influential presses of the State, that my views on this subject will not be acceptable to a majority of the members of this Convention."[35] For Hamilton, Davis, or any other staunch Unionist, anything less than a constitution reflecting the state's loyalty to federal authority would be unacceptable. Indeed, President Johnson's liberal approach to the question of amnesty for former Confederates had drawn the ire of Texas Unionists since its introduction on May 29, 1865.[36]

In Johnson's mind a simple oath of amnesty allowing maximum participation by the whites of the conquered Southern states was sufficient for the rebuilding of loyal civil government. His May 29 proclamation thus demanded that those persons who had participated in the war take only an oath of *future* loyalty to the Union and allowed even high-ranking former Confederates the option of seeking amnesty via a presidential pardon.[37] Because the oath was administered at the county level, Hamilton and others were dubious from the start, for such a relaxed interpretation of Reconstruction would put the bulk of control into the hands of the very people to be Reconstructed. This logical absurdity had kept Hamilton on edge long before his message to the convention delegates. In his Proclamation to the People of Texas on July 25, 1865, for example, he had cautioned citizens not to take the oath in bad faith.[38] And his suspicions were well placed, as the composition of the body of delegates at the convention makes perfectly clear. E. J. Davis was similarly aware that Johnson's approach to amnesty allowed for the presence of too many political enemies. On February 12 Davis called for the removal of those who Johnson had demanded secure a special presidential pardon to gain amnesty (such as those who had violated a previous oath of allegiance to the Union, high-ranking Confederate government officials, and those holding more than $20,000 in property).

The measure was submitted to committee, where it subsequently languished for the duration of the convention.[39]

Despite controversy over the loyalty of the delegates, some issues would draw little debate at the convention. With limited discussion on the floor and seemingly not much more in committee, the general sense of urgency in addressing the problem of frontier protection was widespread. On February 20, James E. Ranck of Mason County introduced a resolution (requesting federal assistance against perceived threats from Native Americans) that was referred to committee and subsequently passed the next day.[40] The resolution, reprinted in the *Southern Intelligencer*, conveyed a sense of doom and desperation:

> Whereas, within the last six months whole families of loyal citizens of the U. States have been shamefully and brutally murdered by Indians upon the northwest frontier of Texas; and, Whereas, a large number of women and children have been carried into captivity by those remorseless savages, whose depredations upon life and property are daily becoming more frequent and bold; and, Whereas, the protection of the frontier from depredations by hostile Indians has always been, and is now, a matter of great importance to the people of Texas; and, Whereas, a large portion of our northwest border is now, and has been for several months, almost entirely at the mercy of hostile Indians; and, under the force of existing circumstances, is likely to remain in that unfortunate condition until United States military posts have been re-established along the frontier border. . . . Now, therefore, Be it resolved by the Delegates of the loyal people of the State of Texas in Convention assembled, That his Excellency, Andrew Johnson, President of the United States, be, and he is hereby respectfully solicited to take into immediate consideration the present deplorable conditions of the frontier people of Texas, and to render to them the early and efficient protection of which they are in so much need.[41]

The frontier violence James Throckmorton had witnessed in his youth fueled both his conservative perspective on race and his unwavering commitment to the white settlers of the frontier.[42] But a closer examination of the facts of frontier violence and the need for federal protection during the first years of Reconstruction creates a handful of political questions.

Along with his conclusion that 1865 to 1869 represented the worst of times for frontier protection in Texas, David Paul Smith noted the strategic predicament faced by the US Army, which would by the end of the decade be reduced to less than forty thousand officers and men. Despite the desperate cries for relief on the frontier, military authorities could not escape the reality of post–Civil War violence in the more densely populated interior. As Phil Sheridan (commanding the military division of the Gulf, which included Texas) noted in his annual report of 1866, positions on the salience of frontier protection versus maintenance of law and order in the cities seemed to break down along partisan lines. By that time Hamilton had been replaced as governor by the democratically elected Throckmorton, and Sheridan was fully aware of each of the men's perspectives on the matter. Sheridan, who did not hold the people of Texas in high regard and vice versa, surmised that the scourge of Native American depredations was likely exaggerated:

Governor Hamilton, the provisional governor, was clamorous for more troops, and in several communications to me asserted that the civil law could not be carried out; that freedmen would be killed and Union men driven from the State without military support, which I gave whenever it was possible. Governor Throckmorton, the present governor, wants all the troops moved from the settled portions of the State, asserting that the civil law was all right; that justice would be done to freedmen, Union men, and our soldiers in the courts. But justice was not done. . . .

During the last six months Indian depredations have taken place on the remote frontier. Their extent is not defined as yet, but they are not very alarming, and I think that the governor has to some extent been influenced by exaggerated reports, gotten up, in some instances, by frontier people to get a market for their produce, and, in other instances, by army contractors to make money.

It is strange that over a white man killed by Indians on an
extensive frontier the greatest excitement will take place, but
over the killing of many freedmen in the settlements nothing
is done.[43]

Historian Robert Wooster concluded that Sheridan's report of exaggerated claims could only serve the purpose of drawing troops away
from the interior, thereby freeing Throckmorton to manage civil
affairs on his own while satisfying the frontier constituents he held
so dear.[44] And while utilizing exaggerated threats may have been
politically effective for Throckmorton upon assuming the governorship, at the time of the 1866 convention, there was little doubt as
to the seriousness of the situation for the Texas populace. Frequent
media accounts of murder and kidnapping made the situation very
real and very urgent.

Other issues at the convention, such as the end of slavery and
the nullification of secession, also drew little initial opposition but
would subsequently create a slew of new controversies requiring
complex solutions. Emancipation and nullifying secession were
included in Hamilton's message for the delegates, and despite the
reality of secession's illegality, almost immediately the question of
war debt repudiation drew controversy. For the Unionists, and for
observers in the North, declaring secession illegal meant any debt
incurred in the name of the secessionist cause was similarly unlaw-
ful. For secessionists this opened a piñata full of problems, as all
transactions conducted in Confederate currency would become
meaningless and thus complicate local economies.[45] Out of this
would come an even broader debate known as ab initio, which
would have declared all acts of the secessionist government null
and void. This would have resulted in countless land transactions,
marriage licenses, and legislation over railroad charters losing their
basis in law. The resultant compromise voided only laws passed in
support of the Confederate cause and retained all laws that did not
contradict the US Constitution. While this proved satisfactory for
Throckmorton, Davis and other Radicals were incensed.[46]

Even more damning in the eyes of the Unionists was the convention's treatment of the freedmen. Article III, Section 1, of the 1866 Texas Constitution excluded "Africans and descendants of Africans" from suffrage, and few of the protections for freedmen that Hamilton had advocated in his message to the convention would be realized.[47] The right of Black Texans to testify in court, a point which Throckmorton firmly opposed for its implication of equal legal status with whites, was compromised in Article VIII, granting the legislature the power to extend it to African Americans as necessary.[48] In all the convention fell well short of what Hamilton, Davis, and others sought for civil rights. This prompted a call from the Unionists for division, a special exception allowed under the statehood provision of 1845, which allowed Texas to divide into as many as five different states. Such a move would have granted quicker readmission for loyalist regions, and likely given more prominent Unionists, like Davis, a political advantage.

In Carl Moneyhon's analysis, the constitution of 1866 did little more than make the minimum number of amendments to the 1861 constitution needed to gain readmission.[49] On March 31, with the convention winding down, Hamilton warned the convention that their intractable stance on civil rights would likely result in the new constitution's undoing. *The Texas Republican*, reprinting a report from the *Henderson Times* a month later, said,

> Gov. Hamilton, in his speech to the Convention, denounced its members, among other things, for not placing the negro, politically, completely upon an equality with the white man, their refusing to give the blacks any portion of the school fund, and making no provision to allow them the right of suffrage. He charged them with having taken an oath upon the holy evangelists which they had violated, and told them that they would go down to their graves as perjured men; that the negroes were their inferiors only in education, but that in moral honesty, patriotism, and loyalty to government, they were infinitely their superiors.[50]

New battle lines were already being drawn. The fight between North and South was over, but a new one defined by conservative versus

Ever faithful to his Collin County constituents, James Webb Throckmorton
was a reluctant Confederate. Over the course of the war and Reconstruction,
his initial opposition to the cause was eventually replaced by a passion
for aggravating Union military authorities whenever possible.
1991/137-068, courtesy of the Texas State Library and Archives Commission.

Radical would determine what reconstructed Texas would look like.
For the conservative elements of East Texas, such an affront by the
forces of Radicalism expressed in Hamilton's speech could only
be interpreted as a call to arms. With the convention finished and the
June elections looming, both sides were emboldened, for no partici-
pant or observer imagined that Reconstruction was over.

Throckmorton Takes Over

With the convention over, the next order of business was deciding who would wield power in reconstructed Texas. Elisha Pease was nominated for governor by what became the Union Party, as provisional governor Hamilton had reached the point of exhaustion. The conservatives nominated James Throckmorton, a move quickly attacked by critics. While he may have been a hesitant Confederate who had once bravely stood up to the unruly mob that raced toward secession, his service as president of the constitutional convention had, for many, been indicative of a pattern of behavior that was an impediment to readmission and Reconstruction. On one level, his hardline stance on Black suffrage was sure to upset the Radicals. But on an even deeper level, his devotion to Union principles had become suspect, as he had seemingly done nothing to prevent the obvious shortcomings of the constitution of 1866 that would ultimately prolong Reconstruction.[51] Unsurprisingly, the *Texas Republican* wasn't shy in its advocacy for what became the conservative Union ticket, with Throckmorton nominated for governor and George Washington Jones, another Unionist turned reluctant Confederate, nominated for lieutenant governor: "It would be a great misfortune to the State and to the country, if by any means a radical should be elected. Taking the situation of affairs as we find them to exist, we this week hoist the names of gentlemen of known conservative views, whose chances of election seem to us the best. In taking this course, we intend to cast no reflection on the merits of other conservative gentlemen already in the field. We are laboring to defeat radicalism, and we believe the union upon this ticket will do it."[52] A week later, reprinting from the *Galveston News*, the *Texas Republican* cautioned its readers to avoid falling into a state of apathy when the fight was so far from finished: "THE RADICALS – Quite a full vote of conservatives in Texas will be needed to neutralize the multitude of Mexican votes which the Radicals expect to introduce along the Rio Grande. We understand that Pease expects immense majorities all along down from El Paso to the Boca. It has often been the fate of a large, apathetic and honest party to be beaten by one which was much smaller but compact and unscrupulous. We warn the conservatives that there is danger in their apathy."[53]

The election of 1866 in Texas became almost a proxy for the events shaping the national debate over Reconstruction. With Throckmorton as a loyal devotee of the soft approach to Reconstruction, allowing for quick readmission while neglecting a number of civil rights issues, and Pease commonly perceived as a Radical, the ideological split mirrored that of President Johnson and the Radical Congress. It is important to note that although Pease was perceived by the opposition as being a Radical, he was not ideologically in line with Hamilton and Davis with regard to race.

As a former governor and devoted Unionist, Pease had political clout, but contrary to popular belief among Texas media outlets, he didn't support universal suffrage for formerly enslaved people.[54] In fact, historian Elizabeth Whitlow's biography of Pease notes that his devotion to the institution of slavery put him far outside of the supposed Republican mainstream. Serving as a clerk in the Constitutional Convention of 1836 at the height of the revolution, it was Pease who personally drafted the language allowing for slavery in the soon-to-be Republic of Texas. According to Whitlow, private correspondences reveal his continued devotion to the institution during his governorship from 1853 to 1857, primarily based on a sense of economic practicality.[55]

In a perfect demonstration of the news media formulating the myth that then became reality, these ideological points about Pease were buried amid the rush to play upon the racial fears of white voters. "Pease is a Hamilton man and Hamilton is an unequivocal negro equality man, and the people of Texas cannot be forced to swallow this damnable doctrine," reported the *Dallas Herald*, reprinting from the *Crockett Sentinel*.[56] As reprinted in the *Dallas Herald*, the *San Antonio Herald* was even more dramatic:

> The handful of Radicals in this State are very moderate in their pretensions. They only require the people of Texas to get down

on their knees before them and humbly acknowledge that they have been fools for the last twenty years; that they never had the least idea of the true meaning of the Constitution and the rights of the States who formed it; that they have just been constantly encroaching upon the liberties of the Northern people, and have always been wrong in all their controversies with them; that they must abuse all the men whom they have heretofore trusted and honored, and praise and vote for men in whom they have no confidence, men who have no sympathy for them, no regard for their interests or feelings, who wish to degrade and oppress them, who love the little finger of a negro more than the whole body and soul of a white man, that they must cease to think of act for themselves, and become the mere tools for the immaculate Radicals to work with for their own profit and glory.[57]

This single-sentence rant demonstrated the conservative determination to disparage the loyal Unionists as Radicals while hopefully preserving key elements of antebellum society through the election of the conservative ticket. Pease, to his credit, accurately predicted that the election of Throckmorton would automatically make Texas suspect in the eyes of the North.[58] Pease consistently preached in his campaign that readmission without further demonstration of change to satisfy Northern observers was a fantasy.

Austin's *Southern Intelligencer*, while endorsing Pease, also foresaw the problems that conservative victory would bring the state in the process of Reconstruction. "Dr. Throckmorton was not originally a secessionist, but he has not been very consistent in his course, is in bad company and has no experience as Governor," reckoned the editors. "He might make a very fair Governor under Jefferson Davis, but he don't suit for one under Andrew Johnson."[59] Pleas for moderation to the will of the national government in the name of quick and lasting readmission were steamrolled by the tide of racial fears and conservative hyperbole, which Throckmorton wholeheartedly encouraged. Ultimately, the election wasn't close, with Throckmorton taking 48,631 out of 60,682 votes.[60] His dominance in both Harrison and Collin Counties was absolute. Once again, it would be easy to point to this result as the product of elite puppet masters, but this would ignore the chief factors that had brought political change and shaped Texas culture through 1866.

The loss of the war and the loss of the antebellum social framework as manifested in granting civil rights to Black Texans had clearly transformed the political culture of Collin County and reinforced that of Harrison. Within a single year, the culture had moved from a weary acceptance of reality at the war's end to one of continued resistance to federal authority. In Collin County Republican editor James Waller Thomas found himself increasingly relegated to the fringe of popular opinion—a point that his rival publication in Harrison County could not help but emphasize in the wake of Throckmorton's landslide victory: "Collin county, the home of Gen. Throckmorton, gave an overwhelming vote for him, notwithstanding the efforts and cunning of the McKinney Messenger, a radical paper, published at the town of McKinney. Throckmorton's vote was 1044; Pease 144; the remainder of the vote being about in the same proportion. This result mush be particularly mortifying to the editor [Thomas] of that redoubtable sheet, and we trust will do him good."[61] To conservatives Throckmorton represented the end of the perceived transgressions committed by the North against the former Confederacy, and his landslide victory demonstrated that most white Texans believed they could still preserve an element of Confederate honor.

Texas was not alone in its stubborn renewal of the political fight. Across the South other states were similarly electing and installing civil governments comprised primarily of former Confederates. What the media outlets championed as a natural right for the state— the ability to preserve local control by electing whoever the white voters saw fit—stood in direct opposition to the will of the increasingly incensed congressional majority, which was fighting both the conquered states and President Johnson, who had done little to discourage the states. Republicans increasingly feared that they had won the war but lost the peace. So in addition to the pressing state issues that Throckmorton and the Eleventh Legislature faced when they arrived in Austin in August 1866, the Texas government was already on shaky ground. Again, the national debate was heavily intertwined with events at the local level in Texas, as Throckmorton expressed his admiration of Johnson during his inaugural address on August 9, 1866: "His [Johnson] generous policy has endeared him to the great mass of the people, in every party of the country. This liberality has deeply touched the tenderest chords of the Southern heart."[62]

As expected, Throckmorton emphasized the monumental nature of the work faced by the newly established civil government of Texas and professed a newfound sense of loyalty to the United States. Never one to forget the constituents of Collin County, Throckmorton emphasized frontier protection in his address: "In the event, a sufficient number of troops cannot be procured from the Government [Federal], for the protection of the frontier, I shall not hesitate to urge expenditures by the States for this purpose. The people of that region, have already suffered with a patience and fortitude truly commendable." This message was by no means new for Throckmorton, who had a long track record of aggressive support of the expectations of his loyal constituents. At the same time, despite Throckmorton's platitudes about patriotism to the American Union and his invocation of the names of numerous founding fathers, there is an unmistakable sense of Confederate pride in his address. While encouraging the legislature and the people of Texas to move forward, there is an implicit framing of an us-versus-them divide: "Under the most trying of circumstances, the people of the South have shown a constancy and devotion, rarely equaled, to a cause considered by them as sacred and holy."[63] Cultural theorists agree that political subcultures hinge upon their opposition; therefore an appeal to Confederate pride, even when it is implicit, can only be interpreted as a rallying cry for Throckmorton's loyal base of support.

Naturally, race remained on the minds of all, and we can once again get a sense of what would become a political tactic for the conservatives. If the position of Throckmorton and the more extreme conservatives was to stand firm against Black suffrage and only accept a bare minimum of civil rights protections, then it was necessary to build a political facade of paternalism. Throckmorton said, "The day is not far distant, in my judgment, when the black people will be convinced that their truest friends are those with whom they have sported in youth, and have cared for them in their infancy."[64] For Throckmorton the dividing line between the factions vying for the hearts and minds of the freedmen had the benevolent conservatives on one side, promising protection and employment, and the opportunistic Radicals on the other, seeking only the Black vote and oblivious to their need for protection.

In the Eleventh Texas Legislature, Collin County was represented by John Kendall Bumpass in the Senate, and Edward Chambers in the House of Representatives. Charles Clark Coppedge represented Harrison County in the Senate, while Robert Garrett and Samuel J. Richardson served in the House. All five were Confederate military veterans. Richardson had even been a member of the Knights of the Golden Circle, the clandestine precursor to the Ku Klux Klan devoted to the preservation of slavery.[65] Following Throckmorton's recommendation, the legislature intentionally chose not to act on the Thirteenth Amendment, eliminating slavery nationally, and they rejected the Fourteenth Amendment entirely. For the conservative majority in the legislature, granting citizenship rights to formerly enslaved people while a number of former Confederates remained disenfranchised was simply too much to swallow.[66]

It took little time for the Eleventh Legislature to offend the sensibilities of congressional Republicans. Faced with what the legislature saw as nothing less than the complete destruction of their economy and way of life, the establishment of the Black Codes in Texas set the stage for future segregation and restricted civil rights and established control over Black laborers. Similar measures were adopted across the South, with the final result being the establishment of an institution that was just short of being slavery.[67] Barry Crouch notes that throughout much of the early historiography, there was a consistent sense of the moderation with which Texas approached the Black Codes relative to the other Southern states, with early scholars such as Charles Ramsdell acknowledging their implementation as "harsh" but also "necessary both for the good conduct and for the protection of the negros for whom alone [they were] intended."[68] Historians Seth Shepard McKay and T. R. Fehrenbach professed similar statements. These proteges of the Dunning School were molded by the social and racial norms of their times, and although Texas's Black Codes might have been a bit more moderate than those implemented by other Southern states, the result was still a level of control over Black labor that Randolph Campbell characterized "as near to slavery as a free man might be."[69]

   As the name implies, the Black Codes were not a singular piece of legislation but rather a series of frequently draconian and always discriminatory laws adopted from the end of the war until Congressional Reconstruction. Along with what some early historians saw as acceptable measures for guaranteeing a perpetual source of labor in the face of a loss of Texas's economic base, the laws also encroached into Black social, legal, and political life. Throughout the South the Black Codes regulated labor, court testimony, litigation and criminal penalties, and vagrancy, as well as including the necessary punishments to ensure adherence. And while short-lived before the congressional assumption of control over Reconstruction, the legacy of the Black Codes would haunt Texas and the rest of the South for a century. For example, the House and Senate journals of the Eleventh Legislature provide few details regarding debate over a bill passed on October 30, 1866 "requiring Railroad Companies to provide convenient accommodations for freedmen" other than to say it was taken up and passed.[70] The lack of elaboration can only be interpreted as common acceptance among the legislators of what would ultimately be the seed of racial segregation and the Jim Crow era.

   But in many ways, it was the choice of Oran Roberts as US senator that set off the Republicans in Congress.[71] In fact, perhaps even more fundamental for Radical critics than the greater South's rejection of

civil rights and installation of Black Codes was the very makeup of
the state governments that had been assembled under Presidential
Reconstruction. German-born publisher and critic of all things slavery
and secession, Ferdinand Flake did not hold back his outrage over
the selection of Roberts for the US Senate: "Judge Roberts, as is well
known, was not only one of the most prominent secessionists, but was
the President of the Convention of 1861, which took, or attempted to
take the State out of the Union. He was also Colonel of the Confederate Army. It is no secret matter that these are the chief recommendations he possesses for the high place of senator. Neither eloquence
nor commanding talents are claimed for him by his warmest friends.
But he was and is the representative of the class most obnoxious to
the Government of the United States."[72] The other US senator chosen
was David G. Burnet, an old-school veteran of the Texas Revolution who, like Throckmorton, had opposed secession only to later
become absorbed by the Confederate tide, which in turn developed
into a strong distrust for Republicans. Randolph Campbell notes
that the installation of former secessionists into positions of power
under the Throckmorton government was prevalent at all levels as
local governments, county governments, and district judges statewide
were predominantly former Confederate officers.[73] Ultimately neither
Roberts nor Burnet were allowed to serve due to the restrictions of the
Ironclad Oath required by the Reconstruction Act of 1867.[74]

Throckmorton Falls Apart

Ever faithful to his constituents, if not simultaneously seizing the
opportunity to rankle federal authorities, Throckmorton prioritized
frontier defense and began requesting additional troops while
vowing to raise a state force should the federal authorities fail to
provide support, a promise delivered by the Eleventh Legislature,
at least on paper.[75] In November 1866 the legislature authorized
the creation of a state militia for frontier protection, but no officers
were appointed and the militia dissolved along with Presidential
Reconstruction. The divide between state and federal authorities

was growing, and Throckmorton's own ideological development had culminated in his assumption of the role of resistant contrarian, unwavering in his defense of states' rights and committed to frustrating federal authorities at all fronts.

By Spring 1867 Throckmorton's governorship was in peril as Congress began taking a more aggressive tack in the Reconstruction process. The question of Union loyalty and Southern intractability had finally pushed the Republican-controlled body to its limit, and the first of the Reconstruction Acts was passed on March 2. One month earlier the *Texas Republican*, while decrying the continued injustices and humiliations being heaped upon Texas by Reconstruction, took the opportunity to heap sarcasm on their perpetual rival, the *McKinney Messenger*, which had endorsed stricter congressional control over Reconstruction: "The McKinney Messenger of the 18th [January], contends that there has been no loyal government since secession, and that there can be none until Congress organizes, faces, and fashions one. Of course such a government will be delightful to contemplate. It is hoped that he [James Waller Thomas] and his sable brethren, whom he is endeavoring to aid Congress in reconstructing, will have a happy time of it."[76]

The first Reconstruction Act declared the new governments of the Southern states illegitimate and split the South into military districts pending their adoption of new, more satisfactory constitutions.[77] Tennessee was the only Southern state exempt from this, as they had adopted the Fourteenth Amendment the year before. The Fifth Military District, encompassing Texas and Louisiana, was placed under the control of General Philip Sheridan. Sheridan chose General Charles Griffin, staunch supporter of the Union, the Republican Congress, and the Freedmen's Bureau, to assume control of Texas.[78] Sheridan's influence on the course of Texas Reconstruction cannot be overstated, as he was firmly allied with Elisha Pease and shared a less than harmonious relationship with Throckmorton. Charles Ramsdell's initial history of postwar Texas pinpoints the Reconstruction Acts as something of a breaking point, although given

Throckmorton's performance up to this point, it would be difficult to argue that former Confederates had ever been cooperative with the Reconstruction process. For Ramsdell the first Reconstruction Act was nothing less than martial law and an overt attempt to remove the leading political elites of the day from positions of power that were otherwise legitimate. According to Ramsdell, "It was expected by the framers and advocates of these measures [the Reconstruction Acts] that the negroes and their white radical friends would control the states, thereby insuring 'loyal governments.' "[79]

Whatever impressions Texas political leaders might have had regarding ulterior motives on the part of the Radicals, compliance with Congressional Reconstruction was required. Motivated by a genuine desire to protect freedmen and Unionists, as well as a determination to enlarge their political base by making possible a Republican Party in the South, Congress turned to the United States Army to implement its will.[80] The civil government elected following the constitution of 1866 was now considered provisional, and the district military leadership was charged with ensuring the election of delegates for another constitutional convention. Universal suffrage regardless of race was mandatory, and the first legislature elected would be required to pass the Fourteenth Amendment.[81] While the continuing policy of Congress did little to affect the voting rights of rank-and-file former Confederates, the shock of political equality for formerly enslaved people sent some Texas communities into an existential crisis not felt since before the war.

Congressional Reconstruction meant, for many Texans, the breaking of a promise they assumed they had from President Johnson. Robert Loughery reflected on the first Reconstruction Act's breach of the constitutional promise of the Tenth Amendment and saw this as the moment in which the soft hand of the conquerors became pronounced vengeance:

The Congress of the United States have passed a bill, or enacted a law, ostensibly for the "more efficient government of the rebel

States," but really to embarrass and cripple our industrial and mechanical enterprises, to injure us financially, to harass and goad us individually and collectively, to degrade us morally and socially, to oppress us politically, and to establish in our midst eventually a government only preferable to anarchy; and which, we very much fear, will lead to it, or at least to the inauguration of a reign of terror similar to that enacted during the dark days of the French revolution, when that nation "got drunk on crime to vomit blood."[82]

From Loughery's perspective any sense of peace with honor following Appomattox had been hijacked by Radicals in Congress over the subsequent two years, which called into question why the South had ever laid down its arms at all. Loughery followed up his editorial by insisting that "the Union of States has been sundered, and the last tie that bound them as one has been riven."[83] This assertion would form the basis of the historical myth making that characterized the early Reconstruction histories. In fact, well into the twentieth century, as Texas sought to reform and remold its cultural identity, Congressional Reconstruction was framed as an aggressive maneuver carried out by Yankee hardliners that could only be purified or "redeemed" once the military occupation was finished.

Throughout the spring and into the summer of 1867, in a last-ditch effort to satisfy the military authorities as a means of maintaining his grip on power, Throckmorton began to take a more aggressive tack in controlling the behavior of government officials at the county level who were either refusing or simply unable to check the rampant violence being committed against formerly enslaved people. However, the rift between Throckmorton and Griffin and Sheridan was too much to overcome. A supplementary Reconstruction Act of July 1867 gave military authorities the power to remove state officials as they saw fit, and Sheridan, deeming Throckmorton "an impediment to reconstruction," ordered the governor's removal from office.[84]

The oldest and most experienced of the Reconstruction governors,
Elisha Pease's attempts to fulfill his duties as provisional governor with
a sense of moderation would win him few friends on either side.
1/102-440, courtesy of the Texas State Library and Archives Commission.

Pease Takes Over

Charles Ramsdell's general argument regarding the developments
of 1867 leading to the provisional governorship of Elisha Pease is
that military officials (Sheridan and Griffin) were frequently operating unilaterally, making them a potentially more dangerous enemy
to the status quo than the Radical Congress itself.[85] However biased

Ramsdell's work may be, the military district chiefs were most definitely empowered to act as they saw fit, as they were crucial to congressional plans regarding Reconstruction in Texas and the rest of the former Confederacy. More recently, historian Gregory Downs argued that the entire notion of Reconstruction hinged upon the US military being able to act with impunity as it overrode state authority. Faced with the almost certain prospect of continued resistance after Appomattox, US authorities understood that enforcing the results of the war and protecting some semblance of civil rights hinged upon controlling the South through military force. Theoretically, this meant that US authorities had no choice but to continue treating the events of Reconstruction as a continuation of the war itself.[86]

For the Southern people, the outrages of Reconstruction were viewed as a betrayal of what they assumed was a settled peace. For US authorities surrender of Confederate forces was not the same thing as a settled peace, and therefore district commanders were obliged to conduct Reconstruction in a military manner. For example, in Texas continuing violence toward freedmen and Republicans was having a destabilizing effect and could not escape Griffin's notice. Griffin's so-called Jury Order of April 27, 1867 effectively barred former Confederates from jury service while guaranteeing jury rights for freedmen. The *Texas Republican's* reprinting of the order came under the simple but very telling headline, "Another Military Order: White Men Still on the Downward Grade."[87]

Gauging the policy ramifications associated with maintaining a government of loyal Confederates is difficult, but some general assessments can be made. Reconstruction violence, which would become a major issue in the Constitutional Convention of 1868 and during the Davis administration, has been categorized as racially or politically motivated, and sometimes both. As the historiography developed, so too did the perspective on the efficacy of the army's presence as an occupying force. The earliest writings did not probe deeply into the social-psychological impact of the military presence in the state. That the occupation was hated by whites is understood and expected given the circumstances. But interpretations regarding the conduct of the military and the impact it had on further consolidating an already resistant political culture have often changed.

Barry Crouch notes postrevisionist William Richter's relatively conservative argument that military commanders had a strong political incentive to guarantee Republican success at all fronts.[88] This would, in turn, inspire within devoted former Confederates a sense of victimhood not too far removed from the sense of intrusion felt at the time of the secession crisis, when states' rights were perceived to be under assault. This feeling of vulnerability at the hands of their Union conquerors would subsequently shape the historical memory of Reconstruction and serve to refashion postwar Texas identity. However, much like the critical moments leading to secession, the preponderance of evidence suggests that heavy-handed intrusion on the part of the military authorities was a necessary reaction to increasing instability. Gregg Cantrell argues that Reconstruction violence had subsided a bit in the first half of 1867, even with the passage of the first two Reconstruction Acts and the transition to Congressional Reconstruction. He also concludes that high levels of violence resumed with the removal of Throckmorton from office and continued to rise until the election of 1868, suggesting a strong link to the changing political times.[89] The same can be said for the Freedmen's Bureau, which consistently drew the wrath of even the most mildly conservative media outlets throughout the period. The contentious viewpoints on the military presence offered by historians as the field developed are important, for they demonstrate a state culture, and a maturing field of study, that was coming to terms with its past.

The purge of ex-Confederates from state government continued, and overwhelmed Pease's term as provisional governor. While for some observers Pease as governor may have been nothing more than a puppet of Yankee tyranny, even Charles Ramsdell expresses a certain admiration, acknowledging him as "the most moderate of all those who had the confidence of the military authorities."[90] Assuming office on August 8, 1867, Pease was immediately placed in an unenviable position as Republicans began pressing him to plead with Griffin and Sheridan for the removal of local officials deemed unsatisfactory. The political motivation was twofold, for quick readmission and the disenfranchisement of future delegates to the constitutional Convention were at stake, and Pease generally complied.[91] *The Texas Republican* similarly interpreted the removal of Throckmorton and his replacement with Pease as a harbinger of things to come: "It shows clearly and conclusively what they have to expect from the present extraordinary and anomalous misrule."[92]

After a brief pause in September following Griffin's death, Pease continued to establish a sense of ideological unity across Texas government under General Joseph J. Reynolds that increasingly drew the objections of many whites in both Harrison and Collin Counties. Coupled with the legal protections offered by the second Reconstruction Act, guaranteeing the African American vote, an exhaustive effort to register as many freedmen as possible for the early 1868 election of delegates for the constitutional convention on the part of Texas Republicans was driving an even deeper wedge between conservatives and Radicals.[93] The concerted effort to remove conservative elements from state government ended when President Johnson replaced Sheridan as commander of the Fifth Military District in fall 1867 with General Winfield Scott Hancock, who staunchly disagreed with Congressional Reconstruction and sought to reestablish the primacy of civil government over the military.[94] However, much was accomplished during the brief time that Pease, Griffin, Reynolds, and Sheridan worked together, and Republican hopes for the 1868 election and subsequent constitutional convention were high.

1868

While Republican momentum was growing throughout late 1867, on a more local level the people of Collin County were becoming further and further enculturated with ex-Confederate conservatives, and any sense of Unionism that had shaped public opinion prior to secession was disappearing. Special Order No. 195, which had been issued on November 1, 1867, had allowed Reynolds to remove over four hundred county officials statewide.[95] Collin County was no exception to this, as the elected county judge, county commissioners, and sheriff were all replaced with appointees deemed more appropriate. Up to this point, Collin County had not been a hotbed of resistance and was generally quiet and compliant. Late 1867, however, saw the beginning of a four-year conflict known as the Lee-Peacock feud. The feud was a series of hostilities surrounding progressive Union League supporter Lewis Peacock and ex-Confederate officer Robert Lee that resulted in a dozen deaths and (rightly or wrongly) lumped Collin County into the category of lawless backwaters that the army authorities were trying to clean up. Stambaugh and Stambaugh note a military report sent to Reynolds conveying the public's impression of Lee and the ongoing violence; as this observer concluded, "Lee seems to be the most popular man in this section of the country, and I am sure that the citizens of that neighborhood would not only give him all the aid in their power, but will even help him with force of arms if necessary."[96] For Collin County the spirit of reconciliation was gone, and the prewar Unionism that had motivated Throckmorton and the people he represented was similarly extinguished.

The dictates of Reconstruction had guaranteed a constitutional convention that would be controlled by the Republican Party, as demonstrated by the results of the February 1868 election of delegates. With most ex-Confederates either disenfranchised through the military authority's interpretation of the Reconstruction Acts or simply refusing to vote as a matter of principle, the election of delegates ultimately hinged upon the Black vote.[97] The sense of dread felt among the white conservatives of Harrison County (where they were now a legal and political minority) was obvious. In anticipation of the election for the convention, the *Texas Republican* continued to stoke the fires of racial doom: "The white people of Texas will never consent, in our judgment, to negro suffrage in any form and if the Convention fails to take the broad ground in favor of a *white man's government*, it will fall short of public expectation, and impair confidence in its action."[98] While Loughery's opinion is easy to summarize as typical nineteenth-century racism, he was correct in his assessment that public confidence would be undermined, and the fires of hate would power many white conservatives through the coming years of Republican control.

Meanwhile in Collin County, a new crosstown conservative rival had challenged James Waller Thomas's *McKinney Messenger* in the form of the *McKinney Enquirer*, run by former Confederate captain John H. Bingham.[99] Responding to the racism spouted by his increasingly relevant competitor, James Waller Thomas devoted several columns to excoriating the *McKinney Enquirer's* interpretation of events on election day. First, the *Messenger* quoted the *Enquirer*: "When the fifteen or twenty negroes formed upon the square, and were served with tickets by a white face and with whoops of exultation marched off to the polls, who failed to recognize the assumption of the negro, and the condescension of the whites who thus dealt with them, as well as those who, as yet, deny the faith and remain the background." Then, Thomas combatively replied:

> Ah! Enquirer, had you kept a vigilant watch to the rear of your office, during the election you might have witnessed a sight that would have sadly shocked your poor, weak nerves. You might have seen two white skinned conservatives, with tickets in their hands, (maybe they had tears in their eyes, but we are not sure of this) pleading with certain sable descendants of Ham to vote the "white-man's ticket," so-called. And will you believe it, Enquirer, after all this "condescension" on the part of the white faced conservatives, the hard-hearted Hamites marched to the polls, not with whoops of exultation, but quietly and soberly, and voted the union ticket! What further evidence do we need of white degeneracy, or black ingratitude? Poor Enquirer![100]

Despite the alarmism coming from Democratic media outlets, the conservative fear of a unified party of Radical Republicans and their freedmen allies was not based in reality. The Republicans would indeed dominate the convention and guide the creation of the new Texas Constitution, but Republican cohesion was anything but certain. Carl Moneyhon points out that the factions within the Republican Party were significantly more varied in their positions on the fundamental issues of the day: the legality of wartime and postwar legislation (the ab initio controversy), development of transportation, education spending, civil rights, frontier protection, and the provision of law and order. This factionalism gave the Democratic Party a louder voice than their numbers would warrant, as the Republican factions frequently spent their energies opposing one another. Most Republican delegates favored transportation improvements and continued settlement of the frontier, but only minimal protections of civil rights and suffrage. Ideological variations among the Republican factions were typically based in sectionalism. For example, future convention president E. J. Davis by then was part of the group most receptive to equal rights. Moneyhon notes that Davis was chosen to represent Nueces County, where African Americans represented a small fraction of the population. Therefore, Davis could afford to take a progressive stance on equal rights without causing controversy among his constituents. By contrast, James Flanagan of Rusk County did not hold back in his antagonism to civil rights, as freed Black people represented the better part of his section's labor force and fears brought on by emancipation continued to grip his constituents.[101]

Electing delegates for the 1868 Constitutional Convention took place in February, with the convention itself starting June 1, 1868. If James Waller Thomas's response to the criticisms of the *Enquirer* were particularly antagonistic, it was likely because he was elected to represent Collin County, indicating his continued influence despite the cultural realignment of the county.[102] Harrison County's representatives included two of the ten African American delegates elected to the convention. Mitchell Kendal and Wiley Johnson were both formerly enslaved men who had been voter registrars for Harrison County, and Kendal would subsequently serve in the Twelfth Texas Legislature as part of the Republican majority coalition. The changing demographics of state leadership further antagonized Harrison County's Robert Loughery, who had dim hopes for what he called a "mongrel Convention" and urged organization and resistance on the part of conservative whites.[103]

Thomas, on the other hand, appealed to his readers' sense of patriotism and want of security and stability through quick readmission to the United States. In the same issue attacking the *Enquirer*, the *McKinney Messenger* pleaded for acquiescence to federal authority as a means of regaining statehood and control over civil affairs:

> Politically we stand now precisely where we stood in the stirring times preceding the late rebellion. We were then for the constitution, the union and the enforcement of the laws. We are for the same things today. The constitution may change, but the duty of the citizen to render a cheerful obedience to them, not as they were, nor as he thinks they ought to be, but as they *are*, must ever remain the same. Especially is this duty obligatory upon the people of Texas at the present time. Having no voice in the national councils it is impossible for them to change or in any way to affect the national will, unless, indeed, by their obstinacy they should bring upon themselves harsher terms than those already imposed.[104]

Thomas's appeal for cooperation in the name of regaining statehood was firmly in line with his prewar Unionism. However, whether his sentiments embodied the culture of Collin County going into the convention is dubious. That Thomas still commanded respect in North Texas is certain, as demonstrated by his election as a delegate. But with more conservative voices disenfranchised owing to their previous allegiance to the Confederacy, the choice of Thomas as a delegate to represent Collin County may have been a hollow victory based on his reputation as an honest advocate for the people of the borderlands rather than a continued voice for the political culture at that time.

The Reconstruction Convention of 1868 faced a number of political challenges when it was called to order on June 1, 1868. Provisional Governor Elisha Pease encouraged the delegates to pursue free public schools for all children, grants of land to promote immigration, and continued promotion of internal improvements in transportation.[105] But by the time of the convention, disorder and lawlessness were impossible for even the most avid conservative to ignore. Cantrell notes that violence spiked around the time of the February 1868 elections, and while it marginally subsided, he supports Moneyhon's contention that parts of Texas remained in a state of virtual war by the summer. The first reports of the Ku Klux Klan from the Freedmen's Bureau showed up in May, and political and interracial violence would play a prominent role in the actions of the convention.[106] Varying perceptions of the violence and the steps necessary on the part of the convention to address it, along with the continuing general questions of civil rights, would do little to help the strength of the Republican coalition as factionalism threatened to tear it apart. Meanwhile, along the frontier, maintenance of law and order similarly continued to frustrate federal efforts.

Frontier protection since 1866 had improved, although the regular army's success in guarding the lives and interests of white frontier colonists remained open to interpretation. With the rehabilitation of military outposts and redeployment of federal troops, the Texas frontier was somewhat stabilized by the second half of 1868, although prolific frontier historian Robert Utley was sharply critical of Generals Sheridan, Griffin, and Reynolds in their preoccupation with Reconstruction matters to the detriment of the prevention of violence between Native Americans and whites. In Utley's view top army brass did not appreciate the threat to the frontier, resulting in a minimal operational approach that did little to address the scale of the problem.[107] In his reports Reynolds noted that secret organizations were operating in Texas to "disarm, rob, and in many cases murder Union men and negroes, and, as occasion may offer, murder United States officers and soldiers. . . . The murder of negroes is so common as to render it impossible to keep an accurate account of them. . . . These organizations are evidently countenanced, or at least not discouraged, by a majority of the white people in counties where the bands are most numerous. They could not otherwise exist."[108] That Reynolds was left with little choice but to protect the interior while the borderlands remained vulnerable demonstrates the near futility of the military's task. Continuing violence in 1868, exacerbated by the arrival of the Klan and their apparent endorsement by the white Texas population, forced a withdrawal from the frontier "to such an extent as to impair their efficiency for protection against Indians."[109] Reynolds's report further supports Robert Wooster's contention that claims of violence being perpetrated by Native Americans were exaggerated to draw troops away from Reconstruction matters for political purposes. The intertwined nature of violence in the interior and violence on the frontier would subsequently lead the Davis administration to take drastic actions.

Once called to order, the convention's first order of business was the election of leadership. E. J. Davis was nominated for president of the convention by Morgan Hamilton, representative of Bastrop and brother of Colossal Jack.[110] Despite Davis's wartime distinction among Texas Unionists, he was generally viewed as a moderate, likely owing to his law experience, which many hoped would make him an unbiased adjudicator. In a message to the convention read on June 3, 1868, Provisional Governor Pease noted the tenuous nature of his position. He declared the state of the provisional government as being one of "extreme difficulty and embarrassment," and expressed his hope for the legitimacy to be gained through the convention and the constitution they would create. He also pushed for solutions to the rampant violence afflicting the state, nullification of legislation passed in aid of the rebellion, an end to payment of debts incurred in aid of the rebellion, civil rights, taxation for the establishment of free public schools, and the temporary disenfranchisement of former rebels in order to gain readmission.[111] Violence and lawlessness reigned as the most pressing issue, and two days later a special committee was established to address it.[112]

The early resolution for the creation of the Committee on Violence and Lawlessness is indicative of how bad the instability had become. The preponderance of violence in the state since 1865 carries enormous significance. It is evidence of both continued resistance and the uphill battle the moderate and Radical elements of the convention were facing when trying to assemble a consti- tution that would be agreeable to enough people to gain readmis- sion. The early historians, the revisionists, and the postrevisionists have presented every conceivable explanation for the ongoing violence, but for the Committee on Lawlessness and Violence, in a report issued to the convention on July 2, 1868, the truth was inescapable:

> This great disparity between the numbers of the two races killed, the one by the other, shows conclusively, that "the war of races" is all on the part of the whites against the blacks. The evidence in our possession also shows that a very large portion of the whites murdered were Union men, and that the criminals, with remarkably few exceptions, were and are disloyal to the Government. We are, hence, directed to the hostility of feeling entertained by ex-rebels against loyal men of both races, for the discovery of the cause of a large propor- tion of these outrages.[113]

For Davis there was no question that the violence was tied to seces- sion and continued resistance. From 1865 to the time of the conven- tion, just under 1,000 homicides had occurred, and a disproportionate number of the dead were formerly enslaved. The following day Davis thus offered a resolution to send two liaisons to Washington, DC, to address Congress on the state of low-level war in Texas. The appointed men were instructed to press Congress on the organ- ization of a loyal state militia to be controlled by the provisional government.[114] More than any other issue that would later impact E. J. Davis's time as governor of Texas, his approach to lawless- ness and violence and the measures he would take, including the creation of a state police force, would elicit the angriest response from conservatives and moderates, and cement his name in the early Texas Reconstruction histories as a tyrant.

That the Constitutional Convention of 1868–1869 completed anything is a small miracle. Four factions of Republicans and a small contingent of Democrats frequently led the proceedings in unanticipated directions. Adjourning from late August until the beginning of December to ensure peace and stability during the 1868 general election, the convention would last until February 1869.[115] Some elements of what would ultimately become the 1869 constitution were expected. Acceptance of the Fourteenth and Fifteenth Amendments to the US Constitution, universal male suffrage regardless of race, strict protections for Black laborers, encouragement of immigration to the state, and a statewide education system were all adopted, signaling a Republican effort (however disjointed) toward progressivism in the face of conservative resistance. These measures stood in stark contrast to the constitution of 1866 but did not reflect the seemingly interminable debate over questions like ab initio and state division.

The ab initio controversy was ultimately settled through a committee proposal from A. J. Hamilton, who by this point had grown increasingly at odds with Davis. It nullified legislation in aid of the rebellion but protected governmental measures over routine domestic concerns that would have otherwise created a bureaucratic nightmare had they been dissolved. State division in the name of ensuring quick admission for regions of the state willing to act in accordance with the rules of Reconstruction elicited strong reactions across party lines, and while Davis favored it, the matter was ultimately left to Congress to decide, and it never happened.[116] The most significant themes of the 1869 constitution were centralization, progressivism, and submission to federal authority. Davis's early endorsement of education over railroads and strong law enforcement measures to protect freedmen and Unionists were earning him a reputation as the face of Texas Radicalism.

The radical shift of tone from 1866 to 1869 is apparent in article I, section 1, of both documents. Like the Texas Constitution of today, both begin with a bill of rights, a stylistic choice that is unmistakably Texan. Section 1 of the 1866 constitution read, "All political power is inherent in the people, and all free governments are founded on their authority, and instituted for their benefit; and they have at all times the unalienable right to alter, reform or abolish their form of government, in such a manner as they think expedient."[117] While not expressly addressing any specific issue of legislative importance, this statement revealed the ideological tone that ultimately led to the dissolution of the document. Its insistence on the perpetuation of states' rights, using the Tenth Amendment to the US Constitution as its foundation, had done nothing to win the favor of the Radicals of the North. The same passage in the 1869 constitution, on the other hand, expressed both subservience to the US Constitution and a spirit of agreement: "The Constitution of the United States, and the laws and treaties made, and to be made, in pursuance thereof, are acknowledged to be the supreme law; that this Constitution is framed in harmony with, and in subordination thereto; and that the fundamental principles embodied herein can only be changed, subject to the national authority."[118] More than any other Texas constitution, that of 1869 also codified a more centralized approach to government. Executive and judicial appointment powers for the governor (discussed further in chap. 4), state level control over labor, and a more specific and overt attempt to create a state managed system of education all signaled a departure from previous decentralized arrangements of power.

In late 1868 in Collin County, expressions of discontent over the centralization of power at the cost of local control, as well as continued disenfranchisement of former Confederates, were increasingly leading to personal attacks on their own delegate, James Waller Thomas. The dramatic cultural shift of Collin County was on display as opinion moved from righteous indignation over the perceived loss of local autonomy to full-on vitriol directed at the unapologetic Unionist. Responding to criticism from the upstart *McKinney Enquirer*, the *Messenger* rebutted in defense of Thomas, "Come now, gentlemen, be quiet. It isn't manly to squall so, when you are hurt. Time will heal your wounds, and convince you that you did not know what was for your own good. As for the delegate [Thomas] to the constitutional convention from this county, he is likely to survive your misrepresentations and abuse. He is not ashamed that he did not follow your master [presumably Throckmorton] in his opposition to the government, and aid him and you in arraying against it the good people of Collin." The commentary concluded with a defense of Thomas's character: "Nor is he so wanting in self-respect as to pander to a corrupt public sentiment for the sake of a short lived popularity. His past history abundantly proves that he is not a political aspirant; that he engages in no machinations for power, and that while he respects public sentiment when it is right, he utterly disregards and condemns it when wrong."[119] The obvious message in this commentary, although not written by Thomas himself, as he was busy with convention duties, is that he was putting principles above public opinion. But public opinion in Collin County was not what it had been in 1861, his election owing at least in small part to the disenfranchisement of former rebels, who probably would have voted against him.

In February 1869 the constitutional convention came to a close without a complete document. Having reconvened with funding provided by a special tax in December, the convention had lasted 150 days in total, roughly triple the length of the 1866 convention, and at approximately three times the cost.[120] The document submitted to the people for ratification was an assemblage of proposals from the convention. Anticipating the difficulties of ratification, both the *McKinney Messenger* and the *Texas Republican* began campaigning months in advance. When the *Messenger* reportedly claimed that several Democratic newspapers had announced their support for the new constitution, the *Republican* fervently agreed with the *Rusk Observer* that such claims were false:

UNTRUE – The Messenger, Radical, published at McKinney, claims that 13 Democratic papers have announced their determination to support the new constitution. *This is utterly false*. Not even the Houston Telegraph, a paper which has talked more about this matter than any other in the State, will

support any constitution that does not enfranchise rebels –
Rusk Observer

Of course this is utterly false. The Telegraph has said the
people would accept a "fair constitution," but who, except
the extremely sanguine editor of that paper, anticipates such
a result? We object in this connection to the term "rebel."
There are no "rebels," as we are aware of, in the county to be
enfranchised.[121]

Ultimately, despite confusion over the convention's adjournment,
increasingly bitter rivalry between Republican factions, and a host of
protests from delegates, the constitution of 1869 was ratified by the
people in summer 1869.

Robert Loughery and the *Texas Republican* were aware of the
implications for self-determination brought by the new state supreme
law. While advocating for a Texas Democratic Convention to combat
the almost certain Radical juggernaut that would be seeking statewide
office after the constitution's ratification, the *Republican* expressed
what it saw as a sacred mission to protect the old order of dual
federalism: "The principles of that party [Democratic], as to the
origin and powers of the government, are as true today as they were
when in periods of tranquility they presented a stern and unyielding
opposition to the exercise of all doubtful or implied powers by the
Federal Government, with the intention of averting the very evils
that are now upon us."[122] By June 1869 the cracks in the facade of
Republican unity were on full display for the people of Texas. Now
in the process of moderating his positions in hopes of attracting
progressive Democrats to aid in his future ambitions, Jack Hamilton
joined Pease in not attending the Texas Republican Convention, held
in Houston by the publisher of the *Houston Union*, James G. Tracy.
With a preponderance of Black delegates and in the absence of
two of the state's most notable Republicans (and the ones with the
greatest crossover appeal), the convention was widely interpreted as
dominated by Radicals and nominated E. J. Davis as the Republican
nominee for governor.[123] The national Republican Party, having no

reason to suspect otherwise and having no intimate knowledge of Texas politics, assumed the choice of Davis was unanimous for the Texas Republican party, and lent him all of their support.[124]

Even among traditionally Republican Texas media newspapers (which were growing fewer in number) there was little fanfare for the convention as the absence of Hamilton and Pease signaled a lack of desperately needed unity as the party worked toward ratification of the constitution, readmission, and electoral victory after the restoration of civil government. Simultaneously, the *McKinney Messenger* was losing its influence in Collin County, despite Thomas's election as a delegate to the constitutional convention the year prior. Typically devoting full columns to rebutting the indictments of rival publications, the *Messenger*'s fall from favor coincided with the rise of its conservative rival, the *McKinney Enquirer*. Of the Republican Convention, the *Messenger* reiterated unflattering reports from the *Austin Republican*, noting that, "The Tracy Convention is a complete failure" on the first day, and that, "The Convention today is more of a farce than yesterday."[125]

In June 1869 Robert Loughery ceased publication of the *Texas Republican* and merged with the *Jefferson Daily Times*, itself a notable proslavery, states' rights–oriented publication, to create the *Weekly Times and Republican*.[126] While the political culture of Harrison County had changed dramatically with the enfranchisement of African Americans, Loughery retained a position of influence statewide throughout Reconstruction, and in time would return to journalistic prominence in Marshall.

Was the factionalism destroying Republican unity at what should have been their finest hour the result of power politics between the state's elites? Or were the myriad of regional differentiations simply too great to form a successful coalition that would support Reconstruction? For rank-and-file citizens on the ground, issues like security, taxes, and race were ubiquitous sources of daily stress, pushing them further and further to ideological extremes. For political leaders such as Hamilton, Throckmorton, and Pease, doing right by the people

Reviled in the early histories of the era as the embodiment of Yankee aggression, E. J. Davis's reputation has been slowly rehabilitated in recent decades. A Unionist possessing a sense of justice without vindictiveness, Davis's realistic and pragmatic approach to Reconstruction put him at odds with the rapidly changing political culture of Texas. *1987/173-23-F23-11, courtesy of the Texas State Library and Archives Commission.*

of Texas while also working to satisfy federal authorities was a ceaseless juggling act beyond the capacity of any individual. As he pursued power over state affairs, Edmund Jackson Davis, capable parliamentarian and respected attorney that he was, could not have foreseen the ultimate futility of his efforts.

Chapter 4

The Davis Regime

If the ideological shift of borderlands communities like Collin County seemed to coincide with the personal evolution of men like James Webb Throckmorton, then so too did the events of war and Reconstruction shape the character of Edmund Jackson Davis. The common image of the man conjured by the Texas mainstream (Democratic) press was nearly synonymous with that of Yankee Radicals like Thaddeus Stevens, but the reality was far less egregious. The early histories of Texas Reconstruction, while anything but kind to Davis, still acknowledged the difficulty of the situation he was placed in. Radical circumstances forced him to act radically, and Davis, like all Republicans, was demonized by the dominant political culture as the source of all sufferings.

The Gubernatorial Campaign of 1869

The race for Texas governor in 1869 was, predictably, a proxy for Reconstruction itself amid the changing tides of political culture in Collin County. President Ulysses S. Grant strongly endorsed Davis's candidacy, which gave a certain legitimacy to the otherwise unremarkable Texas Republican Convention in Houston. At the same time, the growing rift between General Reynolds and Jack Hamilton, as well as Elisha Pease, finally burst wide open when the latter two refused to signal Republican loyalty and participate in the convention. For Reynolds, Hamilton's refusal to cooperate and compromise with the Davis faction of his party spelled doom for the Republicans in Texas, and he informed Grant of his concerns in a private letter.[1] Nonetheless, Grant's favor of Davis grew as his administration began removing federal officeholders at the state and local level who were opposed to Davis.

Elisha Pease, increasingly incensed by Washington's enthusiasm for Davis and the removal of Hamilton supporters from the ranks of Texas government, resigned from office. The *Houston Tri-Weekly Telegraph* speculated as to the cause of his resignation, "Perhaps too, after Gen. Reynolds threw himself into the hands of the Radicals it became difficult to harmonize the civil with the military administration, in our abnormal half military, half civilian form of government."[2] Pease biographer Elizabeth Whitlow contends that Reynolds's strong endorsement of the Davis ticket and criticism of Pease's failure to work with Radical factions, along with the placement of Radicals in federal positions, convinced Pease that he had lost the federal support necessary to function effectively. The provisional governor thus resigned from office.[3]

Whatever the personal or political reasons, Carl Moneyhon notes that Pease's departure signaled two options for the voters: Davis, who dutifully obeyed the federal government that was perpetuating the military presence in the state; or Hamilton, who wanted to end the occupation as a matter of reestablishing Texas's autonomy.[4] The media revulsion against all things Radical grew accordingly, as the split between Hamilton and Davis became the new battle for the soul of Texas. The *Houston Tri-Weekly Telegraph* summarized the controversy as the election neared: "It is astonishing that Texas Radicals have not been able to see the utter foolishness of their course. They could have done nothing that could make their defeat more overwhelming than the very thing they have done. While professing to be very liberal, they have shown themselves bitterly proscriptive, by having our officials removed because they support Gen. Hamilton. Thus do they make their professions a mockery."[5] Without major party support, Hamilton campaigned as a more moderate choice than Davis. Davis, and the Republican convention that had nominated him in June, were now synonymous with Radicalism, and the more conservative media outlets of the state were predicting success for Hamilton. Davis campaigned by defending himself against charges of Radicalism while at the same time indicting Hamilton for having sold out his party. He repeatedly emphasized that his stance on the ab initio controversy was an effort to recover money taken from the state education fund and given to the railroads under the Confederate government. By declaring all acts of the legislature under the Confederacy null and void (ab initio), Davis believed that the state could then recover the money, as well as thousands of acres of land that had been granted to speculators. Hamilton and his supporters immediately pounced on this as an effort on the part of Davis to erase every marriage license, land sale, and contract created during the war.[6] Neither Davis nor Hamilton took particularly loud or aggressive public stances on civil rights. Ultimately, Davis would acknowledge that Hamilton was simply more adept at the game of politics, wherever the actual truth lay.

With easily discernable battle lines drawn, virtues became shortcomings and vice versa in the campaign for governor. For the *Houston Tri-Weekly Telegraph,* the political developments of the state amounted to nothing more than a Radical conspiracy, and by this time a vote for Davis meant a vote for Radicalism. The *Houston Tri-Weekly Telegraph* said, "Though Gen. Hamilton was the father and leader of negro suffrage in Texas, the Radicals had managed to sow distrust of him among the negroes, and in the coast counties where the leagues are active, they had lead [*sic*] off the negroes to the support of Davis by making them believe that Gen. Hamilton had sold out to the Democrats."[7] In the same issue, *The Telegraph* endorsed Hamilton for governor and encouraged Davis to withdraw as a matter of duty to Texas. This is a rather telling stance from a media outlet that in 1862 had referred to Hamilton as a "waste of ammunition" and shows the consolidating power of cultural change. There was nothing in *The Telegraph's* track record that would indicate an affinity for Hamilton at all, but in this case, he simply wasn't Davis, which was good enough.

Fortunately for Davis, Texas Democrats did little more than put up a token fight. This was unfortunate for Hamilton, who had hoped to draw Democratic support only to see them effectively abstain from participation. Although Texans would have a choice in the election, the federal government had ensured that it would be a Republican fight. In early October 1869 a state Democratic convention was held in Brenham, and newspaper editor Hamilton Stuart was nominated for governor.[8] Another Harrison County paper, the *Harrison Flag*, decried the Brenham convention as unrepresentative of Texas Democrats, noting a growing sectional divide that was further relegating East Texas interests. Reprinted in Austin's *Tri-Weekly State Gazette*, the *Flag* said:

> The affair at Brenham seems to us little more than a political spree. It is, moreover, remarkable that every candidate for Governor is selected from the West. We think the East is entitled to some consideration. There are now in the field three candidates [Davis, Hamilton, and Stuart] for Governor—all from the West. The West has no right to gag the voice of the people of this section, and if the politicians expect that the East will submit to and endorse everything that is put forth by the cliques which assemble in Austin, Houston, and Brenham, they will reckon without their host.[9]

The Gazette was even less charitable, referring to the Democratic convention as "The Brenham Abortion."[10] More conservative sections of East Texas were clearly feeling the loss of their former political influence, as they were left with no choice but to support the lesser of two evils. For Hamilton this represented an opportunity, for while Davis had made major headway in courting the Black vote and strengthening the prospects for Republicanism, Hamilton would attempt to spin the changing demographics to his favor.

Ultimately, Hamilton could draw neither Black supporters nor wayward Democrats. While never turning away from the enfranchising of the freedmen, he attempted to cast Davis's version of Republicanism as the party of Black rule while trying to appeal to conservative whites.[11] The moderation of his platform (tangible or not) in an effort to become a more conservative Republican movement left loyal Republicans uneasy, and despite the minimal differences between the two on most positions, Davis retained the support of Texas African Americans and the federal government.

Davis's margin of victory in the gubernatorial contest was razor thin, receiving 39,838 votes to Hamilton's 39,055.[12] Statewide, demographics decided the outcome, as Black support for Davis was unified and strong in the face of continued violence and intimidation, while the conservative whites Hamilton hoped to attract simply chose to sit out the contest. Davis, for example, won the predominantly African American voters of Harrison County, receiving 1,847 votes to Hamilton's 570.[13] Republicans similarly dominated the contests for county office. On the North Texas frontier, the people of Collin County, demographically the opposite of their East Texas counterparts, sided with Hamilton by a margin of 723 to 28.[14]

If the landslide results of the gubernatorial election of 1869 weren't the final nail in Republicanism's coffin in Collin County, Davis's actions while in office were. A few media outlets, including the *McKinney Messenger*, expressed cautious optimism based on Davis's previous demonstration of unbiased leadership, particularly over the constitutional convention. As he struggled to maintain his paper's waning legitimacy among local residents, editor Thomas explained: "It is passing strange men will write and even print what they do not believe true. If any ex confederate soldiers voted for General Davis for Governor, they have done nothing of which they need feel ashamed. Governor Davis is a gentleman and a patriot. It is true he is liable to make mistakes like other men, but we know him well enough to feel assured that if he errs he will do so honestly, and with the best of intentions."[15] But his was a lonely voice among the increasingly conservative Texas media, which reviled Davis from the outset. Thomas's political leanings were well-known, and it was also common knowledge that Thomas and Davis were friends, so any attempt to quell fears of the coming Radical administration in Austin among the citizens of Collin County might have been wasted ink. The expectation of a Hamilton victory among Texas newspapers was likely the result of a lack of communication between white and Black communities. The *Houston Tri-Weekly Telegraph*, for example, passed off Black Texans as little more than pawns in Davis's quest for power: "While Hamilton's supporters were thus unorganized and unharmonious, the party organization of the Radicals, effected at Houston, enabled them to march their voters to the polls in solid phalanx, and vote the straight ticket with unquestioned obedience to their file leaders. The colored men turned out with great unanimity, and with alacrity obeyed commands of the [Union] League."[16]

The Davis Administration

With the new constitution ratified by the voters of Texas, General Reynolds having formally handed authority over to the provisional government and a special legislative session called, Edmund J. Davis was inaugurated on April 28, 1870. His inaugural address was focused on reconciliation with promises of representation for all, lest conservative Democrats feel their interests were being forsaken. But suggestions of a coming ideological change in the tone of government was evident in certain parts of Davis's speech. For Davis, assuming leadership of a formerly rebellious state now reentering the Union under terms dictated by the victors, certain inevitabilities had to be accepted before the state could resume moving forward. Slavery was finished and guarantees of civil rights were necessary for readmission, which brought freedom from army rule but also meant new economic and social modes of thinking. Law and order had to be restored quickly, which meant additional unilateral powers

for the chief executive were necessary. Improvements in transportation and education would require additional revenue, which meant
an unavoidable change to tax policy. More than anything, as Davis
stressed to the crowd gathered at the capital, Texas needed a fresh
start and unity of purpose. Davis knew this was a lot to ask in light of
recent history and the steady shifting of Texas culture, and he noted,
"But sensible men can even now agree to accept the situation as they
find it, and after ten years of war and civil disorganization, take a
fresh departure in political affairs."[17]

Historians have long sought to delineate the source of Davis's
personal feelings about taking the reins of power. Removing his
approach to the office from his personal experience during the time of
secession, through the war, and through the first phase of Reconstruction, however, is not possible. More than any other Texas Unionist
involved in politics, Davis possessed an idealism shaped by his war
experience. At the same time, the consolidating political culture that
took Texas out of the Union in 1861 also victimized the opposition of
which he was a prominent part. The state that was so philosophically
consumed with the primacy of local control had also fallen victim to
the forces leading to secession. This was a process that Davis, along
with his fellow Unionists, could ill afford to let happen again: "While
the general government was restrained from all violation of the right
of life, liberty and property, it was conceded that the local government had no such restraint, accordingly local despotism often flour-
ished under the name of State government. There, free speech and
thought was limited by the will of the majority, until individual freedom disappeared. It is not so now, and cannot (it is sufficient to say)
be so hereafter."[18] Here Davis expressed not only the validation of US
constitutional supremacy but also the end of Texas independence in
the sense of how it had existed before 1861. He went on to say, "While
local self-government still remains, it is within the just bounds that
there is supervisory power over all, far withdrawn from local prejudice
and bias, which will temper State action within the limit of security,
freedom, and justice to all."[19] Along with Davis's clear admonition to

former rebels that their dream of state sovereignty would no longer be tolerated in the new America, he is also striking at the political culture that wrought disunion. Under Davis's watch, no longer would the vox populi be the voice of God; rather, the spirit of constitutionalism that focused on the individual in the face of the tyrannical masses would reign supreme. How the people of Texas would adapt to this new reality remained to be seen.

While his inaugural address was relatively brief, his speech to the legislature the following day, April 29, 1870, provided a more specific outline of his policy initiatives and drew political fire from his opponents. The key elements to Davis's plan were the restoration of law and order (including frontier protection), education, and internal improvement. Davis believed the latter two were reasonable Republican solutions to continued state underdevelopment and the roots of lawlessness. His less controversial initiatives involving education and railroads were widely expected, and although they weren't as contentious and represented forward-thinking governance, they would nonetheless stir the passions of the opposition throughout his tenure. The reinstatement of law and order under a civilian government, however, would occupy most of his energies and drain his political capital through the first called session of the Twelfth Legislature. As the people of the borderlands believed themselves to be in an increasingly desperate situation, Davis understood that he was assuming office in unprecedented times, which would require unprecedented solutions: "I esteem this matter of first importance, because, having peace and security for life and property, everything else will follow, of course. I recommend the passage of a law for efficient organization of the militia, embracing all able-bodied males, between the ages of eighteen and forty-five."[20] He followed this with a call for the establishment of a state police force, as well as unilateral gubernatorial powers to react in situations of extreme lawlessness: "These measures will not be complete without such powers are conferred on the Executive as will enable him in any emergency to act with authority of law."[21] For Davis's critics, this controversial measure amounted to nothing less than martial law in the hands of an authoritarian government.

Skeptical Texas newspapers, already dubious of the forthcoming experiment in Radical rule and reflecting traditional American fears of military despotism, expressed astonishment at Davis's proposals on law enforcement. Austin's *Tri-Weekly State Gazette* judged them as autocratic and tyrannical, a sentiment frequently expressed statewide:

> We announce that Edmund J. Davis is paving the way for a centralization of power in the hands of the Governor of the State and the establishment of a despotism in proposing that the Legislature provide for 1st. THE NATIONAL GUARD. 2nd THE ESTABLISHMENT OF MARTIAL LAW IN THE HANDS OF THE EXECUTIVE. Read his suggestions. Will the people any longer dream as to the aims and results of Radicalism and the designs of its leaders! We ask those conscientious Radicals who are actuated by motives springing from their best judgement and who may not see the designs of the leaders to think well and consider the words of Edmund J. Davis and the change he is contemplating. . . . And finally, we ask those Radicals who planned this programme, and Edmund J. Davis as its head, to pause and weigh well the consequences of the establishment of a NATIONAL GUARD and MARTIAL LAW AT PLEASURE OF THE GOVERNOR—pause long and well before they adopt those tools of despotism, those instruments of tyrants.[22]

Houston's *Evening Telegraph* questioned the legality of the exceptional delegation of autocratic power for the executive included in the militia bill: "The constitution clearly contemplates that the power to suspend the writ of Habeas Corpus shall be exercised only by the Legislature, and it never was intended that it should be delegated to the Governor."[23] The *Belton Weekly Journal* was more succinct in its criticism, saying, "Governor Davis spoiled an excellent message by recommending the Martial Law and Police bills."[24]

In Collin County the anger and alarmism expressed by the conservative *McKinney Enquirer* suggested to some readers that Davis's militia and police bills would trigger a violent response. Writing to the editor of the *McKinney Messenger*, one reader pleaded for the state government to acknowledge the impending backlash coming from former Confederates:

> Mr. Editor: Let the President and the Congress of the United States, Gov. Davis and the Legislature of Texas beware, for that rebel sheet, the Weekly Enquirer of this place, in its issue of the 28th ult., in commenting on the militia bill, now under discussion in the legislature, concludes with these words of awful import: "just so sure will the conflict begin."
>
> Is it not surpassing strange that after rebel papers and leaders have been instrumental, as far as they were able, in impoverishing the Southern people, taking from fathers and mothers their dearly loved sons, from sisters their brothers, and from wives their husbands, and when we have in our community, crying for help to sustain them in life, some of the widows and orphans whose husbands and fathers were hung or brutally shot, simply because they would not strike against the country that gave them birth and protection; and after these malcontents, who failed by war to destroy the Union, and with it too much liberty as they asserted and, perhaps, believed, have eagerly sought, and in form at least taken the oath to support the Federal Government, to abide by the laws of Congress and to encourage others to do the same; and further, after the people have said throughout the United States and the State that they do not want those men to rule over them, is it not strange, surpassing strange, that a little rebel sheet in Collin county should threaten, substantially, that if the Legislature dares to pass the militia bill, and its provisions are attempted to be enforced, "just so sure will the conflict begin."
>
> Who will stay the hand of this wicked threatener of the direst of all evils?[25]

With the fearmongering of the state's conservative press driving the population into a frenzy, such an expression of despondency from the minority Republican population made perfect sense, and perhaps further convinced lawmakers in Austin of the righteousness of their actions. The pace at which Davis's policy ideas were enacted by the Texas legislature would make a modern legislator blush with embarrassment. Although some lingering issues involving the establishment of the state school system remained to be resolved, most of Davis's agenda was in place by the time the legislature adjourned in August 1870.[26]

Despite Davis's success in shepherding his bills through the legislature, the common interpretation of his policy actions was less than kind, and he would later pay dearly for his aggressive action. Part of Davis's success in achieving his legislative goals came from parliamentary tactics that some would characterize as forceful, and others as necessary. Either way, he did little to improve his reputation among his enemies. Faced with the prospect of pushing a legislative agenda that secured his own political base (Radicals and Black Texans) in the face of a factionalized majority party, Davis could ill afford to be diplomatic. For example, the Twelfth Legislature under Davis created both a militia bill and a state police force. Debate over the militia bill was particularly contentious and saw an episode that would be repeated in the late twentieth and early twenty-first centuries. Faced with almost certain defeat while opposing the militia bill, the ten Democratic senators and a handful of opposition Republicans chose to walk out of the Senate chamber. This act, according to the rules of the Senate, would break the necessary quorum for Senate work to continue and thus prevent a vote on the bill. The president of the Senate, in turn, ordered the sergeant-at-arms to arrest the dissenting senators for contempt. An investigation was ordered, and eight of the agitators remained under arrest while the militia bill was successfully passed, followed by the similarly controversial bill creating the state police just six days later.[27] Such maneuvering reflected Davis's uncompromising political character, which undoubtedly endeared him to his base, while turning him into an object of scorn among white conservatives.

Unable to comprehend the logic of the dissenting Democratic senators, the *Houston Tri-Weekly Telegraph* was incredulous, presuming the incident was little more than Radical sensationalism while inadvertently predicting the course of events that followed:

> As to the charge that the minority intend to break a quorum, first put out by the Radicals, we gravely doubt it. Our correspondent, Observer has the same impression, as shown in his letter already published, but we think he also mistaken. Such a course would give the Radicals a decided advantage. They would force back just enough to make a quorum and hold them, if need be by force to enable them to carry their measures, and also to expel the absent members. We sincerely hope that the minority will do no such foolish thing, either by leaving for their homes or by resigning. Let them stay and fight the Radicals to the end and thus hold them to a stern responsibility to the people.[28]

Understanding how E. J. Davis, as the face of Texas government, also became the face of Texas Radicalism and therefore a symbol of federal tyranny isn't difficult. The militia bill and state police upset many over their cost, their questionable constitutionality, and the unilateral power bestowed on the governor. Ideologically speaking, this expansion of gubernatorial power came at the expense of local control, which, like so many elements of Davis's administration, went against Texas political tradition. But in a broader sense, by looking at Davis's major policy initiatives individually, along with the justification used by those opposed to them, we can see how Davis's foes were fueled more by a sense of cultural contrarianism than any legitimate ideological motivations.

One example of the opposition's flagrant disregard for deliberative and prudent policy action would be their position on railroads, where the passions of political resistance made them oblivious to their own hypocrisy. Article X of the 1869 Texas Constitution, covering the Land Office, forbade land grants to railroads. Davis had been a vocal supporter of the railroads but conservative in his advocacy and apparently was the only member of the Texas government that had read the 1869 constitution.[29] In his speech to the Twelfth

Legislature, he had acknowledged the widespread prorailroad sentiment among Texans and prioritized the creation of a line from the
Red River to the Rio Grande, with the hope of fostering intrastate
communication.[30] However, Davis was also realistic in his approach
and mindful of the high cost of state support in the past. With little
state revenue presently on hand to fund his initiatives, Davis urged
a conservative approach to railroad development: "The experience
of Texas in subsidizing public works has not been very satisfactory.
We have invested in this way (including principal and interest due
thereon,) near two and three-fourths millions of specie, or its equivalent, and upwards of five millions of acres of our best lands, (worth
fully ten millions more in specie,) and we have somewhat less than
five hundred miles of railroad, which the State has mainly built, (but
does not own or control,) to show for it."[31] Davis advocated a more
free-market approach, with the railroads investing their own financial resources rather than reducing the public domain, which held
enormous future potential for revenue. For his efforts Davis made
enemies of the railroad lobby, which in turn pressured the legislature
to override any vetoes from the governor on railroad development
bills. Davis also lost the support of Senator James Flanagan, formerly
the Texas lieutenant governor. Flanagan expressed his disappointment over the taxes passed by the legislature while simultaneously
berating the governor for his hesitancy to support the railroads.
Moneyhon points out that Flanagan, despite his bluster about taxes,
also held a major financial interest in the Southern Pacific Railroad.
Davis likewise angered Morgan Hamilton, Texas's other US senator,
who coincidentally owned a significant piece of the International
Railroad.[32] With these kinds of friends in his own political party,
Davis hardly needed enemies from the Democratic side. As things
were, Democratic resistance to Davis's miserly approach to railroad
development had already turned most of the state press against him.
For all of Davis's hesitancy, and despite his imploring the legislature to be mindful of retaining Texas public land, most of the railroad development bills passed (over his opposition); as governor he

became the focal point of opposition for many over the higher taxes that resulted.[33]

Another example of a political culture consolidating against its opposition was the creation of a state school system. The state police, itself a relatively small and inexpensive body (less than three hundred officers), had upset some over its cost despite Davis's advocacy of the group simply as a means of quelling unrest when local authorities were unable to do so at a minimum of expense.[34] But it was the omission of a discrimination clause that really shook cultural sensibilities, as the prospect of a Black police officer was a Texas traditionalist's worst nightmare. The same cultural shock was felt over Davis's education plan. Nothing scared conservative Texans more than an educated freedman, and with protections of political rights in place for Black Texans, they had become unified and relatively loyal Republicans. Signed into law in April 1871, the implementation of the centralized state education system took place during that year's congressional electoral campaign and naturally became a flashpoint of controversy. The Black-owned Galveston newspaper, *The Representative*, reprinting an article from the *National Monitor*, summarized the newfound political empowerment felt by freedmen throughout the South: "Let them be educated, then they will shape their own destiny, and will not have need of advice from carpetbaggers of any stripe how to vote so as to protect their rights as citizens."[35] That Davis saw the promotion of schools for Black children as a means to ensure long-term Republican electoral success is fairly obvious and political common sense. At the same time, conservative media outlets had been portraying Black Texans as uneducated since the first days after emancipation. Logic would then dictate that Davis's bill should have won widespread support.

A quick study of the evolving historiography on Texas's opposition to Davis's school bill reveals a repeating process of cultural consolidation focused on resistance to opposition, rather than unified in good sense and policy. Dunning School historians attributed the distaste for Davis's school system to a number of factors, but ultimately settled on anger over state taxes for education. This is not completely unwarranted, as Davis was attacked for every new tax that came along, and the school system was no exception. Revisionists focused more on pure racism at the heart of the controversy, which is also a self-evident point, as white supremacy reigned in both traditionalistic and individualistic sections of the state. Postrevisionist Carl Moneyhon, on the other hand, focuses his argument on political motivations, wherein the Democrats sought to dismantle every aspect of the Radical agenda, no matter the damage they caused to the state and its interests.[36] While such political resistance was certainly palpable, the widespread backlash found in Texas media outlets suggests that resistance to all things Republican was even broader, taking on a widespread cultural character.

Moneyhon's emphasis on politics is compelling, for the record of events post-1872 as Radical power began to dissolve make it clear that the Democrats were willing to place political rivalry over modernization in every conceivable instance. However, this argument is too restrictive, as racially based developments in Collin County prior to the establishment of Davis's school system suggest a larger cultural backlash had been brewing, which was then exploited by the Democrats for political gain. Concurrent with the *McKinney Messenger*'s decline in influence, the conservative *McKinney Enquirer* was gaining readership, validating the argument for greater emphasis on the importance of acknowledging cultural change. In Spring 1870 *The Messenger* reprinted a short comment from the *Enquirer* regarding the establishment of a new school: "We learn that a negro school has been established on the prairie near town, presided over by a genuine, black, greasy, saucy buck negro, who, ten years ago, would have brought $1500, gold. -Enquirer-" *The Messenger*, ever true to its progressive nature, rebutted the *Enquirer*'s racist assault:

> The above paragraph is, to say the least, exceedingly unmanly. The blacks constitute numerically a very small proportion of the population of this county. Had they no other defence, their

very weakness ought to protect them from insult and injury.
The author of the paragraph does not seem to consider that they
are human beings and as such entitled at our hands to encouragement in every laudable undertaking; much less apparently, has he
reflected on the fact that they are citizens, and as such entitled to
the equal protection of the law. We know nothing personally of
the teacher of this school. It is said, however, that he is capable,
and a strict disciplinarian. We hope he is also worthy; and if such
should prove to be the case, it will afford us great pleasure to see
him liberally sustained by the people of his own color, and to
chronicle his success even to a very limited extent, in dispelling
the mental darkness which has so long enshrouded this race.[37]

An expression of racist sentiments in 1870 frontier Texas is hardly
noteworthy. But a mere six weeks later, the aforementioned school on
the edge of town was burned to the ground by arsonists.[38] The acts of
violence and vandalism that had characterized so much of the Deep
South, including East Texas, had taken hold on the significantly less
racially diverse frontier. The self-perpetuating panic of racial doom
had manifested itself in an area with a drastically different demographic makeup than that of Harrison County. The once dissenting
Collin County was now firmly aligned with the conservative elements
of the state.

Due to the enormous political backlash that Davis faced as a
result of the state police and its makeup, the railroads, and the school
system, it was easy for early Texas historians to ignore a number
of things that went right during his time in office. Carl Moneyhon,
one of Davis's chief defenders in the modern era, notes that state
police accumulated an exceptionally good track record of arresting fugitives during its brief existence, only to be overshadowed
by a handful of instances of police abuse.[39] Even Charles Ramsdell,
despite reemphasizing the corruption and unpopularity of the state
police (which was certain), grudgingly acknowledged its necessity.
Ramsdell summarized Davis's unique, and perhaps unwinnable
situation: "In actual fact the liberty and life of every citizen lay in
the governor's hands. It is not easy to prove that Davis consciously

intended to abuse this power; on the contrary it would seem that what others regarded as an abuse he considered a necessary extension of authority."[40] Unfortunately for Davis's political career and historical legacy, actions taken as a matter of necessity in the fight for law and order also established him as the focal point of cultural opposition for the majority of white Texans. Arresting murderers and protecting the racial and political minority fell by the wayside when evaluating the merits of the state police, and the body's mere existence became a symbol of excessive executive power, overcentralization, and a Radical push toward racial equality.

Despite the cultural resistance and exaggeration of the ills of Davis's plan for law enforcement, the first called legislative session produced a number of important policies. The militia bill, technically passed before the divisive creation of the state police, was supported by all as the pressures (or perceived pressures) of the frontier needed immediate action. Davis supported railroad expansion in principle, but was relatively conservative when it came to government land subsidies. His hesitation and vetoes were overridden by a relatively united legislature on this issue, and subsequent legislative sessions saw even more public land pledged in support of the railroads.[41] The bill for establishing a state board of education passed, and had it survived beyond the later purge of Davis's policies, would have done much to improve universal education for Texas children of all races. Still sparsely populated, Texas needed to encourage continued immigration, which the Twelfth Legislature did by authorizing the creation of a state immigration bureau. Had the circumstances that had shaped Texas political culture through the war, Presidential Reconstruction, and Congressional Reconstruction been different, E. J. Davis might have been celebrated as a man of vision who wanted nothing more than to modernize the state.

Implementing the programs of the Republican-led legislature took little time, and incidents of violence throughout the state quickly tested Davis's resolve, the professionalism of the state police, and the impatience of Texas conservatives. The murder of two Black citizens in Hill County in December 1870, for example, inspired little reaction from the local citizenry, the county having already earned a reputation for lawlessness. Likely owing to the social status of one of the suspected murderers (son of the richest man in the county, James Gathings), local law enforcement's response was similarly tepid. Members of the state police were dispatched to Hill County to make arrests only to be arrested themselves, under the pretense of having conducted an illegal search, by a mob of citizens likely led by James Gathings. The officers were released, but Davis had little choice but to proclaim martial law in response to this usurpation of power. The presence of state police enforcing the Davis order only lasted for a week in January 1871, and Hill County stabilized over the subsequent months, but the greater share of the public controversy over the incident involved Gathings and the dispute with Davis over his state police, rather than justice for the murdered freedman and his wife.[42] The fallout from the Hill County fight, along with other incidents, would follow Davis until the day he left office.

The unsympathetic conservative press was relentless in its criticisms. Austin's *Tri-Weekly Gazette*, on the heels of the Hill County fiasco, devoted ample space to its excoriation of Davis. "Time has proved that the lives of the people are not safe in the hands of the State police under the direction of king Davis," the editors proclaimed, "and he must be disarmed of this power to oppress, outrage, imprison, and murder the citizens, by the repeal of the law creating this police army; and it is to be hoped that this legislature, seeing their great error, will have the manliness to do it."[43] A piece from the *Houston Tri-Weekly Telegraph* published in August 1871 in anticipation of the coming election season battered Davis for his unilateral exercise of power:

THE FIRE IS BURNING—Yes the Democratic fire. It is mad from just indignation, and will consume the Radical obstacles in its way. It is manifesting itself all over the State. It shows itself at public meetings, at barbecues, in the virtuous press of the State of all parties, and it burns in the hearts of the people. It is a holy fire, such as burns up vice wherever found. The Radicals have fed it with the militia, police, election, enabling and tax-acts timber. They have fed it by the money subsidy acts to railroads. They have fed it by every act and every step they have taken since they have been in power. It burns and will burn them up.[44]

And the cultural revulsion to the actions of the state police in places like, Hill, Walker, Limestone and Lampasas Counties did remain significant, and the fires of opposition did continue to burn.

In 2012 historian and long-time state archives staffer Donaly Brice convincingly dissected the popularly held conspiratorial viewpoint regarding Davis's master plan for Texas. First, by shocking the citizens of Texas regarding instances of violence throughout the 1868 Constitutional Convention through the Committee on Violence and Lawlessness, Davis could then theoretically achieve the proper level of public concern necessary to implement Radical solutions. The second part of the supposed master plan was the creation of a state police that would become a de facto team of hired thugs that Davis could control at will.[45] This line of thinking took hold in conservative sections of the state. The fact that the state police force was not reserved exclusively for white males only further reinforced a growing perception that Davis sought the most extreme version of Radicalism and authoritarian control. Despite the nickname Negro Police, the state police were actually multiracial and included officers who had fought for both the Union and the Confederacy, although they were predominantly Republican, which was hardly surprising in an era noted for its partisan patronage. While there were acts of violence committed against the state police, the Texas press was far more interested in the acts of violence committed by the force, thus shaping their legacy for generations to come.

In some ways the undoing of Davis and Republicanism in Texas was brought on by factionalism within the party itself. An unlikely oppositional coalition developed as Jack Hamilton spoke out against Davis's police and tax policies, alongside Texas Democrats who were working to reestablish the viability of their own party. Moneyhon goes so far as to argue that Hamilton's efforts to undermine Davis had been occurring since 1868, and it seemed that momentum for the opposition was building rapidly.[46] The oppositional coalition manifested itself in the Tax-Payers Convention of September 1871. Both Jack Hamilton and Elisha Pease were featured speakers, and the Democratic press endorsed their actions, even if it wasn't necessarily a formal coalition between Democrats and oppositional Republicans. Of the tax burden being placed on Texans by Davis's initiatives, the *Weekly Statesman* claimed, "That a great wrong is being done [to] the people of Texas, there can be no doubt. To doubt it, would be the exhibition of an imbecility of intellect, and perversity of spirit, so great as to shock the moral sense of all honest and candid men."[47] In fact, a number of traditionally Republican newspapers had never ceased their enthusiasm for Hamilton, as his reputation for being a devout and progressive Unionist stretched further than that of Davis. Although many Texans were still having difficulty deciding who to support politically, it had become clear whom they did *not* support.

The year 1871 saw all four Texas seats in the US Congress up for grabs and would signal a drastic change in Texas political momentum, as growing numbers of whites returned to the polls, the army's control having ended with the return of a legitimately recognized civilian government. The sense of unity among Democrats that propelled four conservative Democrats to victory in that election is obvious from contemporary media accounts. Further fueling the consolidation of the oppositional party was Davis himself, who, in anticipation of electoral violence assumed control of all police forces for protection at the polls in early October.[48] This attempt to guarantee police protection for all Texans, regardless of color, was turned into a perceived act of autocracy, and the threat served to unify Texas Democrats. Fighting the fires stoked by the changing political culture of Collin County, the steadfast *McKinney Messenger* stood by Davis, printing a letter from a Kentucky transplant who appreciated Davis's aggressive actions in protecting the vote: "The people in this county need severe rules and laws. I wish Governor Davis would issue an order to fine any bully $500 and two years imprisonment for carrying concealed weapons, or even making threats to law abiding citizens."[49] That same issue of the *Messenger* went on to proclaim that complaints and indictments of Davis's so-called tyranny were "grossly incorrect" and that his actions were merely meant to "interdict shouting and riotous conduct immediately at the polls."[50] Unfortunately for Davis, perception is reality. Violence and intimidation at the polls did occur in both 1871 and 1872, yet Davis suffered politically by attempting to address it. At the same time the *McKinney Messenger* was downplaying the significance of Davis's election order, Austin's *Tri-Weekly Democratic Statesman* was openly daydreaming about what the next session of the Texas legislature might bring in response: "As to the impeachment of Governor Davis, we can only say that any man who will undertake that measure will entitle himself to a crown of unfading glory and the everlasting gratitude of a once free people."[51] For all of Davis's best intentions, his autocratic wielding of power was quickly developing into his own undoing.

1872: The Democrats Regain Control of the Texas Legislature

With Democratic victory in 1871, it was clear that the fire of conservative resistance was still burning, and for Davis, looking ahead to the Texas legislative elections in 1872, the result was a grim foreshadowing. Across the South a new policy movement was taking shape that would serve as the precursor for the Redeemer Democrats who would dismantle Davis's legacy and install Texas's painfully flawed constitution in 1876. What some historians have dubbed the New Departure for the Democratic Party was based on building political success from the bottom up, with an acceptance of the temporary reality of Black suffrage and the Reconstruction Acts as fixtures of the new political reality. Addressing this trend, the *Weekly Democratic Statesman* said:

> In fighting the common enemy, an invitation is extended to all good men "whatever may have been their past political

preference, to unite with the Democratic party in removing from place and power those who now control the State Government, in order to release the people from oppressive revenue and unequal taxation, to insure an honest administration of laws and an honest and economical expenditure of the public moneys and to throw the aegis of justice and protection over the person and property of every individual whatsoever in the State of Texas," in the language of the platform itself. We fight standing on that platform, and most earnestly desire that every good man within the broad limits of the State, will come to our help, and the help of the Democracy, to aid in putting a stop to the vice, demoralization, and crime, now daily, if not hourly, perpetrated by the thieves, robbers, and cut-throats, who in one shape and another control the State Government.[52]

The New Departure, at least in the case of Texas, brought a new sense of unity by dropping some of the more hardline conservative positions in favor of a reorganized and refocused Democratic Party devoted to electoral success and reclaiming political victories within the established system.

The ultimate dissolution of the state police was not the only act of revenge against Radicalism sought out by the Texas Democratic Party, but it certainly carried the most emotional and cultural weight. With controversial incidents involving state police officers as ammunition, the Texas press had little difficulty keeping emotions high going into the state elections of 1872. Along with a presidential election, the entire state House of Representatives and one-third of the Texas Senate were up for grabs. Texas Democrats, alongside dissenting Republicans, routinely attacked Davis on the issue of taxes, which immediately put his state education system in jeopardy.[53] Also threatening Davis's legislative accomplishments were accusations of corruption against several of his appointees, including Superintendent of Public Instruction Jacob C. DeGress and Adjutant General James Davidson, chief of the dreaded and feared state police. Unfounded claims of malfeasance against DeGress would later inspire a House investigative committee on the second day of the Thirteenth Legislature.[54] And while DeGress would retain his reputation throughout the scandal, the mere accusation was enough to drag Davis down during the 1872 election. Davidson did even more to bring Davis down, disappearing from Texas altogether after the discovery of significant embezzlement in his office.[55] For the already hostile press, this was a gift that confirmed their brewing suspicions.

The Democratic victory in 1872 saw a transfer of power in both the Texas House and Senate. In so doing it also revealed the changing political cultures of Harrison and Collin Counties. Although the Democratic triumph was not as complete as the 1871 election might have portended, the trends indicating the Republican decline were obvious. Three thousand fewer Republicans turned out to vote in 1872, contributing to the loss of legislative control.[56] With the army moved to the state's frontier, declining Republican voting numbers, less money for effective campaigning as the national party decided Texas was unwinnable, and continuing intimidation and violence at the polls, the days of Texas Radicalism were numbered.[57] Nationally, the Democrats had thrown their support behind Horace Greeley, running for president as a Liberal Republican, as the most likely means for defeating the incumbent Grant. Although Greeley lost on the national stage, Texans supported Greeley, who took 66,455 votes to Grant's 47,426.[58] Also at stake were two new congressional seats resulting from the 1870 census. Democrats Roger Quarles Mills and William Pinckney McLean, both former Confederate officers, cruised to easy victory. Harrison County voters, including many Blacks still staunchly Republican in sentiment, overwhelmingly voted for Republican candidates who lost. Collin County, now firmly Democrat, strongly supported Greeley, Mills, and McLean.[59]

But the most telling development was, of course, the Democratic dominance in the Texas legislature. The Thirteenth Legislature wasted little time when it convened in January of 1873, dismantling everything built under Radical rule. The state police were repealed. An unpopular printing law, which Charles Ramsdell later referred to as little more than creating a Republican propaganda machine, was repealed. The militia act that had empowered Davis's autocratic exercise of power was amended to remove the governor's power to declare martial law.[60] The Texas press wasted no time in proclaiming the dawn of a new era as Davis's legislation was decimated piece by piece. As Brice points out, following the repeal of the State Police Act by the Thirteenth Legislature in 1873, the *Dallas Daily Herald* included a special insert reading, "THE SCEPTER OF THE TYRANT BROKEN! THE CHAINS SHATTERED! THE PEOPLE FREE!"[61] Despite all exaggerations, what Davis perceived as not only proper in his role but also essential for rebuilding the state represented nothing short of despotism in the eyes of the general public, still reeling from the war and clinging to dreams of antebellum life.

Davis Voted Out

The term *lame duck* is normally applied to an executive that his completing his or her tenure in office and unable to seek further terms. Although Davis would run for reelection in 1873, he was essentially completing his term in office with no reasonable chance for reelection. His school system, his conservative approach to railroad development, and his state police force were all long gone. The Texas Republican Convention, held in Dallas in August 1873, reiterated principles that the party believed were sacred and universal: free public schools, equal protection regardless of race, encouragement of immigration, encouragement of railroads (short of land grants), and economy in government affairs. *The McKinney Messenger* lauded Davis's speech officially accepting his party's nomination as "a remarkable and vigorous production."[62]

The Texas Republican strategy in 1873 was, in addition to preserving whatever they could from Davis's agenda, about reframing the contest through a class lens. Republicans now claimed to be the party of the common man while presenting Democrats as representing moneyed interests like large landowners and railroad speculators.[63] Given the Democratic attack on the school system, which would have benefited all Texans regardless of class, and the overly liberal advocacy of railroad interests, this point is difficult to argue with. Unfortunately, the power of cultural forces shaping individual behavior are strong enough to surpass an individual person's critical reasoning. The result is a governmental choice that goes against rational self-interest.

Harrison County, reflecting its demographics, voted for Davis 2,313 to 997 but was ultimately unable to impact the state result in 1873.[64] Collin County, one of the few areas defiant and independent enough to resist the tide of secession years before, voted for Democrat Richard Coke over Davis by a margin of 1,500 votes, a landslide victory for the former Confederate captain who had voted for secession as a delegate to the convention in 1861.[65] Texas Republicans, most notably Davis, had not given up the fight, but the governorship of Richard Coke would be the nail in the Republican coffin and would saddle the state with political changes that resonate today.

The steady decline in influence experienced by the *McKinney Messenger* occurred simultaneously with the changing political culture of Collin County, and James Waller Thomas would struggle for the next two years to maintain a viable newspaper devoted to preserving the voice of the minority opposition. Meanwhile, Robert Loughery was experiencing financial difficulties in maintaining the *Weekly Times and Republican*, which was his merger of the *Texas Republican* and the *Jefferson Daily Times*. As reported by the *Messenger*, in August 1873 he was seeking a partner to keep his publication afloat.[66] The next two years would see Loughery return to prominence with the short-lived *Galveston Times* and the more successful *Tri-Weekly Herald*, again located in Marshall.

Davis Leaves Office . . . Eventually

Much of Davis's downfall was attributable to the loss of political will in Washington, DC, as President Grant and others simply had no more energy to waste trying to stop the cultural tide that had resisted Reconstruction and ended Texas Republicanism. This was also the case in the infamous post-election standoff between Davis and Coke, an incident that Carl Moneyhon believes was heavily exaggerated but nonetheless became part of the collective memory and defined the early historiography. The early histories made much of Davis's refusal to leave office because it reaffirmed suspicions about his character, pointed to a larger Republican conspiracy, and gave the Redeemer Democrats all the ammunition they needed when they got the opportunity to destroy his legacy.

On January 6, 1874, the Texas Supreme Court ruled in the case of *ex parte Rodriguez* that the 1873 election was invalid and unconstitutional because it did not meet the polling station requirements of the 1869 Texas Constitution. The actual basis of the case involved Joseph Rodriguez, a man arrested for voting more than once in Harris County. Rodriguez was represented by Chauncy Sabin and Jack Hamilton, who found himself returning to the Republican fray after his ideological split with Davis a few years before. Sabin and Hamilton argued that the 1869 constitution provided for elections held at county seats and with polls open for four days.[67] Because these requirements were not met, the court held that the election was invalid and Rodriguez should be released. Davis, always a man of the law, interpreted this to mean that he would remain in office, at least in the interim until the legal questions were sorted out and he received word from President Grant. The result was a controversy where the legend became significantly more compelling than the reality.

Despite Richard Coke being inaugurated as governor on January 15, 1874, Davis refused to leave office because of the court's decision, and a crisis of legitimacy briefly ensued. Davis, feeling he was acting in accordance with the law, requested federal troops for protection against a mob of angry Coke supporters. Thomas Benton Wheeler, the mayor of Austin during the standoff, had been previously removed from his position as Travis County attorney during the purge of ex-Confederates deemed impediments to Reconstruction.[68] In a 1907 piece entitled "Reminiscences of Reconstruction in Texas," Wheeler recalled factions of Coke and Davis supporters on the edge of a violent melee, where the forces of good ultimately triumphed when the oppressive forces of Davis backed down. Wheeler's is a personal account told three decades after the fact and clearly meant to demean Davis, Reconstruction, Black Texans, and, to a certain extent, the federal government, while praising Coke and all Redeemer Democrats.[69] Carl Moneyhon's account of the event is characterized by fewer fireworks and describes a Davis who adhered more to the letter of the law than any political passions.

In addition to the *Rodriguez* decision, Davis had other reasonable grounds for refusing to leave office, as his inauguration under the 1869 constitution had taken place on April 28, 1870, which should have given him an additional three months in office. Observing the Fourteenth Legislature gathering in Austin in January, and corresponding with Coke, who was explicitly demanding the delivery of the executive office, Davis's sense that his office was being usurped in an extralegal manner would not have been completely baseless. The Democratic leadership was pointing to Davis's appointment by General Reynolds in January of 1870 as the beginning of his term, while the attorney Davis was considering the matter constitutionally.[70] According to the constitution, Davis had a four-year term beginning with his inauguration in April 1870. Communications between Davis and Coke hint at Davis's heartfelt belief that the legitimacy of his governorship rested on the supremacy of the United States government, above all. On January 17, Davis wrote to Coke, "I, therefore, now propose to you to submit the question of recognition of the legitimate State government to the Executive or Congress of the United States, or to both. As the Executive of the United States is bound, under the Constitution, to sustain the legitimate State Government against domestic violence, this question is a proper one for him to solve. I pledge myself to abide the decision to be thus made, and will advise all good citizens to do the same."[71] Ultimately, despite Davis's questions over the *ex parte Rodriguez* decision and confusion over the official start date of his term, President Grant refused to dispatch the army and Davis abided by his promise to relinquish the office.[72] The larger point of the Coke-Davis fiasco is twofold. On the one hand, the Democrats, who now held a mandate based on the will of the people, believed they were entitled to assume control regardless of legal technicalities,

Predominantly Democrats and ideologically disunified, the delegates to the
1875 convention shaped a document that satisfied few. The final product the
delegates created was so staunchly devoted to economy and limiting power
that it violated many basic standards for a good plan of governance.
1/170-01, courtesy of the Texas State Library and Archives Commission.

and any effort in opposition to such should be construed as illegal and authoritarian. On the other hand, the victors in both war and politics have final say over the shaping of the historical narrative, and Thomas Wheeler's account of the events became the collective memory for a very long time. While James Waller Thomas at the *McKinney Messenger* reprinted correspondences between Coke and Davis, he provided limited commentary on the matter aside from occasional use of the word "usurpation."[73] Meanwhile, Austin's *Tri-Weekly Democratic Statesman* went to great lengths to expound upon Davis's crimes against humanity: "We have nothing to hope or expect from Governor Davis. He will go just as far as he dares go and the Federal government will back. He hates the people of Texas, whom he knows he has injured and offended past all thought of pardon, and he will do the worst he can—mark our words."[74] Davis was not the only Union man to be tarnished in the historical memory, but he became the final symbol of Radical tyranny. After Davis the governor's mansion would not be occupied by a Republican until Bill Clements was inaugurated in January 1979, 105 years later.

Chapter 5

The Texas Constitution of 1876

A lthough Texas's experience in both war and Reconstruction was unique, there were certain commonalities it shared with the Deep South. Relatively unscathed physically and never characterized by a sizable Federal presence, Texans nonetheless felt a comparable sense of loss at their core. This, combined with what many saw as continuing humiliation from the Yankee conquerors throughout the Reconstruction era, was sufficient to consolidate the state's political culture in a manner that did not exist prior to 1861. But political defiance alone does not yield a political culture that is self-perpetuating to the point of permanence. This can only be achieved institutionally, and the tide of public pressure following Radical rule demanded a new constitution.

The period following the downfall of the Davis administration represents the institutional culmination of a cultural evolution begun in 1861. And while it did not result in the perfect realization of the goals of the Democratic Party, it does provide a valuable insight into the natural functioning of a political culture predicated upon resistance and hatred, and very little else. By the time of the Constitutional

Convention of 1875, the very concept of *Radical* had become increasingly amorphous, and the surging conservative Democratic majority had adopted a with-us-or-against-us mentality. Having abandoned the most virtuous practices of good democracy, the convention majority ultimately produced a supreme law that satisfied almost nobody.

Dismantling Davis's Legacy

The Thirteenth Texas Legislature had already undone most of Davis's work before Richard Coke took office. On their second day in session, a bill to repeal the state police was presented in the Texas House of Representatives. Davis's veto was then overridden by the House and Senate on the nineteenth and twenty-second of April, 1873, respectively, and the state police ceased to exist.[1] The Thirteenth Legislature also passed a new school bill that dismantled Davis's program, which had put roughly half of the state's children in school in 1871. Incorporation of new railroads and the provision of public land subsidies also continued despite Davis's wishes and previously mentioned constitutional prohibitions.[2] The Thirteenth Legislature had also seriously considered constitutional revision. The matter found great support in the Texas House of Representatives but did not fare well in the Senate.[3] Despite the common cry from the Texas press, the Senate remained frugal regarding government expenditures in general and practical on the mass psychological effects of frequently rewriting the organic law according to the swinging pendulum of public opinion. The majority (Republican dominated) report from the Senate Committee on Constitutional Amendments noted that: "Our State has had a surfeit of constitutional conventions; three such bodies assembled within seven years would be more than any State could stand. What we now desire is peace, and we submit that the assembling of a body to make radical changes in our fundamental law will not tend to the pacification of our State. There are many other reasons which suggest themselves, and might be given why it is inexpedient at this time to call a constitutional convention, not least of which is the expense such a body would inflict upon our already tax ridden people."[4] Repeated calls for economy and retrenchment would appear later at the convention in 1875 in such a way as to expose Democratic hypocrisy and disunion. Statewide, the level of satisfaction with party leadership, both Republican and Democratic, was waning. Although the people of Collin County had undergone a significant change of public opinion over the course of the war and Reconstruction, little had happened to genuinely endear them to the leadership of the Democratic Party. The populism that would define much of American agrarian life at the tail end of the nineteenth century had yet to develop into any sort of clearly discernible national movement. However, ideologically similar movements were growing regionally and achieving significant popularity for their renunciation of the major political parties in lieu of agrarian interests. Identifying the impact of protopopulist movements at the Constitutional Convention of 1875 is another exercise in differentiating between the myth and the reality of early Texas Reconstruction historiography.

When Coke assumed office after the short standoff with Davis, calling a new constitutional convention was not part of his initial legislative agenda. The great sense of urgency in destroying Texas Republicanism that came from the Thirteenth and Fourteenth Legislatures eventually changed his mind. In his address to a joint session of the Fourteenth Texas Legislature on January 26, 1874, Coke acknowledged an emotional tide demanding a repudiation of Republicanism that went much further than routine legislation: "It is admitted on all hands that the Constitution of Texas must be extensively and radically amended, or a new one adopted in the regular mode in a convention to be assembled for the purpose. The country expects and demands a thorough change in many essential points, not necessary to be enumerated here, of the organic law."[5] The commonly held belief that a new constitution was essential for erasing Republicanism and moving Texas forward under unified Democratic principles had been prevalent since the election of 1872. Early Texas constitutional historian Seth McKay noted that leading Democrats were hesitant to call a convention too quickly, lest they invite federal interference. Yet the belief in its necessity was almost unanimous, despite having no coherent argument for doing so other than the fact that the constitution of 1869 was crafted by Republicans.[6] The Coke-Davis fiasco demonstrated that federal interference was becoming less of a concern as time passed, so anti-Republican passion was considered a sufficient condition for a new constitution. Historian John Walker Mauer noted a lack of public debate found in Texas newspapers concerning the necessity of a new constitution, for the common sentiment was already strongly against the 1869 document. However, the controversy over the best means for doing so fell largely below the public's radar, as much of it was restricted to legislative committees that garnered little press attention.[7]

Coke's noncommittal stance on the issue in his January 26 address illustrates more a lack of Democratic consensus on the best means for drafting a new organic law and less a hesitancy to follow through with dramatic constitutional revision. Suggesting possible methods for reform such as a constitutional convention, extensive amending through a joint legislative committee, or a new document produced by legislative commission, Coke's admonition only hints at his personal preference regarding the potential cost of a convention: "If the desired changes are made in the constitution, the mode in which the result is accomplished does not seem to me to be material, except so far as the expense is concerned."[8] Naturally, the cost associated with a joint legislative committee during a regular session would pale in comparison to that of a new convention. However, the idea of a regular legislative session drafting a new organic law via a commission, an action beyond the realm of any routine legislative business, could only be interpreted as a momentary political passion. Indeed, the House and Senate split on the issue in the first session of the Fourteenth Legislature, with the House endorsing a commission established by the legislature for drafting the new constitution and the Senate preferring a convention voted upon by the people. The House minority report strongly chastised the majority for its "anti-democratic" actions that could only be interpreted as a fear of the will of the people.[9]

Over the course of 1874, pressure for a new constitution grew into a common acceptance that it was merely a matter of when, not if, it would happen. Correctly anticipating the tide of advocacy that would come from the Democratic press, James Waller Thomas at the *McKinney Messenger* focused squarely on his old rival Robert Loughery in his commentary on February 12: "Loughery is the little man who undertook to prove in his paper that the assassination of Lincoln was praiseworthy. Of course he will approve the murder of the State constitution."[10] At this point the *Messenger* was experiencing financial difficulties and advocated against the calling of a new convention for the sake of economy and general apathy among the voters. Reprinting Senator L. D. Bradley's objections to a new convention, the *Messenger* reflected a commonly held sentiment among Republican news sources: "The holding of a convention for the purpose of framing a new Constitution, to be composed of 90 or 120 members, it is estimated, will require a sum of not less than $300,000, and will probably exceed that amount. . . . Practical observation, by those who made the political canvass preceding the last election, has convinced a number of the members of the Legislature that the masses of the people, though sound in sentiment, are tired of elections."[11]

In December 1874, during his short time operating the *Galveston Times*, Robert Loughery took the opportunity to advocate for a new constitution, perhaps even suggesting that it was a foregone conclusion, when commenting on a new usury (lending) law, as reprinted in *The Times Picayune* from New Orleans: "The Galveston Times says: The great majority of the newspapers of the State are in favor of the usury law. Of course, like many other grievances under which the people are laboring, there can be no relief from usurers until a new constitution is framed."[12]

By the second session of the Fourteenth Legislature, Governor Coke had shed any past inhibitions about a new convention when he addressed a joint session on January 12, 1875: "Necessity forced it [the 1869 Constitution] on the people of Texas, and held it on them until the first meeting of your honorable bodies. Prudence and policy, prompted submission to it from then, until this time. No reason exists now for longer submitting to it. The causes which one year ago rendered it imprudent to call together a constitutional convention, have ceased to exist and the time and temper of the people are propitious for the work of constructing a new constitution."[13] State senator, former Confederate lieutenant colonel, and longtime vocal critic of the 1869 constitution David Browning Culberson presented a joint resolution for a constitutional convention later that day.[14] Having passed the Senate and the House later in the session, the measure was subsequently sent to the people of Texas, who were allowed to decide and choose delegates in August 1875.

Voters of Collin County, now firmly enmeshed in the strengthening conservative climate of Texas politics, supported a convention by 1,154 to 88, a resounding statement on their political cultural shift.[15] Despite the reemergent voice of Robert Loughery as the editor of Marshall's *Tri-Weekly Herald* in early 1875, Harrison County, a bastion of Southern tradition before emancipation, now boasted an overwhelmingly Black majority and thus opposed the convention 2,338 to 839.[16] Loughery, like his Democratic newspaper colleagues, had nonetheless hammered home an alarmist message centered on excessive taxation, convincing *Tri-Weekly Herald* readers that if a new constitution were not created, nothing short of storming the Bastille would alleviate their suffering: "From an overflowing treasury, the State is now involved in a debt of millions; from taxation that was scarcely felt, the burden has accumulated, until every species of industry and enterprise feels its crushing weight; and now, with credit impaired, the vast resources of the State squandered or frittered away, the grave responsibility is left the people of endeavoring to arrest the evil, by providing a good government, which, if consummated, will lighten their taxes and bring with it, in the end, renewed prosperity."[17] The new constitution, reasoned Loughery, would erase the last vestiges of Davis and Republicanism, providing for decentralized power, shorter terms of office for state officials at lower salaries, local control over segregated schools, lower taxation and state expenditures, and continuing land subsidies for railroads.[18]

Amplifying the already present cultural forces that had transformed once moderate places like Collin County since 1861, most

Texas newspapers were unabashed, explicit, and ideologically similar in their expectations of the convention. Newspapers frequently stated their platforms along with endless editorializing about specific issues, most of which can be summarized as the antithesis of Radical Republicanism. On August 28, 1875, the *Tri-Weekly State Gazette* numerated its specific policy preferences, each of which carried a deeper ideological significance for the overall structure of the new constitution:

> The election of the Supreme, District, and County Court Judges by the people. A reduction in the number of District Judges, as well as their salaries. The election of the Attorney General, Secretary of State and State Reporter by the people. A reduction in the tenure of office of all State officers, from four to two years.[19] A reduction of State taxes and limitations on the power of counties to tax beyond a maximum rate. A limitation on the power of the Legislature to create State debt. A return to the old road law. Uniform taxation and no exemptions whereby the burdens of taxation shall be increased upon the people. Power in the Legislature to pass a usury law. The Constitution of 1845, a basis of the new constitution. The Legislature to fix by law qualifications of petit grand jurors.[20]

Each of these points was a direct repudiation of Davis's perceived autocracy and a clear plea for a less professionalized government at a reduced cost. Popularly elected judges as opposed to gubernatorial appointments, separately elected executive officers (effectively creating a plural executive), and reduced term limits would each be addressed at the convention and would facilitate the creation of a heavily constrained state government.[21]

Much like the participants in the Secession Convention of 1861, the delegates to the 1875 Constitutional Convention were a snapshot of the Texas political culture at that moment. One delegate had been present at the convention in 1845, and another had been part of the 1866 convention. Eight delegates had been present at the 1861 Secession Convention, and none of the delegates had taken part in the writing of the 1869 Texas Constitution.[22] Ninety delegates represented the people of Texas, 75 of which were Democrat, while a mere 15 were Republican. That split became 76–14 after one Republican delegate resigned.[23] Owing largely to its newfound Black majority, Harrison County was represented by David Abner (one of only five Black delegates at the convention) and Stillwell H. Russell. Collin County was represented by Edward Chambers and John H. "Rutabaga" Johnson, who earned his nickname owing to his connection to the Patrons of Husbandry, or the Grange, the key protopopulist movement of the time. Johnson's reputation as a Granger would earn him widespread attention, and his reputation would in time would be misleadingly applied to the entire body of delegates.[24]

Indeed, the Patrons of Husbandry had been embraced by the residents of Collin County almost from the start. Perhaps in an effort to reclaim the waning influence of his *McKinney Messenger*, James Waller Thomas now published an increasing barrage of Grange-related articles, which dealt with the agrarian issues of interest to potential readers. But while Thomas had previously commanded respect in Collin County, by 1875 he no longer enjoyed the same level of confidence. John Johnson, on the other hand, was considered the very embodiment of the people. Born in North Carolina and growing up uneducated in abject poverty, Johnson was self-made and had even accumulated enough wealth in Missouri during the decades prior to his move to Texas to purchase enslaved people. Always outspoken in his politics, Johnson had served in the Missouri legislature before moving to Collin County at the time of secession in 1861 and served as an officer in the Confederate Army.[25] Revered in Collin County, Johnson now spoke for the individualistic frontier culture in a way that James Waller Thomas no longer could.

Following the credentialing and swearing in of delegates, the first order of business when the convention met on September 6, 1875, was the selection of a president. On the second round of voting that honor was given to Democratic state legislator and former Confederate lieutenant colonel Edward Bradford Pickett of Liberty.[26] Governor Coke's message to Pickett on the second day of the convention emphasized the importance of an "honest, economical, efficient and free government."[27] Robert Loughery's commentary in Marshall's *Tri-Weekly Herald* that same day reiterated Governor Coke's call for economical government: "Retrenchment should be the watchword, and carried out practically in the administration of public affairs. Not that character of petty retrenchments exhibited by the 14th Legislature, which confined itself to diminishing the number of clerks and pages, and of stinting various offices at the Capital to a starving basis, while it squandered thousands of dollars on other purposes of no particular urgency, but an economy that will prevent all injudicious expenditures, and place a barrier to legislative extravagance."[28] Interpretation of the word "economical" quickly snowballed into a matter of serious debate on the third day as the question of a five-dollar versus four-dollar per diem and compensation for delegate travel drew a broad range of opinions.

The majority resolution of five dollars per day in compensation for convention delegates was itself less than previous legislatures, and the cost-cutting spirit was nearly unanimous. The compensation matter became a debate for deciphering the very will of the constituents, with few delegates willing to speak on behalf of the adage that you get what you paid for. William Thomas Green Weaver of frontier Cooke County had been a reluctant Confederate and had presided over the postwar trial of the kangaroo court "jurors" suspected of carrying out the Great Hanging of Gainesville in 1862.[29] His progressive views regarding women's suffrage would later draw criticism from fellow delegates, but on the third day, he reminded the body that their decision would set a precedent for all future legislatures. The delegates were there to reform on the question of taxation, explained Weaver, a matter that included salaries.[30] The folksy witticisms of John Johnson during the compensation debate drew laughs and gave him his "Rutabaga" reputation, but they also revealed the expectations of his constituents back in Collin County. *The Debates of the Texas Constitutional Convention of 1875* summarized his point: "With reference to the rate of pay at which gentlemen could afford to serve the people, as good men as he could be hired in his neighborhood at a dollar a day and board themselves. His constituency did not propose to send men of the highest talent to represent them, because the people had had too much of talent."[31] And indeed, the finagling over what seemed a minor administrative matter for the convention would later have great significance for the Texas Constitution itself. While the pressure of retrenchment brought to the convention by Rutabaga Johnson may have defied good governmental sense, it was nonetheless the product of a cultural shift in Collin County. And while the zeitgeist demanded the economical administration of government, extreme retrenchment was a short-sighted approach to drafting the state's fundamental law and ultimately led to suboptimal final product.

The pursuit of retrenchment impacted numerous elements of the convention while establishing a precedent of such miserliness that it's a wonder Texas was left with a government at all. Republishing a column from the *Shreveport Times*, the *Dallas Daily Herald* on September 18, 1875, sharply criticized the behavior of convention delegates, which would subsequently leave Texas ill fit for modernization:

> Upon the other hand, there are members of the body whom one wonders to see in an assemblage called together by the enlightened people for the very important purpose of framing the organic law of a great and rapidly growing State; men of good intentions, but who have absolutely no comprehension of the work entrusted to their wisdom. They have taken up the cry of "retrenchment and reform," and like parrots they scream it into the ears of the Convention, in and out of season. If a motion is made to allow the members postage stamps, this class, in the interest of "retrenchment and reform," are ready to waste three hundred dollars worth of Convention time in debating a resolution to reduce the number allowed each member two or three stamps.[32]

It is not difficult to ascertain who the subject in question was, as the press's disdain for delegates like John Johnson was growing rapidly. The salience of the Rutabagas in the formation of the organic law will be discussed further below, but the general tide of restriction and retrenchment left a deep impression of underprofessionalization that remains meaningful today.

Nearly a century later, as momentum for constitutional reform was building in the early 1970s, the theoretical significance of lawmaker pay was brought to public attention. Along with an urgent plea that legislative compensation be set by statue rather than constitutionally, the Citizens Conference on State Legislatures (part of the combined effort at Texas constitutional reform) emphasized the importance of the matter for guaranteeing a more professionalized legislature: "Our own view is that it is better, in general, to err on the side of over-compensation in order to make as broad as possible the sources of potential candidates for the Legislature. Such potential breadth of representation and the resulting diversity of views and backgrounds in participating in legislative deliberations seems well worth paying a minimum full-time wage for what may be less than full-time service."[33] When the Eighty-Seventh Texas Legislature convened in Austin in January 2021, they continued to work for a paltry annual salary of $7,200. Although the per diem rate of $210 set by the Texas Ethics Commission dramatically improved overall compensation, it was not nearly to a level that would ensure legislative professionalization on par with comparably sized states. For example, according to the National Conference of State Legislatures, in 2020 California (the only state larger than Texas) legislators earned an annual salary of $114,877.[34] While there was and remains a widespread cultural preference in Texas for the archetype of the citizen-legislator performing their work out of an honorable sense of duty, some fundamental questions arise when considering the ramifications of legislative underprofessionalization in a state with a higher population than Australia.

Political scientist Peverill Squire's analysis of state legislatures utilized the US Congress as a benchmark for measuring legislative professionalism, defined as "the capacity of both individual members and the organization as a whole to generate and digest information in the policy-making process."[35] Squire, the preeminent political scientist on the matter, conceptualized legislative professionalism upon the variables of salary and benefits, time demands of service, and staff and resources. According to his professionalization ranking, Texas moved from twenty-fourth in the nation in 1979 to fifteenth in 2003, nowhere close to the top-rated state, California, but respectable and still fitting for the expectations of the Texas political culture.[36] However, the point of highlighting the development of professionalism in the legislature is not to denigrate the capabilities of Texas's elected officials, nor is it to point out the obvious restrictive demographic nature of a body composed only of legislators who are wealthy enough to independently support themselves for 140 days every two years. Rather, the debate's real significance lay in the constitutional legacy of severely limited government.

Article III, Section 24, of the Texas Constitution covers both member compensation and the duration of regular legislative sessions. This section was amended five times between 1876 and 1991, requiring the normal mechanism of amendment, which included ratification by popular vote of the people.[37] In addition to the expenditures associated with holding elections, this reveals what is perhaps the greatest flaw in the Texas Constitution of 1876: its very structure. Article I, Section 8, Clause 18, of the US Constitution, known as the "necessary and proper" clause, allows the US Congress the flexibility of implied powers that are conducive to the execution of its enumerated powers.[38] In other words, the US Congress fulfills its duty through appropriate means without altering the constitution itself. The Texas Constitution does not contain such a clause and the Texas legislature does not enjoy a similar luxury. The Texas Constitution requires that all powers be enumerated in the constitution itself, requiring a multitude of amendments to keep the government going.

Article XVII lays out the process of amendment, a measure necessary for any constitution, but its significance in Texas is especially important. With the legislature and the governor both constrained by a fundamental law that does not allow for necessary and proper changes or any semblance of implied powers, the only means for changing the law becomes amendments, which voters ratify by a simple majority. In this way the Texas Constitution defies the very simple premise purported by constitutional law scholars that the best kind of constitution is short and vague. The 1875 delegates also failed to take heed of the words of Governor Richard Coke, who explicitly addressed this point the previous year: "It will be found universally true that those State constitutions which contain the smallest number of provisions, which adhere most closely to fundamental declarations, and to the fixing simply of boundaries, leaving the interior to be filled by the enactments of the legislatures, have been the wisest and most enduring."[39]

As amendments have been added over time, the Texas Constitution has come to resemble a code of law rather than a fundamental plan of government. It is ironic that following the conclusion of the compensation debate on the third day, another resolution proposed using the Texas Constitution of 1845 as the very basis for revision, requiring copies be distributed to the various committees designing the new document.[40] While some elements of Texas's first state constitution would be adopted in 1875 (biennial sessions, short terms), the spirit of brevity that has earned the constitution of 1845 praise from scholars was not. The cultural backlash against Radical Republicanism would manifest itself in the extraordinarily restrictive language of the new supreme law, impacting the structure of the three branches as well as local-level policy on tax rates, education, and railroads.

Readers of the 1876 Texas Constitution will note that Article XVII is one of only two articles that contains only a single section, the other being Article II: The Powers of Government. The debate over the means of amendment consumed the twenty-fourth day of the convention, October 2, 1875, and included discussion over the means for calling a new constitutional convention. The original plan allowed for a two-thirds majority of the entire legislature to call for a new convention, a section that President Pickett proposed for removal on behalf of the voice of the people, lest they be bound by a convention they did not support.[41] Alternate versions of constitutional reform and revision were presented, including periodic reviews every ten years, every twenty years, and simply by the will of the people at any time. Pickett's proposal to remove the section carried and the subject was left alone, leaving Texas as one of a handful of US states without the means for calling a convention.[42] Putting aside the obstacles this created for subsequent attempts at constitutional reform, the lack of a mechanism for creating a new convention also creates a philosophical conundrum, as the "inalienable right to alter, reform or abolish their government in such manner as they may think expedient" belongs to the people, at least according to Article I, Section 2, of the Texas Constitution of 1876.[43] This disconnect between ideal and practice is an oft-repeated deficiency in the Texas Constitution, and represents a major part of the structural inefficiency that Texas has survived in spite of. The branches of government as laid out in the 1876 constitution are similarly constrained in a manner that ultimately represents something deeper than a backlash against the Radicalism of Reconstruction. The restrictive nature of the 1876 constitution represents a lack of trust in liberal democracy itself.

The Governor

If the general reasoning for replacing the constitution of 1869 boiled down to little more than its Republican authorship, then the structuring of the office of the governor that took place at the 1875 convention is similarly little more than a backlash against Davis. While the convention's approach to the new constitution would undoubtedly be restrained and a drastic departure from the trend of liberal constitutions adopted in 1866 and 1869, some elements of governmental restraint were already in place. Under the 1869 constitution, many officers of the executive branch were already elected independently of the governor, and the plural executive was already an established part of the Texas political tradition. In fact, the plural executive is common throughout the United States. However, the constitution of 1876 did take the step of further diluting gubernatorial power by making the office of attorney general an elected position when it had previously been an appointed position under the 1869 constitution.[44]

Article IV, Section I, of the 1869 constitution lists the officers of the executive branch: "a Lieutenant Governor, Secretary of State,

Comptroller of Public Accounts, Treasurer, Commissioner of the General Land Office, Attorney General and Superintendent of Public Instruction."[45] Of these, superintendent of public instruction was dropped completely, as Davis's education program had already been dismantled. Article IV, Section 1, of the 1876 constitution lists the executive officers: governor, lieutenant governor, secretary of state, comptroller of public accounts, treasurer, commissioner of the general land office, and attorney general.[46] At the convention it was suggested that the position of secretary of state be made elected, as were all of the other specified offices. This proposal from William Pinckney McLean of Hunt County on the thirty-sixth day of the convention reflected a sentiment that the office of secretary of state, like the other executive officers, needed to be answerable to the people and therefore afforded a proper degree of independence.[47] In a rare moment of farsightedness, the sentiment from the committee on the executive department was summarized by Judge William Pitt Ballinger, who stated that the committee had unanimously agreed that "the governor ought to have in the Secretary of State a man whose relations would be friendly and agreeable to him," and that the low salary of the office made it unjust to put him to the expense of running a statewide campaign for election.[48]

The ultimately unacceptable constitution of 1866 had established gubernatorial terms of four years, but limited governors to serving only eight out of every twelve years.[49] Gubernatorial term limits were abandoned altogether in 1869, but four-year terms were kept. This was changed by the 1876 constitution, which said in Article IV, Section 4, "The governor . . . shall hold his office for the term of two years, or until his successor shall be duly installed."[50] Terms were once again extended to four years by a constitutional amendment in 1972, and to the present day, Texas is one of a minority of states without gubernatorial term limits. Although the general sentiment of the 1875 Constitutional Convention was retrenchment and reform, and although many issues regarding the restrictive nature of the final document generated ample debate, executive term limits were not particularly controversial. By contrast, the debate on compensation for executive officers was frustratingly drawn out and demonstrated the array of opinions on what constituted appropriate retrenchment.

Exhaustive debate over the executive department on October 4, 1875, served to demonstrate the media's exasperation with the members of the Grange, as the spirit of retrenchment evolved into a competition of who could out-retrench who. Following the successful striking of the office of "Superintendent for Public Instruction," the unsuccessful call to make the office of secretary of state an elected position was accompanied by an even more preposterous (and similarly unsuccessful) call to eliminate the office of lieutenant governor.[51] Proposed by Rutabaga Johnson of Collin County, the amendment calling for $4,000 in annual pay for the governor triggered a series of calls for even less pay followed by solid rebuttals, particularly from Fletcher Stockdale of Calhoun County, who had served as governor following the flight of Pendleton Murrah to Mexico before A. J. Hamilton arrived. Stockdale argued that "it was an office requiring the highest order of talent, probity, and integrity, and the very credit of the State, and its future as well as its present honor and glory required that it should not be reduced beyond the figures reported by the committee." Johnson responded that if $4,000 wasn't enough for Coke, he would gladly fill in and serve as governor himself.[52] Johnson's amendment ultimately passed, and gubernatorial pay was set at $4,000 annually, $1,000 less than provided by the 1869 constitution.[53] The political culture of Collin County, as vocalized through Rutabaga Johnson, had little interest in attracting the best talent money could buy. Consolidated in its opposition to Reconstruction and still suffering the ill effects of an economic calamity known as the Panic of 1873, the people of Collin County were not eager to support career politicians, preferring a less professionalized model of citizen-legislators who served as a matter of civic duty.

While analysis of the structure of the executive office offers a great deal of insight into the motivations of the delegates in 1875, it is ultimately an examination of the governor's enumerated powers that demonstrates the extreme spirit of reform, retrenchment, and restriction that dominated the proceedings. Robert Loughery, expressing the general sentiment of the Democratic press on the state of the executive going into the convention, said, "The Executive Department, by legislative sanction, has been invested with authority never contemplated by any well devised Constitution. This has been manifest in the extraordinary powers conferred on the Governor in control of the frontier defence, the printing bill, and other measures of purely legislative character."[54] Once again, this sort of criticism was likely an expression of frustration with the legacy of E. J. Davis and Republicanism, and the predominantly Democratic delegates followed suit in their actions.

In many states the executive power of budget making is a major political advantage. Through 1973 and the push for constitutional reform—the most significant attempt to draft a new constitution in a century—Texas was one of only four states where the governor did not enjoy full authority for budget making. According to the 2020 edition of the *Book of the States*, a reference volume assembled by the National Council of State Governments, the practice of shared budget-making responsibility with the legislature has become increasingly common, with twenty-three states sharing a similar arrangement.[55] The Texas governor enjoys the power of item veto over appropriations, which is a power any US president would kill for. But while the Texas governor today enjoys an increasingly respectable role in budget creation, this has been the result of a gradual evolution, for the initial budgetary powers laid out in 1875 were minimal.

Seth McKay's early analysis of the making of the Texas Constitution notes that "the greater part of the hatred for the radical control, too, had been aimed at the appointees of the governor rather than at Davis himself. This fact caused the people to expect the convention to curtail the appointive power of the governor."[56] This logical assumption was based on the general disdain Texas voters felt for some of E. J. Davis's more progressive initiatives and the repeated assertions of corruption levied at his appointees. For Texas voters and for convention delegates, the instances of corruption (or perceived corruption) involving

Superintendent of Public Instruction Jacob C. DeGress and Adjutant General James Davidson signaled a need to curtail the governor's power of appointment. Article IV, Section 12, of the 1876 constitution describes the governor's appointment powers. Professor Fred Gantt Jr., writing in 1973 as part of the statewide push for constitutional revision, noted that "in making appointments, the executive faces certain limitations. All appointments require confirmation of two-thirds of the senators present, a large number when compared to the simple majority vote that the President of the United States must secure for his appointments."[57] On its own this is not particularly striking, as many states feature a more limited avenue for gubernatorial appointments than that enjoyed by the US president. However, the restrictive nature of Section 12 becomes more pronounced when accounting for the myriad of appointments a Texas governor must make to various boards and commissions. Like other governors, as well as the US president in some instances, the Texas governor is somewhat constrained by the independent nature of some of the boards and commissions to which he or she is responsible for appointing leadership. With staggered six-year terms for officials working on many of these state boards and commissions, the opportunities for a governor to influence policy through appointment becomes more limited. Often the governor of Texas does not get an opportunity to appoint new people to these positions until later in their terms, thus losing any significant advantage for setting an ideological tone across the state bureaucracy. Gantt also noted the unwritten and seldom mentioned tradition of "senatorial courtesy," a practice that similarly takes place in the US Senate, where the larger body will side with the senator of the nominee's home district or state if the senator opposes the nomination.[58] In Texas this practice is applied to senatorial districts.

Modern comparative analysis of gubernatorial power across states began with political scientist Joseph Schlesinger in 1965. His methodology has been modified and regularly updated over the decades as constitutions have changed and political science methodology has evolved. Although more complex approaches have been employed (some utilizing dozens of independent variables), Schlesinger's work, subsequently carried on by political scientist Thad Beyle, has remained the gold standard for ranking US governors according to their formal powers.[59] Beyle's 1968 replication of Schlesinger's Combined Power Index ranked the Texas governor forty-ninth out of fifty according to measures of budgetary power, appointive power, tenure power, and veto power.[60] More recently, Beyle and Ferguson's 2008 version combined the variables of budgetary power, veto power, separately elected officials (the plural executive), tenure, gubernatorial party control, and appointment power.[61] According to this index, Texas was once again surpassed only by South Carolina in the race to the bottom of gubernatorial power, ranking forty-ninth out of fifty. Most political scientists working in the field acknowledge the natural imprecision associated with comparing formal power to power-in-reality, and Texas politics textbooks typically pay special attention to the informal powers a governor can use to his or her advantage. However, popular expectations are often at odds with historical and legal realities, and because of the cultural backlash of 1875, Texas's chief executive is constitutionally weaker than the public realizes. As former governor Allan Shivers once noted, "The Governor of Texas is something of a paper tiger."[62]

The rush to divest the state's chief executive of power, intertwined with the push for extreme retrenchment inspired by the cultural backlash against Davis and Republicanism, left a legacy of deficient regulation and poor governance that Rutabaga Johnson and his Collin County constituents did not anticipate yet were left to bear the burden of. One example of this is the railroads. Beginning during the Davis administration, a fever for expanded transportation infrastructure was felt statewide, opening Texas up to the predatory capitalists who became known as the robber barons. Exemplifying the excesses of the Gilded Age, unrestricted railroad growth in Texas led to calls of mismanagement, misappropriation, unequal facilities, and rate discrimination, inspiring a special breed of animosity from populist organizations like the Grange and the Farmers' Alliance, who felt the railroads did little more than exacerbate socioeconomic division.[63] As early as 1870,

legal relief against railroads in Texas was sought to put an end to predatory railroad practices, but little was accomplished. Calls for railroad regulation throughout the 1880s likewise did little to break the
stranglehold enjoyed by railroad interests in Texas. Implicitly, at least,
the constitution empowered the legislature to act, but lacking any true
power of the sword, that body failed to do so in any meaningful way.
The people of Collin County, exasperated by the false promise of what
the railroads would bring and wrapped up in the spirit of populism,
would elect Rutabaga Johnson as a state senator beginning in 1884. In
an impassioned speech that year, reported by *The Democrat* published
in McKinney, Johnson advocated for control over railroad interests in
the name of the people:

> But now let us come to our own state, the great "Lone Star"
> state of the Union and see if she has done justice between the
> monopolies and the people. First, she has given away 31,500,000
> acres of her public domain to the railroads, and exempted seven
> millions of acres from taxation for twenty-five years. Did she
> stop here? No, sir; she exempted the International railroad, with
> all its fine fixtures, from taxation for twenty-give years.
>
> Now think of what effect these exemptions have upon the
> poor people of our state. The International road was permitted
> by state government to lay her certificates in tracts and bodies
> to suit themselves, and as much as 400,000 acres were located
> in one county. Yes, sir, think for a moment, only four hundred
> and eighty thousand acres of land in Wheeler county and four
> hundred thousand acres of that amount exempt from taxation.
> You see by this that the eighty thousand acres owned by the
> farms of that county are forced to shoulder all the expenses of
> that county for the next twenty-five years, and many other coun
> ties are in nearly as bad a condition. What do you think of this
> discrimination against the people and in favor of a monopoly
> with its millions?[64]

Johnson's attempt to indict the unrestrained capitalism that was holding the rank-and-file citizens of the state hostage, however, overlooks a
major constitutional deficiency that he played a role in establishing.

The most appropriate means for ensuring proper regulation of the railroads was through the empowerment of executive oversight. The Constitutional Convention of 1875 was driven by opposition to the centralization of power that had existed under the Davis administration, with Johnson taking the lead on behalf of a political culture that was myopic in its pursuit of retrenchment. Desperately needed railroad regulation would not come until the establishment of the Texas Railroad Commission under Governor Jim Hogg in 1891. The advocacy of Jim Hogg, along with that of attorney (and former law partner of James Throckmorton) Thomas Jefferson Brown, was essential to the commission's creation. Brown, a strong ally of the Grange and the Farmers' Alliance, would later serve as district judge for Collin County and subsequently chief justice of the Texas Supreme Court.[65] His searing indictments of the railroad industry in Texas were printed in *The Democrat* in 1890:

> It is true that the public pay for all the results of carelessness, extravagance, and dishonesty in the management of the railroads in this state, and, therefore, it becomes a matter of public concern to have them not only honestly managed, but also economically and carefully conducted. It is said that it is none of the people's affair as to how this business is carried on. This would be true if the people did not foot the bills, but so long as they must settle the accounts they should insist upon having something to say in the manner of conducting the business. This can be safely and properly done only through a commission.[66]

That nearly fifteen years were required to right the wrongs of the constitution of 1876 in the realm of railroad regulation was unfortunate. That some of the strongest advocates for railroad regulation would come from Collin County, so heavily absorbed by cultural opposition and the pursuit of retrenchment in 1875, was painfully ironic.

The Legislature

In the American constitutional tradition, the legislative branch enjoys primacy over the executive and judicial branches. At the root of the ancient tradition of democracy, the key function of government is the establishment of law, or legislation. Legislatures are, or should act as, the keystone of the social contract between the people and their government. State governments are granted power through the Tenth Amendment to the US Constitution, and the only real restrictions on their power are the limitations enumerated in their own framing documents. These limitations are, theoretically, imposed upon them by the people themselves (through mechanisms such as constitutional conventions) and therefore state legislatures best embody the will of the people.

As part of the 1973 effort toward Texas constitutional reform, the Citizens Conference on State Legislatures harshly criticized the statutory elements of Article III because of a basic structural and systemic flaw that restricts legislative power beyond what the original framers might have imagined. Because the Tenth Amendment to the US Constitution grants all powers not specifically enumerated for the US Congress to the states, listing the powers of the Texas legislature in the Texas Constitution of 1876 had the adverse effect of restricting it to only those elements that were enumerated. In political science this is known as a positive grant of power, and it leaves the Texas legislature unable to interpret or expand its lawmaking role. The result is a myriad of inappropriate statutory elements that restrict the Texas legislature beyond what might be reasonably expected for a government of its size.[67]

When creating the Texas Railroad Commission, for example, direct attempts by the legislature to establish regulations had failed, underscoring the need for an executive-level solution. The initial piece of legislation in 1891 allowed for gubernatorial appointment of railroad commissioners, but this was challenged in court only a few months later. The validity of the Texas legislature's act was ultimately upheld by the US Supreme Court, but legal questions lingered over the regulation of fares, putting the future of the commission in doubt. Ultimately, owing to the restrictive structure of the constitution, which prevented expansion of legislative power, an enduring Texas Railroad Commission could only be created by constitutional amendment, which did not occur until 1894. By restricting the Texas legislature to such a degree, the delegates to the convention of 1875, who were acting on behalf of an oppositional political culture seeking to liberate themselves from the tyranny of governmental control, opened a Pandora's box of necessary regulations for subsequent generations.

Another example of the constrained nature of the Texas legislature can be found in Article III, Section 49, which places a restriction upon state debt: "No debt shall be created by or on behalf of the State, except to supply casual deficiencies of revenue, repel invasion, suppress insurrection, defend the State in war, or pay existing debt and the debt created to supply deficiencies in the revenue, shall never exceed in the aggregate at any one time two hundred thousand dollars."[68] The debate that Section 49 inspired among the delegates in 1875 was, much like the earlier lengthy discussion over delegate pay, something of a proxy for the ideological tone of the constitution itself. Modern constitutional law scholars (including those who worked toward constitutional reform in 1973) understand the dangers implicit in such a narrow-minded approach to state debt, and some delegates at the time were similarly aware of the pitfalls. During the debate over state debt on September 29, 1875, Justus Wesley Ferris of Ellis County, attorney and cofounder of Citizens National Bank, noted the similarities in the clause to the constitution of 1845 but also noted that "it was impossible to anticipate what might occur in future years. In case of the failure of crops, fire, or robbery of the Treasury, the clause as it stood would leave the State without resource."[69] Charles DeMorse, notable editor and Granger representing Red River County, countered with an expression of severe retrenchment recorded in the Debates of the Texas Constitutional Convention of 1875: "The people had heard enough of having their bonds hawked about Wall Street and sold for 60 cents. As the chairman of their committee had observed, 'once let them get a little into debt and they would soon be at the end of a rope.' If they were compelled to make a little debt it could be paid as it had been in the past."[70] His assertion was countered by other delegates noting the legislature's responsibility for protecting the lives and property of the citizens in the face of invasion or rebellion.

When asked what the state's alternatives would be in the face of an invasion of the frontier, DeMorse responded that he "supposed the patriotism of the people would be equal to the occasion, as it had been before, and that they would defend the frontier without pay," and he was answered by thunderous applause.[71] No statements espousing laissez-faire government in Texas have since surpassed this.[72]

While such a spirit of retrenchment and rugged self-reliance may have resonated with the Patrons of Husbandry, such a tone of restriction was and is not conducive to a good constitution.[73] The Texas Democratic press found themselves increasingly flustered by the overwhelming attitude of restriction at the convention, even though such sentiments had been expressed by Democratic leaders for years with little effect. The *Weekly Democratic Statesman,* for instance, did little to hide its disgust with the trend of limited government and retrenchment at all costs: "That the public is beginning to feel that the constitutional convention is a failure is a fact that cannot be denied."[74] Extreme retrenchment, in the eyes of the mainstream Democratic press, was a momentary political passion that was endangering the convention by forcing delegates to answer to the will of the masses rather than any prudent or deliberate sense of good government that would otherwise be expected from a body that included so many attorneys. *The Statesman*, reprinting from the *Calvert Republican*, focused on Collin County's John "Rutabaga" Johnson as the face of extreme retrenchment at the cost of proper governance:

Out of the ninety delegates in attendance upon the Constitutional Convention in Austin, a very small percent of that body rise above the local politics of the hour, or can get their minds beyond the circumscribed limits of their districts. Mr. Johnson, of Collin county, whether he is a statesman or a backwoods politician, it matters not, as a jokist he is a success, for he has stirred up the bile of the Grangers and Radicals in that body. Every public assembly, it seems, now-a-days, has its clown, and Mr. Johnson might as well assume that role as any one else, as long as the people are unwilling to dispense with it, and are willing to pay five dollars per day for the exhibition.[75]

At the same time, many in the Democratic press began to express concerns over the length of the convention, resulting from the incessant debate over retrenchment, and the rising cost of keeping the body in session. Responding to criticism from the *Houston Tri-Weekly Telegraph* in mid-October, Robert Loughery at the *Tri-Weekly Herald* in Harrison County urged readers to maintain faith in the process:

> Too many men get into all such Conventions who are not qualified by education or experience for the task assumed. Such is the case in our Convention, and with those that are, in every respect, proper members, there existed differences of opinion upon important questions that could only be settled by full discussions. The Texas Convention, as a whole, we are inclined to believe is as able a body of men as has ever been called together in the State. It embraces, we know, many men of eminence that would be an honor to any State. This delay, no doubt, has been in part their work, and in this we think they have acted wisely.[76]

His spirit of optimism was likely fueled by the praise he had heaped on the delegates in advance of the convention two months prior on August 12, 1875:

> We now find that this body will be composed of men representing every class of society, and comprising as much talent as has been found in any similar assemblage that has ever been convened in the State. Nearly every district has elected one or more able men, and among them there are quite a number of large experience and marked ability. They have been criticized very severely even in advance of knowing who they were. Apprehensions have been freely indulged in, that few of them would prepare themselves for the work, that the session will be unnecessarily prolonged, and that when the new Constitution shall be offered to the people, it will be found so disjointed, incongruous, impracticable, and containing so many objectionable features that it will be promptly rejected. If ever a body of men has been called together that ought to be stimulated to exercise the most laborious, patient, and enlightened investigation to frame a Constitution which will be regarded as a model of Statesmanship, it is this Texas Convention.[77]

Whether Loughery was attempting to save face or genuinely believed in the capabilities of the delegates, it was becoming increasingly obvious that the convention was losing sight of its mission.

Historian John Walker Mauer saw the curtailment of the legislative power of the purse as something even greater than an attempt to revive the antebellum governmental order, for there was evidence of drastic constitutional change happening nationally, not just in the South. For Mauer the impetus for creating the restrictive Texas Constitution of 1876 was as much a product of the economic times and the subsequent populist backlash as it was a reaction to Reconstruction. Mauer presented a classification scheme of state constitutions that is helpful for delineating between liberal and restrictive constitutions. Mauer identified restrictive constitutions as those containing limiting provisions in four categories: a strict ceiling on taxes, explicit limits on public debt, the prohibition of public aid to private enterprise, and controls on the use of tax revenue.[78] According to Mauer, "The 1876 document broke with the liberal tradition that had dominated all earlier constitutions. . . . The restrictive Texas Constitution placed controls on state government in all four key areas of financial functioning and also on local government in two of these areas. In addition, the 1876 document set maximum salaries for state officials and prohibited the legislature from passing many categories of legislation as special or local laws."[79]

In addition to the costs associated with the convention, which were short-term, the ill effect of retrenchment and restriction placed upon the Texas legislature that resulted from a political culture forged by the challenges of secession, Civil War, and Reconstruction would stifle Texas progress long-term. Despite the media's attempts to lay blame on the Grange (discussed further in chap. 5), the limitations of the 1876 constitution in a much larger sense stemmed from the consolidation of Texas into an indisputably traditionalistic political culture. The common experiences of the preceding fifteen years had erased the political diversity that characterized the antebellum years. Like many Southern constitutions written between the conclusion of the war and the early part of the twentieth century, the Texas Constitution of 1876 is a break from the liberal tradition of strong institutionalization that had defined state constitutions prior to the war.

The Judiciary

The primary goal of any constitution when establishing a judicial branch is to ensure strength and independence. The purpose of separating powers, from the Enlightenment to the present day, has always been to establish a system of checks and balances wherein no single branch could exercise a level of control to the detriment of another. Traditionally, this has proven difficult when establishing a judiciary, which lacks both the power of the purse and the power of the sword, a point clarified by Alexander Hamilton in *Federalist*, no. 78: "The judiciary on the contrary has no influence over either the sword or the purse, no direction either of the strength or of the wealth of the society, and can take no active resolution whatever. It may truly be said to have neither force nor will, but merely judgment; and must ultimately depend upon the aid of the executive arm even for the efficacy of its judgments."[80] Like Articles III and IV, establishing the executive and legislative branches, Article V lays the foundation for a judicial branch based on the philosophical leanings of the time. In 1875 Texas was only thirty years old as a state, still underpopulated, and primarily rural with little industrial development. Unfortunately, this lent itself to the building of a judiciary over time in a piecemeal fashion, establishing new courts as necessary according to population changes. When given an opportunity to wipe the judicial slate clean and begin anew, the delegates to the constitutional convention were instead directed by the cultural pressures of the moment, a vox populi predicated upon opposition to the unholy forces of Republicanism and obsessed with economy.

As a result of determination to be guided by contemporary political culture rather than sound legal philosophies, Article V of the Texas Constitution of 1876 suffers from structural flaws that have undermined the spirit of retrenchment that was supposedly guiding the framers. For the people, particularly those represented by the more vociferous advocates for retrenchment (Collin County), the structure of the judicial branch has produced both unexpected long-term costs and less-than-optimal administration of justice, as the structure of the Texas court system is virtually inaccessible for laypersons. That such a plan for the judicial branch would be so readily endorsed by the people most adversely affected by it demonstrates the strength of the consolidated Texas political culture by 1876. As of 2014 Texas has approximately three thousand elected and appointed judges, an excessive amount that reflects the convoluted nature of the Texas Constitution.[81] Law professor Allen E. Smith, writing in 1973 as part of the constitutional revision effort, emphasized in his critical analysis that "Texas reputedly has more judges than any geographical unit in the English-speaking world, including all of Great Britain."[82] Although this claim is difficult to confirm with absolute certainty, the excessive number of judges in Texas makes the system's efficiency instantly suspect in the eyes of any legal analyst brave enough to dive into the state's Byzantine legal organization. A model state judiciary is ideally characterized by clear lines of jurisdiction and an easily understood hierarchy. The Texas judiciary suffers from both practical and symbolic faults, and its overall deficiency can best be summarized through examination of two dimensions—structure and selection.

Texas is currently one of only two states (the other being Oklahoma) with a bifurcated supreme court—one for criminal appeals and one for civil appeals. This approach to establishing a court of last resort would draw an immediate red flag from any novice comparative politics scholar, as it removes the symbolic power of a unified court that undergirds state legitimacy. The impetus for creating the two-headed Texas Supreme Court lay in practical concerns of the moment. By 1875 the still-singular supreme court established by the constitution of 1869 was faced with a backlog of approximately 1,600 cases, a constitutional outrage for anyone stuck in prison awaiting appeal.[83] And the people of Texas were fully aware of the ongoing miscarriage of justice at the time of the convention. In the early days of the convention,

Robert Loughery acknowledged the need for reform, with an emphasis on both retrenchment and decentralization of power: "Our entire judicial system, civil and criminal, needs revision, and can be so changed as to cost less than half what it does at present. We ought to have fewer District Judges, and a different character of county justices, with more enlarged powers."[84]

The final product created by the 1875 convention established a three-person supreme court to deal with civil appeals and a three-person court of appeals to deal with criminal cases. More than the establishment of the other branches, the judiciary drew the broadest and least unified collection of opinions from the delegates in 1875, resulting in an arrangement that was considered suboptimal by all. Historian James Haley, writing in cooperation with the Texas Supreme Court Historical Society, said, "After the crucible of debate and compromise, the convention produced a new format for the judiciary that, although it passed, was warmly espoused by no one."[85] Like Articles III and IV, Article V in practice operates more as a code of law rather than a constitution. Subsequent calls for reform of the myriad of courts in Texas in order to create a more streamlined and efficient system have been met with the same obstacles facing those seeking executive and legislative reform. By strictly adhering to the 1876 constitution's enumeration of powers, it becomes difficult for any legislature to reorganize a judicial mess like that in Texas. It also worth noting that restructuring the court in 1875 had little impact on the size of the judicial backlog faced by either the supreme court or the court of appeals.

Judicial selection in Texas, as established in 1875 and as it still stands as of this writing, was clearly developed as a backlash against the Davis administration. The constitution of 1869 gave considerable power of appointment and removal of justices to the governor, with advice and consent of the legislature.[86] When drafting the constitution of 1869, the delegates were aware of the extensive removal of judges, as well as county and local officials, by the military authorities (Griffin and Reynolds) in the name of Congressional Reconstruction, and thus granted greater powers to the chief executive. This is perhaps another example of the Republicans designing a system with the implicit belief that they held a mandate from the federal government allowing them heavy-handed, top-down, centralized control over state affairs. Knowing the enormous political and cultural crisis the state underwent over the lifespan of the 1869 constitution, it was only natural that the delegates would create a new document that would simultaneously place judicial selection in the hands of the people while weakening the governor.

The Texas Democratic press strongly endorsed this course of action. In response to initial reports coming from the Judiciary Committee in September, *The Weekly Democratic Statesman* supported a system of judicial elections while simultaneously advocating for restricted suffrage, lest legal decisions fall into the hands of formerly enslaved persons:

> Upon one single point the whole Convention is an unit [*sic*], that one-third of the counties of Texas are not in a fit condition, while universal suffrage is the absurd policy of the State, to create for themselves local courts. In Northern and Central and Western Texas where the people, and not the rabble, are supreme, the masses have declared that they preferred a judiciary elective by the people; but since the government of Texas is now and must forever remain a white man's government and there is no danger of wrong if the judiciary be creative by its chief magistrate and legislature, it is commonly asserted that if no other recourse be presented, the judges shall be eligible by the Legislature, the Governor nominating. But another scheme has been defined which may accomplish the purposes of conservatism, and at the same time be universally approved. The judges will be elected by the State at large or by districts so defined that there will be no danger that the ermine will be worn by one unworthy of its stainless honors.[87]

The author's choice to omit East Texas from the list of regions ruled by the people rather than the "rabble" was obviously based on race. Areas like Harrison County, with its African American majority, were not fit to make decisions of such a monumental nature, whereas the predominantly white Collin County, now heavily consolidated and recast in the traditionalistic political subculture, was perfectly qualified. That one of the principal voices opposing poll taxes when the matter came up for debate the next month was John Johnson only underscores the nature of a political culture blindly opposing the perceived evils of its opposition rather than deliberately pursuing good public policy. Johnson was always unabashed in his defense of the poor citizens of Collin County, many of whom could not afford to pay a poll tax.

The widespread cultural sentiment against the centralization of power in the hands of the executive led to the establishment of partisan elections for judicial positions. While the unified supreme court and inferior district courts were filled by gubernatorial appointment in 1869, Article V of the 1876 constitution only allowed for appointments in order to fill vacancies.[88] Partisan elections of judges (a practice only followed in Texas, Alabama, and Louisiana) is nearly universally condemned by both American legal scholars and foreign nations that have adopted elements of the American judicial system for the same general reason.[89] Electing judges removes the principle of political insulation that characterizes the US judiciary, and automatically creates a court system that is accountable to the general will instead of legal precedent.[90] With the extra incentive of needing to satisfy a political party, candidates for judicial office, like candidates for a legislature, must endure the process of campaigning and fundraising, thus calling into question their objectivity. For voters, most of whom are unfamiliar with a candidate's qualifications, the natural impulse is to vote according to partisan label. As all Texas judges above the municipal level are elected, the result is a judiciary that is easily purchased, leaving rank-and-file Texans without an impartial system. As former chief justice of the Texas Supreme Court Wallace Jefferson put it, "Judicial elections force judges to raise money from lawyers and litigants; they give voters the false impression that party affiliation or persuasive television commercials are an adequate substitute for merit; they undermine the Founders' concept that judges rule not according to popular will, but to advance the rule of law."[91]

In addition to issues of structure and selection, the 1875 convention again went into exhaustive and predictable debate regarding judge's salaries at the highest level on the fifty-eighth day, with pleas for retrenchment dominating. General Lawrence Sullivan (Sul) Ross's lengthy admonishment to the convention that administration of justice was carried out by men and therefore the optimal system would employ the best available (and therefore paid) men was countered by John Johnson, who felt that $2,500 in annual pay was sufficient for any judge.[92] Although Johnson did not get his wish regarding judicial salaries, the $3,550 in annual pay dictated by the constitution of 1876 was still well below the $4,500 allotted by the constitution of 1869.[93] A week after the convention had adjourned, Harrison County's Robert Loughery vented his frustrations about the new constitution by directly attacking a Grange journalist from the *Tyler Reporter* who advocated Johnson's plan: "This is the animus of that demagogism that placed all that is parsimonious and mean ingrafted in the New Constitution. Suppose a Judge can live on $2,500, is he to receive only a bare living? Is that a fair renumeration for his talents, the expense, and the years of study required to render him fit for a position on the bench? . . . This ignorant rutabaga, blatherskite of the Reporter, no doubt thinks $2,500 amply sufficient, and that the Judge ought to save at least $1,500 out of the $2,500."[94]

The Model Constitution

At the tail end of the nineteenth century, as the Gilded Age was coming to a close and a heightened sense of the people's role in maintaining governmental and business accountability took hold, signaling the dawn of the Progressive Era, the National Municipal League (now National Civic League) was founded with the goal of tackling patronage and corruption at the local level. With an eye on electoral reform and promoting civil society, one of the National Municipal League's great achievements was the development and proliferation of model city charters and model state constitutions. The general argument of the National Municipal League, and similar nonpartisan reform efforts, was that state constitutions ought to be modeled on the federal constitution, with a focus on brevity, and devoted solely to the structure of government instead of the details of policy.[95]

While the model constitution did enjoy brief popularity following its final publication in 1968, with a number of states adopting elements to improve their supreme law, the Texas Constitution, founded on the basis of the whims of the vox populi rather than according to sensible public policy, remained in place. The model constitution did, however, serve as an ideal benchmark for the reform efforts of the early 1970s, and some of the most basic elements of its design for governmental structure were highlighted as examples of how the delegates in 1875, in their rush to redeem Texas from the tyranny of Radicalism, got things woefully wrong.

In an effort to preserve the spirit of the citizen-legislator, which was a natural outgrowth of the evolving political culture of places like Collin County at the time, Article III, Section 5, of the 1876 constitution called for biennial sessions, a break from the 1869 constitution, which had dictated annual sessions.[96] The assumption of the delegates in 1875 was that the allowance for special sessions called by the governor would be adequate for the state's needs. Section 4.08 of the National Municipal League's model constitution suggests, "The legislature shall be a continuous body during the term for which its members are elected. It shall meet in regular sessions annually as provided by law."[97] In 1973 the Citizen's Conference on State Legislatures emphasized this point, and blasted the Texas Constitution's limitation on special sessions, which only allows them to be called and address an agenda set by the governor, thus limiting the control of the legislature itself.[98]

On a broader scale, the model constitution also addresses the greatest flaw of the Texas model: its structural limitation on power. The omission of a necessary and proper clause similar to that of the US Constitution, as well as the enumeration of legislative powers, has led to a proliferation of amendments, rendering the Texas Constitution indecipherable. According to the example from the National

Municipal League: "ARTICLE II: Powers of the State Section 2.01. Powers of Government. The enumeration in this constitution of specified powers and functions shall be construed neither as a grant nor as a limitation of the powers of state government but the state government shall have all of the powers not denied by this constitution or by or under the Constitution of the United States."[99]

In 1972, as Texas voters were being asked to approve the calling of a new constitutional convention (which they did), longtime *Dallas Morning News* analyst Sam Kinch Jr. wrote, "Slowly but surely, Texans have amended their Constitution into a contradictory and complicated document that confounds courts and lawyers and, in a number of ways, inhibits the effectiveness of state, county, and municipal governments. If it continues, scholars predict that by the year 2001 the Constitution will have been amended 345 times."[100] Kinch's projection ultimately underestimated the scale of unbridled constitutional growth necessary to keep Texas running. By September 2001 the Texas Constitution had been amended 390 times out of a proposed 567 amendments.[101] As of this writing, the Texas Constitution has been amended over 500 times, with approximately 700 amendments proposed by the legislature. The cost in time and resources spent on amending the constitution since 1876 is beyond calculation, but it is safe to assume that it has long surpassed the expectations of any of the entrenchment-minded delegates in 1875, who were more intent on responding to the passions of the day than in creating a government that could effectively respond to the long-term needs of its citizens.

Chapter 6

Texas Redeemed

C elebrated as a link to the past, Alberta Martin of Enterprise, Alabama, passed away at the age of 97 in 2004. Having lived in poverty most of her life, she was quickly granted a pension by the Alabama legislature when her status as the last surviving Confederate widow was revealed publicly in the mid-1990s.[1] Had Alberta Martin lived in Texas, it would not have been a problem, as the last provisions guaranteeing Confederate pensions were not removed from the state constitution until November 1999. The constitutional amendment removing the provisions was the ninth and most recent amendment to Article III, Section 51.[2] Each amendment proposed by the legislature was submitted to the voters for ratification, creating enormous administrative costs. And Article III, Section 51, is only one section of a document that has grown to excess and become ultimately unknowable for the people it is meant to serve.

The seemingly inconsequential debate over delegate compensation in the opening days of the Constitutional Convention of 1875 set a precedent for the decades that followed. Seldom in the history of democracy have voters enthusiastically approved pay raises for their elected officials, and in a political culture like Texas, the resistance to proper compensation has been even more pronounced. Of the twenty-seven proposed amendments to Article III, Section 24, twenty-one were rejected by voters, and it was not until 1991 that the twenty-seventh proposed amendment was ratified, creating the Texas Ethics Commission, which is charged with setting per diem pay for legislators.[3] And while attempting to amend a single section twenty-seven times may seem excessive (the US Constitution has only been amended twenty-seven times in its 235-year history), it pales in comparison to the evolution of Article VII. One of the more obvious policy deficiencies of the 1876 constitution, Article VII of the Texas Constitution covers education and has been amended fifty-five times out of a proposed ninety-two amendments. This is not a criticism of Texas lawmakers, who have done the best they can within the limits of the system, but rather an indictment of a constitution that is structurally deficient and grounded in the shortsighted mistakes of the past.

Redeemer Democrats

Although vague and beyond perfect classification as a movement, the Redeemers, or Redeemer Democrats, were a political coalition of white Southern Democrats unified in their opposition to carpetbaggers, scalawags, enfranchised Blacks, and civil rights. For the Redeemers the tenuous coalition of Unionists, African Americans, and those seeking to fully rejoin the American nation, along with support from vindictive Radicals in Washington, DC, had kept people like Davis afloat and perpetuated the injustices being done to the Southern people during Reconstruction. It naturally followed that only a similarly unified white conservative coalition could undo the damage of the Davis years and restore the natural order of political elitism that characterized a traditionalistic culture. Historian Patrick Williams identified the Democratic legislative victories of 1872 as the watershed moment of Texas redemption, carrying an even greater significance than the reactionary 1876 constitution itself.[4] However, Williams also acknowledges that the work of the Redeemers was a drawn-out and incremental process.

While wealthy landowners and Southern Democratic political elites were undoubtedly significant in giving the Redeemers a voice, the larger cultural movement was defined first and foremost by what it opposed. In August 1873 Austin's *Weekly Democratic Statesman* called for popular unity to answer the Radical coalition and restore Texas and the South to its previous glory:

> To redeem the country and restore an honest government, nothing, then, is needed but a union of all the elements opposed to Radicalism, and a free expression of the people's will at the coming elections in several States and at the Presidential election in 1876. How can that union be most easily effected? That is the important question. It must be admitted at once that much of the largest portion of the opposition to the Radical party is made up of Democrats, and that they combine more zeal and energy, a more bitter feeling and a more uncompromising hostility to Radicalism than can be found in any other portion of the opposition.[5]

This quote illustrates not only the primacy of opposition to Radicalism as a motivating factor but also a sense of the scattershot Democratic ideology. Although some specific pleas for policy change unified the Democrats in 1875 and 1876, a lack of ideological consensus is apparent. The lack of Democratic unity that manifested itself before, during, and after the Constitutional Convention of 1876 went far in affirming for some the Republican argument that the Democratic party was elitist and out of touch with rank-and-file Texans. Indeed, the emergence of political forces (including the Grange) dissatisfied with Democratic leadership would characterize the second half of the 1870s, and in the eyes of the Democratically dominated Texas media at the time, and subsequently the first wave of Reconstruction historians, represented a challenge to Democratic dominance that was as threatening as that posed by the Republicans.

The Grange

A long-standing myth regarding the 1875 Constitutional Convention is the unanimity of the Patrons of Husbandry, otherwise known as the Grange. The Grange was a national interest group of farmers first

established in Texas in 1873, and the commonly accepted version
of events in early histories was that Grangers (who made up nearly
half the membership of the convention) pushed for a more agrarian-
focused document, to the detriment of Texas's industrial development
and progress in general. For example, Ralph Smith's 1939 history of
the Grange in Texas highlights the presence of Grange membership at
the Convention:

> The Grangers performed their master work in the constitutional
> convention of 1875, one-half of whose members were Grang-
> ers. Their demands for "retrenchment" found expression in the
> provisions setting small salaries for public officials. Their home-
> stead article, a provision instructing the legislature to protect
> from forced sale a certain portion of the property of all heads of
> families was the work of the Grangers. The restrictions that they
> placed on levying education taxes has necessitated the continu-
> ous amending of the Constitution in order to provide a system of
> free public education for the state. The influence of the Grangers
> in the convention is also very noticeable in those articles relating
> to railroads.[6]

Their preferences for lower taxes, lower salaries, less spending, and
shorter terms for state officials supposedly won the day at the convention and set Texas on a course of perpetual underdevelopment.[7] While
many of the policies created at the convention suited the members
of the Grange, historian Patrick Williams noted several questionable
conclusions that became part of the legend. Much of what was later
attributed to the Grange was actually part of the larger Democratic
plan for the state.

In his address to the Texas legislature upon taking office January 26,
1874, Richard Coke summarized the expectations of the people, and
the loose Democratic platform: "It is justly expected by the people of
Texas that the new administration of the government will be marked
by the strictest economy in all its branches. The people in the late
canvass received our pledge to that effect. I suggest the importance
of the closest scrutiny of all expense incident to the public service,

and tender you my cordial cooperation in reducing them to the lowest figure consistent with the public interest."[8] When Coke made this statement, the Grange had only existed in Texas for a little over six months and was a long way from reaching its peak of political influence. His position was in line with the mainstream Democratic Party's continual critique of Radicalism, particularly the fiscal practices of E. J. Davis. In fact, differentiating between Grange positions and those of the Democrats becomes even more problematic when examining the official platform of the Texas Democratic Party as established in September 1873, merely two months after the Grange's establishment in the state. The unanimously agreed-upon platform, as submitted by platform committee chair and former member of Jefferson Davis's cabinet John H. Reagan used language such as "high salaries for a large and useless number of officers" when indicting the Radical education program and a promise of an "honest and economical expenditure of public monies" in the conclusion.[9]

In its formation at the national level, the Patrons of Husbandry's emphasis on nonpartisanship was both practical and philosophically necessary. From a practical standpoint, mobilizing a mass interest group for the purpose of promoting a sector of the economy (agriculture) meant they could not afford to discriminate politically. The genesis of the Grange lay with principal founder Oliver Hudson Kelley's appointment to the US Department of Agriculture by its first commissioner, Isaac Newton, in 1865. Kelley had been enlisted for a fact-finding mission on the status of southern agriculture by Newton, who wrote, "The relations of the Southern States with the Government for several years having prevented this Department from obtaining the usual statistical and other information from those States, and a prevailing desire for reliable information being manifested on the part of the people, I have determined, with the advice and authority of his Excellency, the President of the United States, to appoint you an Agent of this Department, to proceed immediately through the States lately in hostility against this Government, to procure such information, and report the same to this Department for publication."[10]

As Kelley was touring cotton plantations in South Carolina, he noted the advantage he enjoyed by being a Freemason, which went far in eliciting the hospitality of planters otherwise indifferent to the queries of a federal agent. This proved to be the seed for the Patrons of Husbandry as a fraternal organization. Philosophically, much like the Freemasons, political partisanship was fundamentally at odds with the mission and spirit of the Grange. In a circular issued in 1868, after the establishment of the Grange as a national organization, Kelley clarified the point for all current and potential members: "We ignore all political or religious discussions in the Order; we do not solicit the patronage of any sect, association or individual upon any grounds whatever, except upon the intrinsic merits of the Order."[11]

Political scientist Roscoe Martin noted in his early analysis of the Grange's activities in Texas that actions and statements on the part of the group were frequently interpreted as political by critics, who failed to delineate between advocacy on the part of a non-partisan interest group and overtly political actions being conducted by an organized party. Martin stressed, "It will be noted that the objects as stated above do not include participation, either direct or indirect, in politics. In fact, the leaders of the order were at some pains to explain that the Grange must not be dragged into politics; and a penalty was set upon any subordinate grange which might attempt to capitalize the name of the Grange as a political weapon. Members were permitted, nay, encouraged, to take an active part in politics, but it was in their capacity as citizens that they were to do this, and not as Grangers."[12]

The myth of Granger derailment of the proceedings at the Constitutional Convention of 1875 was propagated by the Democratically dominated press, and in many ways predated the convention proceedings by several years. For example, in one of the *Weekly Democratic Statesman's* many scathing diatribes against Davis in 1872, the paper established a tone of oppositional outrage based on the two-party paradigm: "In the first instance, E. J. Davis is a usurper . . . he is loathed, scorned, and held in supreme contempt by the people of the whole United States; he has suppressed free speech, the writ of habeas corpus and levied oppressive taxes under the power of military rule upon unprotected communities; he has attempted to debase the noble men of the State, and place them in the power of bloody minded demons, who would perfect his will."[13] Amid such a list of grievances, it's almost reasonable to forgive the Texas press for their hypocrisy in criticizing Davis and the Republicans over the tax burden. When a governor is accused of employing "bloody minded demons," the natural assumption is that anything the oppositional party does is better than the alternative.

Republican tax policy during the Davis era had provided the press with sufficient ammunition to frame the Democratic Party as the party of the people, at least from the perspective of an opposition party building momentum for political victory later. Actions by the Twelfth Legislature in 1870 had established state property taxes while giving discretion to county governments to do the same, resulting in a 300 percent hike.[14] Davis's sense of fulfilling the state's destiny of social and economic change mandated by the national powers of Reconstruction would not come cheap, particularly with regard to education. In his message to the Twelfth Legislature on April 29, 1870, Davis said, "It is not possible, under the circumstances, to make even a fair approximation to an estimate of the expenses of our State government in the future, but it is safe to look to a very large increase of expenditure, even with the greatest care and economy."[15]

Thus, within the confines of the narrative established by the partisan press: Democrats good, Republicans bad. But for the Grangers, who were nonpartisan and aware of the Democratic Party's long-standing vocal opposition to the Radical tax plan, actions spoke louder than words. This fiscally centered and nonpartisan mindset characterized the Grangers at the convention. Without declaring loyalty to either side, they focused solely on policy objectives rather than partisan aims. Unfortunately, this also set them up as the perfect scapegoats in the eyes of the Texas media and subsequent historians. Similar results from the convention of 1875 on salaries and term lengths would be attributed to the Grange, despite Democratic endorsement of the same positions in the years prior.

Patrick Williams's analysis of roll-call voting at the convention also demonstrates a lack of Grange unity. For example, the convention decided against monetary grants to railroads while sticking with land grants as a means of encouraging development. This can hardly be attributed to the Grange, as nobody at the convention was arguing for grants of money, and so the final choice was between land grants for development or nothing at all.[16] The Texas Democratic Party platform established in 1873 advocated the liberal provision of land grants for internal improvement:

> That the Democracy of Texas adhere to their past policy of developing the material resources of the State, and fostering the best interests of the people, by encouraging the construction of railroads. That to this end, and to encourage the investment of capital in such enterprises, we favor the granting of liberal characters to companies able to build such railroads, and of donating to such companies alternate sections of the vacant lands, under proper restrictions, and with such provisions of law as will protect the people against oppression and unreasonable exaction, until each section of the State has its equal proportion of railroad facilities.[17]

Amid the political finagling of Tom Scott and the Texas and Pacific Railway to secure lucrative deals from the federal government and several Southern states, it was Collin County's John Johnson who tipped the convention in favor of railroad interests. Despite the certainty of the Democratic press that Grangers unanimously opposed railroads, it was Johnson who reaffirmed the Democratic Party's own stance on liberal assistance for railroads, as explained in the *Weekly Democratic Statesman*:

> The cession made last Saturday by the Convention is not only munificent, confirming all former grants, but there can be no need for future action at the hands of the Texas legislatures. The ordinance extends the time, within which Tom Scott must

build the road to Fort Worth, to the close of the next session of
the Legislature which will not adjourn until after the road will
be built to the point beyond which restrictions and conditions
cease to operate. Strange, too, this ordinance was offered by Old
Rutabaga himself, Mr. Johnson of Collin, whose horror of railways, when he first appeared in Austin, was deemed absolutely
sublime. What the people of Texas will say of all this queer
concatenation of curious, liberal and illiberal policies and declarations affecting railways involved, in the action of the Convention, remains to be seen.[18]

As a historical trend, the Grange's influence over Southern state
constitutions is incontrovertible. A protopopulist movement that
predates other Gilded Age agrarian movements, the Grange still exists
today, although their political influence was strongest in the 1870s.
John Walker Mauer notes that postponing any effort toward holding a
convention in the early 1870s likely opened the door for Grange dominance by 1875 for several states.[19] What then, was the dominant force
shaping events in 1875 in Texas? Mauer argues that the Texas Constitution was shaped by the common interaction of forces influencing
constitutional development nationwide: the effect of Reconstruction
politics, state economics, and rational self-interest (this is where the
Grange would fall), and the influence of restrictive constitutions in
the North, which were used as models.[20] However, in addition to
his legal argument about a growing national trend toward restrictive, rather than liberal, state constitutions, Mauer still attributes a
great deal of influence to the Grange, citing their resentment of the
Democratic leadership for financial practices that differed little from
their Republican predecessors.[21] The Grange's influence, however,
becomes clearer when looking at the course of events through the lens
of political culture.

   Carl Moneyhon notes that despite heavy Grange representation at
the convention, the general substance of the document (limited state
government, devolution of power from state to local authority, limited
power to tax) was ultimately agreeable to the mainstream Democratic
party as well. The popular vote of ratification in February 1876

was 136,606 to 56,653 in favor, indicating support well beyond the Grange's influence.[22] The Democratic criticism of Radicalism, particularly the Davis administration, was based on an impression of overtaxing and overspending. With little change to this course of action occurring between the time the Democrats seized legislative control in January 1874 and the convention in 1875, the Grangers had free rein to push the concept of limited government to the extreme. In response the Democratically dominated press of Texas focused their criticisms of the ongoing constitutional debates on the Grange. But, as seen from Williams's points and the historical contradictions presented above, it is impossible to blame the final product on the Grange. Instead, the Grange was merely a scapegoat for the damage that resulted from Democratic disunity. Ultimately, with the Democratic Party ideologically disjointed and the influence of the Grange under question, there is only one common denominator: the opposition itself. Blacks, Republicans, Radicals, Carpetbaggers, and Scalawags—or rather the opposition to this motley collection of bogeymen—influenced the Texas Constitution of 1876 more than any other force.

The most frequently cited example of Grange influence in the formation of the Texas Constitution is the issue of poll taxes. Both in the press and on the convention floor, the Grangers were accused of allying with the Republicans in opposition to poll taxes. But a vital historiographical point made by more recent historians strongly diminishes the significance of the Grange at the convention. The twenty-ninth and thirtieth days of the convention, October 8 and 9, 1875, saw extensive debate suggesting an alliance between the Grange and the Republicans (as well as the African American delegation) at the convention seeking to prevent poll taxes. That such a debate would ensue and elicit strong reactions from Grangers and accusatory non-Grangers illustrates the precedence that political parties took over the development of a good organic law in 1875.

Inspired by the suggestion of a "holy alliance"[23] between the Grange and the Republicans in the *Austin Statesman* on the morning of October 8, 1875, the first order of the day was an ill-fated attempt to expose Grange subversion of the Democrats' larger anti-Radical agenda. The state press had been largely in favor of a poll tax as a means for preventing "negro rule," a sizeable portion of the Democratic Party agreed, while the Republican minority was unanimous in its opposition, likely owing to the Black base of support it enjoyed. Ultimately the pressure for a poll tax failed, and it was Rutabaga Johnson of Collin County—delegate for frontier farmers of small, hardscrabble homesteads who would be similarly impacted by such a voting restriction—who found himself at the center of the controversy.[24] According to the *Debates of the Convention, 1875*, Johnson stated that, "The more they attacked him the stronger would be his conviction that he was right."[25] The nerve of Johnson to openly defy the Democratic establishment in its righteous quest to erase the legacy of Radicalism severely irked the Democratic press, regardless of the best interests of his constituents.

In fact, Democratic media objection to the Grange predated the convention and was loudly articulated to such a degree that their bias became the official record. This historiographical disconnect was exposed on two different fronts by Joe Ericson in 1963 and Patrick Williams in 2002. Williams contended that the Grangers received the blame/credit for defeating the poll tax measures in large part because Seth Shepard McKay's early analysis made such an argument. However, McKay's entire point was taken from the *Austin Daily Democratic Statesman*, October 8, 1875, and in turn established by him as fact despite numerous objections on the convention floor from self-professed Grangers on October 8 and 9. Francis M. Martin of Navarro County, who would indeed later establish himself as a notable Texas populist, strongly objected to the notion of any "unholy alliance"[26] between the Grangers and minority elements. His impassioned denial of the charges levied by the *Statesman* was recounted by the *Debates in the Texas Constitutional Convention of 1875*: "He was a Granger, and so were his two colleagues from the Ninth District, and if anyone asserted that he or either of them had entered into a compact with the minority or anyone else, he had most foully lied. He knew no Granger on that floor as a Granger, and did not know that any Granger had concerted with a minority, but no Granger could control his vote or action. The charge was infamous."[27] While Grangers opposed the poll tax, they were also joined by fourteen non-Grange Democrats who feared disenfranchisement for their loyal white agrarian constituents.[28] Despite considerable evidence disputing any claims that the Grangers were a unified front or possibly in league with Republican elements, the misinformation disseminated by the press became history.

Ericson acknowledged mistakes made in McKay's early history as well, but with a focus more on the Grange's supposed numerical dominance. According to Ericson's analysis of convention demographics, the delegates consisted of thirty-three lawyers and twenty-eight farmers.[29] This differs from McKay's account, which counted forty-one farmers and twenty-nine lawyers.[30] Ericson notes that many of the lawyers owned land and would conveniently declare themselves farmers when politically convenient. Perhaps unjaded by politics at the time of his writing, McKay did not account for the natural shiftiness of men whose livelihood relied on getting votes. Thus, it becomes next to impossible to discern with absolute certainty who comprised the largest bloc of delegates. Ericson's source is available biographical information he used in assembling his own dissertation. By comparison, McKay drew his conclusions regarding Grange numeric dominance solely from a report in the *San Antonio Herald*, August 5, 1875.[31]

The myth of Grange dominance at the convention endured for generations of historians, but it would be rather unfair to attribute this historiographical legacy exclusively to McKay's methodological choices. To assign credit to McKay alone for building the legend would be to ignore the evidence he had available. Texas media accounts, through their partisan perspective, opposed the Grange from the very beginning as a potential threat to Democratic unity. That the debate over the supposed Grange-Republican conspiracy at the convention was spawned by the *Statesman* should come as no surprise, as the Austin paper had been vocally opposed to the Grange's very existence from the start two years earlier: "Who is R. A. Baird, of Fort Worth, [founder of the Texas Grange] who is trying to make trouble in the Democratic party of Texas by organizing Granges to interfere with Democratic nominations? . . . No better 'people's party' is wanted than the Democratic party. Look out for tricks to divide the Democracy and create confusion. We have no need of Granges in Texas. They are one of the Northern patent political inventions to break up the Democratic party."[32] For the mainstream press, the Grange represented a threat to Democratic ownership over the rural bloc, which meant everything for a state like Texas. As the *Statesman* added:

> It is said that we are opposed to the interests of the farmers. This is untrue in every respect, as we have frequently avowed and explained. But we are strongly opposed to a farmer's party as distinguished from and in opposition to the old Democratic party. We insist there is no necessity for such a party in Texas, and that the Democratic party is all sufficient for the time and circumstances, and that it will attend, as it always had, to the best interest not alone of the farmers, but of all classes, as a great and true party should. We think the Granges will run into politics and the formation of a farmer's party, hence we oppose them.[33]

The Democratic fervor for partisanship over policy still ultimately won the day, even if complete dominance wasn't possible. The truth is that Texas, over the course of war and Reconstruction, had achieved a more consolidated and unified political culture than what existed prior to the Civil War. The historical record of the Grange's Reconstruction-era position on race further diminishes the legend of their conspiring with minority groups at the time of the convention and thus subverting the creation of a good constitution. Charles Postel, prominent historian of American populism, noted that for political expediency in the 1870s, the Grange intentionally remained silent on the controversial question of race, despite their underlying mission of seeking class equality. Postel explained:

> The Grangers studiously avoided the questions of racial equality, at least in public. Rather, they promised a vision of national reconciliation that would move the country beyond the old sectional

quarrels and restore equality and harmony between the states. No one in Washington or beyond misunderstood the double meaning of such a promise: on the one hand, the Grange wanted no part of the black struggle for equal rights; and on the other hand, it was sending an offer of solidarity to the white planter class of the South. The advocates of white supremacy quickly recognized a potent ally. By the early 1870s, the Grange had become a refuge for rural white power across the former Confederacy.[34]

Even though accusations of conspiracy and Grange-led plots to subvert Democratic control blossomed in the press, the suboptimal and regressive product presented to the people of Texas for ratification was the result of nothing more than ideological disunity.

On the surface education might serve as another example disproving the myth of Grange dominance at the convention. Nationally, the Patrons of Husbandry were explicitly apolitical, and prohibitions against partisan speech at local meetings were included in the group's bylaws.[35] But as the nation's premiere agricultural interest group, seeking not only to reconcile differences between North and South in the postwar environment but also to remove class barriers by empowering the nation's farmers, the Grange's status as a politically oriented group could not be avoided. Although strongly in favor of government funding for higher education in the form of state universities (ideally for the purpose of promoting agricultural science), the Grange rarely advocated government spending for primary education, despite widespread illiteracy among the farmer class throughout the South. In Mississippi in 1874, for example, the state Grange urged the governor to eliminate the office of county superintendent of education, a move made in the name of retrenchment that was even more extreme than the stinginess on display at the 1875 convention in Texas. Records from the Tippah County, Mississippi, Grange in spring 1875 unambiguously argue that freedmen should pay for the education of their own children, rather than burdening white farmers with additional taxes.[36] Postel maintained that the Grange's disconnect from the plight of the freedmen, from education to basic civil rights, was more than just political pandering to prospective members, asserting that the group was actually deeply embedded with white nationalist paramilitaries and unified in opposition to Reconstruction.[37] Whether a similar devotion to the subversion of national authority and civil rights existed in Texas is unclear, but the preponderance of evidence does not remotely support the notion of Grange-Republican or Grange–African American collusion on the question of government support for education.

The spirit of retrenchment over education in Texas followed a similar pattern to that of Mississippi, with the quick elimination of the office of superintendent of public instruction on October 4, 1875.[38] The impassioned speech of Colonel Richard Sansom, a Democrat representing Williamson County, given five days earlier against the intrusive nature of a government empowered to mandate the education of children, has a clear agricultural tone about it: "A system of public free schools to be supported by taxation is not adapted to the condition or wants of the people of Texas. The State is barely thirty years old, and its first settlement by English speaking people dates back only a little over fifty years. Its present condition is like that of a young man with small capital just entering upon the business of life, with broad but undeveloped fields of enterprise stretching into the distance on every side."[39] Sansom was not alone in his concerns that Texas was too sparsely populated and generally underdeveloped to support a free education system at the state level. The final diminishment of state-operated public education demonstrates a consensus between the Grange and the non-Grange Democrats. The Republican State Convention in January 1876, while denouncing the new constitution as a whole, also pinpointed education policy as a particular disappointment. One adopted resolution included the words, "the late Democratic Constitutional Convention of this State has, by its action, made the maintenance of the public free schools in this State, in case the new constitution is adopted, an impossibility."[40] Despite all attempts to pass the buck, the destruction of public education in Texas, which disproportionately impacted rural children, both Black and white, was the product of a Democratic party focused primarily on anti-Radicalism.

Perhaps sensing their own culpability in allowing a great opportunity to slip away, Texas Democratic newspapers were already at work washing their hands of the document prior to ratification. Their party, in its parliamentary ineptitude and unified only in its opposition to Republican Radicalism, had taken the better part of three months, from September 6 to November 24, 1875, to fashion a supreme law that they knew was deficient. So blinded by fear and hatred of villains like E. J. Davis that they failed to concoct any better ideas for governance, the Democratic press focused on positioning the minority as the driving force behind the constitution's shortcomings, despite that minority enjoying only fourteen of ninety seats at the convention. In January 1876, just prior to the ratification vote, the *Weekly Democratic Statesman* posed a series of questions: "If a constitutional convention restricts the power of the legislature beyond all precedent, what opinion did it have of our legislators? If it provides that a minority can ratify the new Constitution, what confidence did it have in the people? If it provided that any legislature having a majority of two-thirds could amend out of the new Constitution all that is good as well as what is bad, and have it ratified in ninety days, what reliance did it have in the Constitution?"[41]

The Democrats' handwashing did not go unnoticed by Texas Republicans. Prior to the Republican State Convention in January 1876, the *Houston Tri-Weekly Telegraph*, as reprinted in the *Panola Watchman*, accurately predicted Republican policy at the convention by reporting on a local meeting in Austin: "The Radicals hold a Convention tomorrow to send delegates to Houston. A platform has been prepared, to be submitted at Houston, which declares in substance: That the new Constitution did not suit the Democratic politicians who made it, and who only compromised upon it to avoid the discredit of showing themselves unable to make a Constitution; that it is our purpose to let the Democratic politicians be responsible for their own work, and to carry out the alternative they have chosen to adopt, without any assistance, direct or indirect, positive or negative, from us."[42] Although this resolution was not adopted by the convention in Houston, the *Telegraph's* liberal use of the phrase "in substance" does help to give their prediction a hint of truth.

Called to order in Houston on January 12, 1876, with Davis as chairman of the state committee, members of the Republican State Convention adopted a platform condemning the Democratic constitution, calling special attention to issues like education for such criticism: "Because the said Constitution seeks to cheat the people with specious provisions in relation to schools, while it utterly fails to secure an efficient system of free schools, which is the greatest necessity of the State, the surest guaranty of progress, and the best defense of liberty."[43] As reprinted in the *New York Times,* in addition to education policy, the Republican platform also included criticisms of the constitution's establishment of the judiciary, perceived opposition to immigration, perceived opposition to internal improvement, weak frontier defense, and tax policy. Unfortunately for the Republicans, and ultimately the people of Texas, the die was cast. So powerful was the tide of anti-Radicalism among newspapers and the culture itself that the truth mattered little, and Texas Democrats were enabled to write the early history of Reconstruction and the constitution of 1876 however they saw fit.

Ratification

That the people of Texas were being offered a choice between bad and worse in 1876 was a foregone conclusion months prior when the convention was still in session. That the people of the frontier, consumed like their representative Rutabaga Johnson by a zeal for retrenchment would vote against their own interests was less certain. The *Weekly Democratic Statesman,* commenting in early November 1875, expressed the attitude of the Democratic press that while the results were increasingly suboptimal, the scourge of Radicalism had to be eliminated: "The Mexia Ledger says: 'With the school law killed, virtually, the suffrage law framed to suit demagogues, laws driving away capital, immigration snubbed, thus early in the session, how can the friends of progress, sound policy and justice, hope for a Constitution the people will approve? We predict that when the new Constitution is submitted to the people, they will spew it out.' We cannot yet concur in all this with the *Ledger*. However absurd and objectionable in many of its features, this new code, it may still be properly preferred to the existing Constitution."[44]

Owing to a massive demographic change by the time of the ratification vote, Harrison County had become a different place politically by early 1876. As Campbell notes, "On February 15, 1876, Texans overwhelmingly ratified the new constitution and elected state and local officers under its terms. Harrison County's Republican majority was on the losing side of virtually every contest that extended beyond the community's borders. They carried the county against the constitution 2,713 to 1,036 and voted for all of the unsuccessful Republican candidates for state offices."[45] Harrison County had become a Republican stronghold due to its Black majority and remained "radical" long after the government in Austin was redeemed. At the same time, Robert Loughery remained a powerful voice in Democratic politics, not just in Harrison County but statewide. His series of commentaries in January and February 1876 preceding the ratification vote demonstrated two relevant points: One, his endorsement of the new constitution and encouragement of its ratification by the voters hinged primarily upon the opposition and the supposition that anything less than ratification was the equivalent of Radicalism. While his commentary on January 29, 1876, highlighted specific points that Loughery saw as political victories (biennial sessions, limited public debt, lower taxes, and a new preamble), his ultimate argument for ratification by the people hinged upon a classic phrase that has plagued democracy since ancient times: the lesser of two evils. From the *Tri-Weekly Herald* in late January 1876: "Latterly the ardent friends of the new Constitution have exhibited more wisdom. Unable to answer the arguments adduced against it, they have concluded to advocate its adoption as a choice of evils. This is the present position of that able and usually logical paper, the Waco Examiner. This is the true and only defensible ground."[46] Secondly, his strong endorsement, while not bothering to acknowledge the foregone conclusion that his home of Harrison County would vote against ratification, reiterated the existence of a racial barrier preventing even the slightest amount of communication between the two sides. Overall, compared to many in the Texas Democratic press, who encouraged ratification even if it meant voters holding their noses while doing so, Loughery was noticeably less critical of the document. Instead, Loughery accepted the document as a malleable frame of government, adaptable to future needs through the process of amendment.

At the same time, Collin County had become conservative while mostly eschewing the political establishment. The myth of the Granger-Republican alliance persisted through to the last day of the convention, with many delegates still believing that John Johnson of Collin and Stillwell Russell of Harrison were in cahoots. The legend would persist in the history books, and Johnson's own behavior did much to perpetuate it. Unable to resist the opportunity to take a victory lap on behalf of the people of Collin County, marginalized politically since 1861, Johnson's remarks were noted in the *Debates in the Texas Constitutional Convention of 1875*:

> Mr. Johnson, of Collin, rose to a question of privilege. He had been assailed in that body and throughout the whole State. Some one had sent the report to his home paper that he had chosen to sit among the negroes in the Convention. He would like to know what member of the Convention had done this. He had had to take the seat he had drawn, thought he would have preferred to be somewhere else. He had carried every point he had started out with when he left his county. They had "fit" the opposition carefully and beaten them. There were thirty-six lawyers in that body, but they had been superior to them. They had beaten the talent of the Convention all along the line.[47]

The February 22, 1876, *Galveston News* reported voting results for the constitution, as well as the governor's race wherein Davis was attempting to regain office, "McKinney, Feb. 21 – Collin county, official: For constitution, 2824; against, 157; Coke, 3131; E. J. Davis, 2."[48] Although it is impossible to determine, it is entirely likely that one of the two votes for Davis came from *McKinney Messenger* publisher James Waller Thomas. That the constitution contained elements detrimental to their own interests mattered little for the political culture of Collin County. The results highlighted the remarkable changes in formerly individualistic Collin County and Harrison County, which had before the Civil War stood as a bastion of traditionalistic Southern culture.[49]

Reform

The deficiencies of the Texas Constitution have not escaped notice. While attempting to create a document that would limit the scope of government, the Texas framers unknowingly set up a document that could only grow to excess, defying the spirit of retrenchment altogether, and Texas lawmakers have not been oblivious. When the most serious attempt at constitutional revision came in 1974, even finding a mechanism of initiating reform proved difficult. Article XVII did not originally contain provisions for calling a new constitutional convention, so an amendment was presented to the voters, which they overwhelmingly approved. Voters in 1974 understood the quagmire the constitution had become, for in the twenty years preceding the convention of 1974, the bulk of the growth of the Texas Constitution was amendments to amendments.[50] Initially authorized to work for ninety days, the Constitutional Convention of 1974 was extended by an additional sixty days, only to fail by three votes to achieve the necessary two-thirds majority required to send their document to the voters. The political accusations flew, with some arguing in favor of maintaining the limited power of the Texas executive branch, which was a key philosophical feature of the 1876 constitution. Most, including convention president Price Daniel Jr., attributed the failure to the influence of organized labor, which had virulently fought against the new constitution on the grounds of its right-to-work provision.[51] Wherever the truth lay, the constitution of 1876 remains in effect today and is so convoluted that it is accessible only to the most devoted of constitutional law scholars and sleep-deprived graduate students.

Measuring Political Change

In 1993 political scientist Joel Leiske noted that Daniel Elazar's initial classification scheme of political subcultures was not based on a particularly rigorous statistical methodology by today's standards.[52] Elazar's work argued that political subcultures are established in identifiable geographic areas due to migration patterns, the perpetuation of cultural patterns due to shared ethnic and religious values among people who settle in the same area, and the process of enculturation for those who don't share the same old-world values. Space for subjective interpretation abounds in Elazar's work, and any sort of comparative predictive power is based on past behavior, which can be problematic for identifying change, no matter how lumbering. In other words, Elazar's theory is limited in its power to understand and explain how entire cultures experience ideological shifts. Yet Elazar's work remains a fixture in political culture literature, and his classification scheme is one of the few culturalist ideas of its time that has achieved staying power in mainstream higher education. Following in the footsteps of Elazar, scholars developed a more refined concept of political culture in the late 1980s through the 1990s, and the genre remains vibrant in political science today.

At the beginning of the late twentieth-century renaissance of political culture, political scientists Richard Ellis and Aaron Wildavsky's 1986 analysis of the cultural roots of the Civil War hinted at reactionary cultural forces pushing the South toward secession with an exaggerated fervor beyond the scale of any genuine political or social threat from the North. The examples of Harrison and Collin Counties in Reconstruction represent something similar. Ellis and Wildavsky broke from the dominant paradigms of the time used to outline the causes of the American Civil War by presenting abolitionism as its own political culture. Encompassing more than just two cultures (North and South) defined by drastically different patterns of economic development and divided by their stance on slavery, Ellis and Wildavsky's conception of the roots of the war brings the abolitionists to the forefront. Although previous theories had accounted for the impact of fringe extremists creating a false sense of emergency for the larger culture, in turn fostering a snowball effect that quickly subsumed the larger populace and making war inevitable, Ellis and Wildavsky took their cue from anthropology and defined cultural types based on two variables: grid and group. The grid spectrum measures the degree to which an individual's behavior is shaped by social cues. The group dimension measures the extent to which an individual's life is absorbed by group membership.[53] Using these two variables, the authors defined a hierarchal culture as one where authority is institutionalized to a high degree and inequality is justified in the name of social harmony. Strong boundaries preserve differences between races, and the result is a cultural type not far removed from Elazar's traditionalistic type defined two decades earlier.

This classification scheme can be applied to Harrison and Collin Counties. For Harrison County, modeled upon the plantation-style economy of the Deep South, hierarchy was a way of life. Randolph Campbell's demonstration that the initial Anglo settlers in East Texas found conditions perfectly suited to the climate and soil conditions necessary for plantation agriculture confirms the applicability of Zelinsky's theory of first effective settlement to the region. To maintain a way of life keeping with the Deep South tradition, a rigid sense of social/racial hierarchy was necessary, and the commentaries of the *Texas Republican* and *Tri-Weekly Herald* demonstrate that this was perpetuated well beyond the Civil War itself. On the other hand, owing to a completely different social, racial, and economic order, Collin County in 1861 was significantly less hierarchal, having no practical reason to embrace a comparable level of group identity. However, by the end of Reconstruction, Collin County had fallen in step with the rest of the state culturally. Ironically, the new voting power of African Americans had the opposite effect in Harrison County, which temporarily remained a Republican stronghold in an overwhelmingly Democratic state.

It would be easy to point to the hierarchal traditional culture of the South and explain its incompatibility not only with the developed non-enslaving North but also with the very philosophical tenets of the American founding. The day enslavers successfully defended their practice as a social good (at least in the minds of Southern whites who otherwise had no reason to support the practice) was the day the divide between North and South became so entrenched that only a war could solve it. But at the same time, it is important to account for the oppositional culture, which can likewise escalate tensions.

For Ellis and Wildavsky it was the abolitionist movement as a veritable culture that exacerbated the already uneasy social and economic duality that defined the United States during the first part of its history by forcing the cultures of the North and South to articulate their positions, fostering violent conflict.[54] On the other side of the war, the staunchest of former Confederates similarly fanned the flames of discord during Reconstruction, thus forcing Texans to choose sides. But at the same time, while extreme elements played a role in escalating conflict in Reconstruction Texas, clearly discernable cultural change took place that was even greater than the extremist influence. The natural process of enculturation, political socialization, and the psychological effects of losing a war changed the face of Collin County between 1861 and 1876 from dissenting Unionist to die-hard rebel. The experience of these counties before and during Texas Reconstruction, therefore, is an exceptionally useful case study for both historians and political scientists because it demonstrates how behaviors change on the mass level, something not easily accounted for through quantitative modeling.

Negative Polarization

The fallout from Reconstruction and the adoption of a regressive constitution set Texas on a course of perpetual underdevelopment that the state was fortunately able to avoid, but it took generations to do so. Carl Moneyhon noted the virtual abolition of the state education system along with limited improvements in frontier protection under Democratic leadership after Reconstruction. Simultaneously, Texas Democrats strongly favored railroad interests through extensive land grants, in turn favoring wealthy interests, while the loss of state educational support disproportionately impacted poor rural districts.[55] The seeds for this legacy were readily apparent at the time of the Constitutional Convention of 1875, and there was little reason for any objective observer of public policy to expect different. Put simply, without taking away from Moneyhon's eloquent and nuanced assessment of the state during the Reconstruction era, the masses that supported the Texas Constitution of 1876 got exactly what they wanted, even to their own detriment. In political science, this is known as negative polarization or negative partisanship.

Political scientists describe negative partisanship as a mass psychological phenomenon wherein a significant portion of voters dislike the opposition to such a degree that it outweighs any positive feelings they harbor for their own side. This dislike is potentially so palpable that it can also outweigh reservations about the leadership or direction of their own side, along with good old-fashioned common sense.[56] The term gained prominence in analysis of the 2016 US general election, notable for featuring two presidential candidates that generally polled unfavorably among all voters. However, while a proper scientific name for this sort of development may not have existed in Reconstruction Texas, the phenomenon was very much on display.

On October 11, 1875, the delegates of the constitutional convention were deep in discussion about Article VII, "Education: The Free Public Schools," with a focus on Section 3 and the question of proper taxation.[57] Policy concerns included even distribution of the free school system statewide (which Johnson of Collin County supported, but which was opposed by many others), sources of revenue (in particular the level of poll tax), what portion of the state revenue would be devoted to education (ultimately they settled on one-fourth of state revenue), and the usefulness of having a state education system at all. One of the more illuminating comments on the spread of negative polarization in Reconstruction Texas came from George M. Flournoy of Galveston. Flournoy was a college graduate, an attorney, a former Texas attorney general, coauthor of the declaration of the causes of secession, and a former Confederate officer.[58] His argument against the free public school system was summarized in the *Debates in the Texas Constitutional Convention of 1875*:

> Mr. Flournoy said he was opposed to any system of public free schools supported by taxation. He contended that no free government could levy tribute on the citizens to force education on the children. Massachusetts and other states had been held up as having magnificent schools, sustained by their respective states. Were those people any happier, wiser, or more virtuous than those of Texas? Nay. He would venture the assertion that there lived no more virtuous, intelligent, and prosperous people than Texans. They were the peers of any people. They had no right to invade the mansion of the parent and take from him or her their bright-eyed child, and turn him over to the State. Whenever they should do that they could do anything. When that was done the science of free government was trodden under foot; the liberties of the country gone.[59]

In their single-minded quest to keep taxes low regardless of the long-term ramifications, the delegates created a deep class division by underfunding rural schools, which in turn had the effect of enshrining agriculture as the state's leading economic sector—to the detriment of future industrialization. At the same time, the dilution of the free school system drove an even deeper racial wedge, as literacy rates among African Americans remained around 45 percent through 1900.[60] Flournoy's statement, which was absent any of the objective logic normally expected from a constitutional framer, summarized the motivation for a policy direction that would obviously do the people of the state more harm than good. Yet, lest the blame for Texas's constitutional tragedy fall entirely upon the head of a single delegate, it is worth remembering that Flournoy was just one of many at the convention who had fallen into the trap of negative polarization, all of whom were speaking on behalf of the political culture that elected them.

Post-Reconstruction Harrison County

With Reconstruction complete, and a constitution in place designed to perpetuate agricultural interests over industrialization, many landowners began to return to positions of political prominence. Although slavery was gone, the instillation of the so-called Black Codes in Texas during Throckmorton's tenure in 1866 had effectively tied freedmen to the land and solved the immediate labor problem for landowners. In 1874 the practice of sharecropping was further enshrined with the Landlord and Tenant Act under the Fourteenth Legislature, which gave landowners the right to seize property from tenants in order to ensure repayment of debts, while giving zero control to the tenants.[61]

The basic model of sharecropping became further institutionalized following Reconstruction, and a clearly discernible hierarchy developed wherein sharecroppers at the bottom, with no capital and only their labor to offer, were frequently required to pay landowners up to half of the crop they harvested. Naturally, this had the effect of permanently tying sharecroppers to the land, as the debt they incurred would be more than they could possibly make. This de facto form of economic slavery carried hints of feudalism and disproportionately impacted freedmen and the economics of predominantly Black counties. By 1880 Harrison County had one of the highest tenant farmer populations in the state, accounting for approximately 60 percent of the county's entire population of farmers.[62] Randolph Campbell noted that the overall decline of Harrison County's economy after the war was likely attributable to the preexisting dependence on slavery along with its unfortunate geographic location, rather than the impact of Reconstruction politics. Relative to other counties that suffered economic stagnation after the war, Campbell notes that Harrison County African Americans did surprisingly well considering they entered into the market economy with no wealth at all.[63]

Politically in post-1876 Harrison County, we catch a glimpse of how conservatives worked to manipulate public opinion by targeting the county's Black majority. In the buildup to the 1878 election, the work of the Radicals to protect Black interests in an uncertain social and political environment was flipped. As Campbell explained, propagating the myth of the Texas carpetbagger proved an effective way to convince Black voters that they were simply pawns in the Radical struggle for power. Additionally, emphasizing fears over taxes and the disproportionate burden being carried by the poor went far in convincing Black voters to abandon the Republicans.[64] In Harrison County the Redeemers, now branded as the Citizens Party, managed to engineer a significant swing in favor of conservative candidates despite an actual increase in Black voter turnout. The politics of fear had triumphed. The Republican Party was relegated to the political wilderness in Texas until the 1960s, when ideological splits over civil rights finally disrupted Democratic dominance.

Collin County

As the economy of North Texas expanded, so too did the fortunes of Collin County, with McKinney serving as the commercial heart. The meager 4,371 cotton bales produced in 1870 had exploded to 22,145 bales in 1880, although corn remained the most widely grown crop.[65] The 1872 arrival of the Houston and Texas Central Railroad (in a grand ceremony hosted by James Throckmorton) finally connected McKinney with the rest of the state and literally put the city of Allen on the map.[66] Additional rail connections came throughout the 1880s, and Collin County prospered.

However, like much of the South, the statistics revealing impressive growth also have a hidden side. While the overall value of farms increased statewide into the Progressive Era, individual and family subsistence farming became a much more difficult enterprise. National economic crises like the Panic of 1873, along with falling land prices, resulted in greater debt and mortgages for people in areas like Collin County. The growth of railroads due to generous land grants from the Texas legislature did much to help commercial farms and the burgeoning manufacturing sector but drew cries of monopoly from rank-and-file farmers. The result was the continued growth of farmer unity. From the Grange to the Farmers' Alliance to the People's Party at the height of the Populist movement, Collin County was very much a part of the Progressive Era's push for more equitable opportunities for rural Americans.

Along with neighboring counties such as Dallas, Collin County's ultimate suffering at the hands of Congressional Reconstruction was more a matter of perception than reality. Aside from federal intervention in the Lee-Peacock feud of 1869–1870, there was little visible presence of Northern authorities during Reconstruction, and the return of the regular army to the northern Texas borderlands eventually ended the perceived security threat posed by Native Americans. Although McKinney did have a local Ku Klux Klan organization, their activities were few, probably owing to the relatively small percentage of African Americans in the area.[67] Given the absence of any genuinely tangible Union affront to the cultural sensibilities of the people, understanding Collin County's shift from Unionism to conservatism is a matter of understanding the natural dynamics of political culture. Isolated on the fringes of the frontier, the people of Collin shared information with each other as it trickled in. The result is a group of people developing a narrative on their own, with the more extreme elements influencing the natural tendency toward polarization. Texas-style conservatism of the 1870s, much like the war of the decade prior, had little to offer the people of Collin County, yet they embraced it based on the perceived threat of Northern hostility.

A. J. Hamilton

Colossal Jack Hamilton's postgovernorship career was spotty. Despite his shift away from Radicalism to a more moderate ideological position, his mere association with the Republican Party following his loss to Davis in the 1869 race for governor left him isolated. Hamilton biographer John L. Waller, writing in 1968 and toeing the historiographical line of his era, strongly suggested interference in the 1869 race on the part of General Joseph J. Reynolds to guarantee victory for Davis. Waller even goes so far as to suggest that Hamilton felt cheated

for the remainder of his life.[68] His activism in opposition to Radicalism resulting in the Tax-Payers Convention of 1871 was likely meant
to earn him a modicum of support from centrist Democrats, which it
did not. At the same time, his continued public criticism of the Davis
administration left him with no friends among the Radicals. In the
political wilderness, Colossal Jack was too far removed from his legal
career to resume practice, and he found himself adrift.

His participation in contesting the results of the 1873 gubernatorial election would prove to be his final public act. The very basis for
attempting to declare the 1873 election illegal in the case of *ex parte
Rodriguez* was its violation of a constitutional provision mandating
elections at county seats with polls open for four days. Hamilton
himself was the author of this provision to the 1869 constitution, so his
involvement in defending Rodriguez made sense, even if his indirect
defense of Davis and the Radicals did not.[69] When the decision of *ex
parte Rodriguez* did nothing to stop the Democratic Party, which was
empowered with a mandate from the voters, Hamilton's reputation
was ruined, and he settled on his farm outside of Austin. He did not
get to see the final victory of the Redeemers and the final disgrace of
the Republicans as he died at home in the spring of 1875. Remarking
on his passing, the *Weekly Statesman* said, "He loved Texas with a
most fervent zeal, and this love, while it led others to the reverse,
impelled him, as the breaking out of the Confederate war, to quit the
South. He spent the period which encompassed that eventful struggle at the North, and when it was ended he came back to Texas as
its provisional Governor, and instead of exercising the powers of the
conqueror, dealt out justice and leniency to her people."[70] His funeral
was widely attended by supporters, both Black and white, as well as
Governors Coke, Pease, and Davis.

James Throckmorton

Under the General Amnesty Act of 1872, James Webb Throckmorton
was allowed to return to public office. Although unsuccessful in
his attempt to reclaim the governor's office in 1878, he was elected

to the US House of Representatives in 1882, 1884, and 1886 and performed his duties with relative mediocrity according to historian Kenneth Howell, frequently taking leave due to ill health.[71] Another short-lived attempt to run for governor followed in 1892, and when that failed, Throckmorton's political career ended with a whimper. Howell credited Throckmorton's fervent racism with setting back race relations in Texas for years, and indicted the former governor for using his political influence to promote railroad development while simultaneously serving as an attorney on the payroll of the Texas and Pacific Railroad.[72] Contrary to popular belief, Throckmorton County, in north-central Texas was actually named after his father, William Edward Throckmorton, an early settler in the area. There was likely a political motivation for the honor, as Throckmorton County was established by the legislature in 1858, while James Throckmorton happened to be serving in the Texas Senate.[73] Owing to his open opposition to secession, avowed white supremacy, and Reconstruction obstinacy, Throckmorton enjoys a legacy today that the word *complicated* is insufficient to explain.

Elisha Pease

Elisha Pease, having split from the mainstream Texas Republican party following his dispute with General Reynolds and later leading the anti-Davis Tax-Payers Convention alongside A. J. Hamilton, found himself drawn back to the Republicans in 1874.[74] His opposition to what he perceived as Radical despotism under military controlled by Reynolds had led to his involvement with the Liberal Republicans, for whom he served as the delegate for Texas at their 1872 convention. Although reconciled with Davis in 1874, Pease did not seek out positions of leadership, instead deferring to Davis and others, preferring a more hands-off role.[75] In 1879 he accepted a federal appointment as customs collector at Galveston from President Rutherford B. Hayes. In 1881, in an attempt to extend a bipartisan olive branch to an old foe, Governor Oran Roberts nominated Pease to serve on the first board of regents for the constitutionally established University of Texas. It was a position of honor that Pease likely would have accepted had his nomination not drawn the opposition of an overwhelming majority of Democratic senators in the Texas legislature, still angry over Pease's Unionist past.[76]

E. J. Davis

Despite the fireworks associated with his acrimonious departure from office, the relegation of the Republican Party in Texas to the fringes of the political scene, and his family's immediate financial needs, staying absent from the public eye was not an option for E. J. Davis. Carl Moneyhon noted that Davis's legacy of service to the Republican Party, along with overwhelming support from Black Texans, gave him a firm mandate of control over the party that he clung to throughout his remaining years.[77] Although nominally run by new blood in order to help the Republicans reorganize, reconsolidate, and reassess their strategy for the state, the party began to strategically choose its electoral battles as Davis remained an omnipresent force. When he finally spoke publicly at the Southern Republican Convention in Chattanooga on October 15, 1874, it was to give an honest and objective assessment of the state of affairs in Texas under Democratic rule. According to the *New York Times*, which covered the event, "Gov. Davis declared that since January there have been over 600 homicides in his State. He did not make the mistake of ascribing all these crimes to politics, but, on the contrary, said comparatively few were due to that cause; but the general lawlessness proven by these startling statistics was, he said, a proof of the utter inefficiency, if nothing worse, of the Democratic State Administration. He dwelt at length on the mismanagement of all public affairs in the State, and of the corrupt and reckless waste of its resources."[78] Likely armed with little historical context regarding Davis's governorship, the *New York Times* reporter, who was otherwise hostile to the convention's proceedings, was rather generous in his appraisal of Davis, noting his moderate tone and honesty. But well-received speeches do not translate into action when the speaker is a political pariah. Indeed, under the Democrats, the very issues that Davis had worked so tirelessly for—free labor, the state educational system, a basic guarantee of civil rights, and law and order to end lingering violence—had disappeared along with Republican relevancy.

In many ways Davis served as the prototypical Texas Republican during Reconstruction in the first phase of the historiography. Exaggerated perceptions of tyranny, a false sense of racial doom, and hostility to all things Union (with which he became synonymous) led to his demonization in the early histories, and it has only been in recent decades that he has been redeemed as a man of principle and vision. When he passed in February 1883, the *Weekly Democratic Statesman* magnanimously found a common humanity with the individual previously so reviled: "Sadly the Statesman tells the tale, for while it has harshly criticized the acts of the public man and the politician, it bows lowly before death, that holds in its embrace a man who, in the social and friendly relations of life, was a model worthy to be copied after. . . . He was a gentleman of culture and refinement, courteous, gentle and refined in his bearing, devoted to his family, true to his friends."[79]

John "Rutabaga" Johnson

Aside from accusations of his conspiring with the Black delegates at the convention, John H. Johnson was unconcerned with opinions of the Democratic press. Less than a month after the convention had concluded, directly below a commentary curiously titled, "Ratify! Ratify! Ratify!" the *Weekly Democratic Statesman* continued its personal assault on Johnson, referring to him as a "hairy vegetable" similar to the one that gave him his nickname. The *Statesman* continued: "In fact, Rutabagaism in the Constitutional Convention was planted, cultivated, watered and garnered by men entirely outside of the Democratic Party."[80] For Johnson this was the greatest endorsement he could have imagined, and his disdain for the party establishment made him a celebrated figure in Collin County for the remainder of his life. He embraced the nickname "Rutabaga" from the start, and even went so far as to use it in his signature on public documents. The people of Collin County never forgot his fighting spirit. For while his extreme pursuit of retrenchment may have been ill-advised for the state in the long run, his devotion to farmers' interests from homestead exemptions to poorly paid state officials made him beloved at home. The people would later elect him to serve in the Eighteenth and Nineteenth Texas Legislatures as a senator for the Seventeenth District, including Collin and Denton Counties. When he died at age 80 in 1899, the McKinney paper *The Democrat* noted his funeral commanded one of the largest corteges the city had ever seen and that "from the thoroughfares of this city a most familiar figure has disappeared. The home circle loses a friend indeed."[81]

Robert Loughery

In his short biographical piece on Robert Loughery, editor of the *Texas Republican*, historian Max Lale noted that in the nineteenth century, "The press was largely a personal, not an institutionalized element of society, inasmuch as readers tended to read an editor, not a newspaper."[82] Along with his political impact, Robert Loughery's influence on Texas journalism was significant, and he is remembered alongside Charles DeMorse (whom some have called the Father of Texas Journalism) as one of the great newspapermen of his era. After ceasing publication of the *Republican* in 1872 and serving as editor of the *Tri-Weekly Herald,* he worked for both the *Jefferson Democrat* and the *Austin Statesman.* He later received a diplomatic appointment from Democratic president Grover Cleveland in the 1880s. Despite his firebrand reputation and his public expectation that the people of Texas would never cease the fight, Loughery accepted the war's result and backed reconciliation, encouraging his fellow Harrison County citizens to follow suit. But the man who once called Sam Houston a "traitor" remained a tireless conservative and states' rights advocate until his death in 1894.[83]

James Waller Thomas

By the time the 1876 constitution was ratified by Texas voters, the *McKinney Messenger* was already gone. James Waller Thomas, friend of Sam Houston and E. J. Davis and fearless advocate for Unionism, had finally ceased its publication in 1875.[84] This followed multiple attempts on his life, one of which, in 1871, nearly killed his daughter, an incident the rival *McKinney Enquirer* couldn't help but make light of: "Mr. Jas. W. Thomas, editor of the McKinney Messenger, has been shot at several times on account of his Republicanism, but the Ku Klux can't hit him. We believe a light scratch would wake him up and do him good. His paper, like several other Republican sheets in Texas, needs improvement."[85] The *Weekly Democratic Statesman* similarly belied Thomas's strength of character in 1873 when his name was being rumored for Davis's cabinet: "Poor Thomas is weak as water, and afraid of his shadow. Some time ago, he got a notion into his head that the Democrats wanted to assassinate him, like Brutus and others did Julius Caesar. But he is in no danger. Such men live a long time. Should he, however, by some accident happen to be made Comptroller, he might die of fright in the course of a few months."[86] A more suitable summation of the state of Texas journalism in the Reconstruction era would be difficult to find, for Thomas was one of the few Collin County residents with the courage to resist the cultural tide that transformed the region, even when his physical safety and that of his family was at risk. Thomas's 1906 obituary referred to him as "a man fearless in the expression of his views under all circumstances."[87] Today, his house still stands as a protected Texas landmark.

Epilogue

When Gabriel Almond and Sidney Verba made their great leap forward in the empirical study of political culture in 1963, the static nature of cultures became accepted in the field.[1] Indeed, observable instances of political change are rare, and Collin County's shift during Reconstruction was a notable natural experiment. With the conclusion of Reconstruction, Texas political culture and identity would remain staunchly Confederate for decades. Political scientist Harry Eckstein's 1988 contention that political cultures have their own inertia that makes them resistant to physical change applies perfectly in this case. Texas has remained saddled with the 1876 document (despite the efforts of well-meaning reformers) because Texas has not experienced political and social turmoil comparable to the Reconstruction era in the ensuing century and a half.

When referring to the 1867 reinternment of Confederate General Albert Sidney Johnston at the Texas State Cemetery, historian Jerry Thompson said, "The single most important feature of the 'lost cause' was the formal sanctification of heroes such as General Johnston through ritualistic acts of public memory."[2] Killed at the Battle of Shiloh, and a passionate Texan, Albert Sidney Johnston was the highest-ranking officer to die in battle on either side during the war. The fight over Johnston's reinternment in Texas had been yet another point of controversy between Reconstruction authorities (General Griffin in this case) and the Throckmorton administration, and understandably so. Griffin was fully aware of what celebrating a Confederate hero like Johnston would mean for public sentiment. The veneration in Texas of Confederate heroes in subsequent years by groups such as the United Daughters of the Confederacy would help to perpetuate the idea of a culture that was indistinguishable from the Deep South. Decades later, the centennial celebrations of 1936 would play a major part in reshaping Texas's collective memory, with less emphasis on antebellum plantation life and more on the courage of the Alamo defenders and the rugged individuality of the frontier. Texans began to embrace their past as not only Southern but also Western. As historian Walter Buenger reflected, "Texans abandoned the limited possibilities and racist ideology implicit in the lost cause and adopted the mantle of progress of the Texas Revolution."[3] But while 1936 was undoubtedly a turning point for Texas identity, the past always shapes the present, and the legacy of the Confederacy still resonates. For in the absence of any traumas as significant as Civil War and Reconstruction, political cultures remain in place.

In summer 2020, as Black Lives Matter protests were taking place nationwide following the death of George Floyd at the hands of a white police officer, a public outcry erupted in historic downtown McKinney, Texas, over a statue of James Webb Throckmorton that stands in front of the old Collin County Courthouse. A petition to remove the statue read, "James W. Throckmorton was not the worst confederate to come out of Texas, but he was a poltroon. He was given many opportunities to fight with the Union for the freedom of all men, but he was only looking out for himself. We, as McKinney citizens, will not have our city defined by a coward who was ultimately removed from office because of his racist policies."[4] The matter was taken up by the McKinney City Council, who commissioned a public survey in September 2020 regarding community sentiment on the statue. Over two thousand respondents, 85 percent of whom were McKinney residents, both Black and white, responded in favor of keeping the statue in place.[5]

Endnotes

Introduction

1. Carl Moneyhon, *Texas after the Civil War* (College Station: Texas A&M University Press, 2004), 199.
2. Charles Postel, *Equality: An American Dilemma, 1866–1896* (New York: Farrar, Straus, and Giroux, 2019), 19.

Chapter 1

1. Gabriel Abraham Almond and Sidney Verba, *The Civic Culture: Political Attitudes and Democracy in Five Nations* (1963; repr., Princeton, NJ: Princeton University Press, 2015), 12.
2. Ronald Inglehart, "The Renaissance of Political Culture," *American Political Science Review* 82, no. 4 (1988): 1203–30.
3. Daniel Elazar, *American Federalism: A View from the States*, 2nd ed. (New York: Harper and Row, 1972), 89.
4. Elazar, *American Federalism*, 90.
5. Inglehart, "Renaissance of Political Culture."
6. Aaron Wildavsky, "Choosing Preferences by Constructing Institutions: A Cultural Theory of Preference Formation," *American Political Science Review* 81, no. 1 (1987): 4.
7. Gabriel A. Almond, *The Politics of the Developing Areas* (Princeton, NJ: Princeton University Press, 1960), 83.
8. Wildavsky, "Choosing Preferences," 7.
9. Ronald P. Formisano, "The Concept of Political Culture," *Journal of Interdisciplinary History* 31, no. 3 (Winter 2001): 394.
10. Ronald Inglehart, *Modernization and Postmodernization* (Princeton, NJ: Princeton University Press, 1997).
11. Robert Putnam, *Bowling Alone: The Collapse and Revival of the American Community* (New York: Simon and Schuster, 2000).
12. Colin Woodard, *American Nations: A History of the Eleven Rival Regional Cultures of North America* (New York: Penguin Books, 2011), 82.

13. Woodard notes that although slavery was still a commonly accepted practice throughout all the American colonies, the particular brand of harshness that originated in Barbados and subsequently Charleston included draconian punishments for enslaved people seeking freedom, from whipping to castration to death. See Woodard, *American Nations*, 86.

14. Woodard, *American Nations*, 101.

15. Randolph B. Campbell, *A Southern Community in Crisis: Harrison County, Texas 1850–1880*, 2nd ed. (Austin: Texas State Historical Association, 2016), 298.

16. Ernest William Winkler, ed., *Journal of the Secession Convention of Texas 1861*, edited from the original in the Department of State (Austin: Texas Library and Historical Commission, 1912), 61–65.

17. Moneyhon, *Texas after the Civil War*, 5.

18. David J. Weber, *The Mexican Frontier, 1821–1846* (Albuquerque: University of New Mexico Press, 1982), 176.

19. Randolph B. "Mike" Campbell, "Harrison County," *Handbook of Texas Online*, accessed June 22, 2022, https://tshaonline.org/handbook/entries/harrison-county.

20. Campbell, *Southern Community in Crisis*, 20.

21. J. Lee Stambaugh and Lillian J. Stambaugh, *A History of Collin County, Texas* (Austin: Texas State Historical Association, 1958), 22.

22. Wilbur Zelinsky, *The Cultural Geography of the United States*, rev. ed. (Upper Saddle River, NJ: Prentice-Hall, 1992), 119.

23. Terry G. Jordan, *German Seed in Texas Soil: Immigrant Farmers in Nineteenth-Century Texas* (Austin: University of Texas Press, 1966), 3.

24. Walter L. Buenger, *Secession and the Union in Texas* (Austin: University of Texas Press, 1984), 8.

25. Zelinsky, *Cultural Geography of the United States*, 13.

26. Ralph A. Wooster, *The Secession Conventions of the South* (Princeton, NJ: Princeton University Press, 1962), 129.

27. Wooster, *Secession Conventions*, 129.

28. Elazar, *American Federalism*, 94.

29. Buenger, *Secession and the Union in Texas*, 10.
30. Elazar, *American Federalism*, 99.
31. Elazar, *American Federalism*, 102.
32. Charles A. Johnson, "Political Culture in American States: Elazar's Formulation Examined," *American Journal of Political Science* 20, no. 3 (August 1976): 492.
33. The demographics of Texas in 1860 support this theory, with immigrants from the upper South settling in places like Collin County and immigrants from the lower South settling areas like Harrison County.
34. Jeffrey J. Mondak and Damarys Canache, "Personality and Political Culture in the American States," *Political Research Quarterly* 67, no. 1 (March 2014): 27.
35. Zelinsky, *Cultural Geography of the United States*, 77.
36. Mondak and Canache, "Personality and Political Culture," 38.
37. Walter D. Kamphoefner, "New Americans or New Southerners? Unionist German Texans," in *Lone Star Unionism, Dissent, and Resistance: Other Sides of Civil War Texas*, ed. Jesus F. de la Teja (Norman: University of Oklahoma Press, 2016), 102.
38. Jordan, *German Seed in Texas Soil*, 109.
39. Wooster, *Secession Conventions*, 133.
40. Jordan, *German Seed in Texas Soil*, 110.
41. Wildavsky, "Choosing Preferences," 4.
42. Kamphoefner, "New Americans or New Southerners?," 109.
43. Indeed, in August 1862 nearly a dozen pro-Union Germans were executed following a sharp skirmish near the Nueces River as they attempted to flee to Mexico. Stanley S. McGowen, "Battle or Massacre? The Incident on the Nueces, August 10, 1862," *Southwestern Historical Quarterly* 104, no. 1 (July 2000): 64–86.
44. James Alex Baggett, "Origins of Early Texas Republican Party Leadership," *Journal of Southern History* 40, no. 3 (August 1974): 448.
45. Buenger, *Secession and the Union in Texas*, 9.
46. Buenger, *Secession and the Union in Texas*, 4.
47. Baggett, "Origins of Early Texas Republican Party Leadership," 441, 448.

48. Bizarro is a DC Comics character known for being a mirror image antagonist to Superman.

49. Carl Moneyhon, *Edmund J. Davis: Civil War General, Republican Leader, Reconstruction Governor* (Fort Worth: Texas Christian University Press, 2010), 8.

50. Moneyhon, *Edmund J. Davis*, 16.

51. Carl Moneyhon, "Edmund J. Davis: Unlikely Radical," in de la Teja, *Lone Star Unionism*, 232.

52. Moneyhon, "Unlikely Radical," 229.

53. Baggett, "Origins of Early Texas Republican Party Leadership," 449.

54. Moneyhon, *Edmund J. Davis*, 60.

55. Moneyhon, *Edmund J. Davis*, 63.

56. James Marten, *Texas Divided: Loyalty and Dissent in the Lone Star State, 1856–1874* (Lexington: University Press of Kentucky, 1990), 66.

57. Carl Moneyhon, *Republicanism in Reconstruction Texas* (Austin: University of Texas Press, 1980), 22.

58. Marten, *Texas Divided*, 67.

59. *Houston Tri-Weekly Telegraph*, September 11, 1862.

60. Frank H. Smyrl, "Texans in the Union Army, 1861–1865," in *Lone Star Blue and Gray: Essays on Texas and the Civil War*, 2nd ed., ed. Ralph A. Wooster and Robert Wooster (Denton: Texas State Historical Association, 2015), 250.

61. Marten, *Texas Divided*, 72.

62. Smyrl, "Texans in the Union Army," 244.

63. Charles Ramsdell, *Reconstruction in Texas* (Austin: University of Texas Press, 1910), 112.

64. Kenneth Wayne Howell, *Texas Confederate, Reconstruction Governor: James Webb Throckmorton* (College Station: Texas A&M University Press, 2008), 5.

65. Howell, *James Webb Throckmorton*, 72.

66. Moneyhon, *Edmund J. Davis*, 88.

67. Buenger, *Secession and the Union in Texas*, 151, 159.

68. Wildavsky, "Choosing Preferences," 5.

69. Ramsdell, *Reconstruction in Texas*, 67.

70. Gregg Cantrell, "Racial Violence and Reconstruction Politics in Texas: 1867–1868," *Southwestern Historical Quarterly* 93, no. 3 (January 1990): 355.

Chapter 2

1. J. L. Greer, in *Reminiscences of the Boys in Gray: 1861–1865*, ed. Mamie Yeary (Dallas: Smith & Lamar, 1912), 285.
2. Howell, *James Webb Throckmorton*, 43.
3. Buenger, *Secession and the Union in Texas*, 62.
4. Moneyhon, *Republicanism in Reconstruction Texas*, 16.
5. *McKinney Messenger*, September 14, 1860.
6. *Dallas Herald*, November 14, 1860; *Texas Republican*, November 10, 1860. Neither Abraham Lincoln nor Stephen Douglas was on the ballot in Texas. Douglas supporters were asked to give their support to Constitutional Union candidate John Bell. Thus, Texas voters chose between Southern Democrat John C. Breckinridge and a fusion ticket. Breckinridge's margin of victory in Texas was approximately 2–1, making Texas his strongest state. Collin County voted 696 for Breckinridge and 424 for the fusion ticket. The Harrison County vote for Breckinridge was closer to the Texas average of 2–1 in favor, with a majority of over 300.
7. Wooster, *Secession Conventions*, 131.
8. Thomas Proctor Hughes of Williamson County, just north of Austin, was the lone dissenting vote from Central Texas. Also of note, five of the seven dissenters of military age at the secession convention would still go on to serve the Confederacy either as soldiers or officers or by raising their own units. Only John D. Rains of Wood County and Joshua Foster Johnson of Titus County refused to support the Confederacy. George Washington Wright of Lamar County would grow to support the Confederacy but was too old to fight. See *Journal of the Secession Convention of Texas 1861*, edited from the original in the Department of State by Ernest William Winkler, State Librarian, Texas Library and Historical Commission (Austin: Austin Print. Co., 1912), 49.

9. *McKinney Messenger*, March 1, 1861.

10. Campbell, *Southern Community in Crisis*, 4.

11. Max Lale, "Robert W. Loughery: Rebel Editor," *East Texas Historical Journal* 21, no. 2 (1983): 3.

12. *Texas Republican*, March 29, 1856.

13. *Texas Republican*, May 26, 1849.

14. Daniel J. Elazar, "Political Culture on the Plains," *Western Historical Quarterly* 11, no. 3 (July 1980): 276.

15. Buenger, *Secession and the Union in Texas*, 64.

16. US Department of the Interior, *Population of the United States in 1860, 8th Census* (Washington, DC: Bureau of the Census, 1864); US Department of the Interior, *The Statistics of the Population of the United States, 9th Census* (Washington, DC: Bureau of the Census, 1872).

17. Elazar, "Political Culture on the Plains," 267.

18. Elazar, "Political Culture on the Plains," 274.

19. *McKinney Messenger*, March 1, 1861.

20. Elazar, *American Federalism*, 128. See also Walter L. Buenger, "Texas and the South," *Southwestern Historical Quarterly* 103, no. 3 (2000): 308–24, who also emphasizes the growing influence of Southern culture in Texas following the Civil War.

21. There were 38,196 acres of improved farmland in Collin County compared to 117,847 acres of improved farmland in Harrison County. This likely should have led to a much higher cash value for farms in Harrison County, but Campbell notes frequent underreporting in the US Census from Harrison County, likely even more exaggerated in the 1870 Census. Either way, the developmental advantage for Harrison County is clear. See US Department of the Interior, *Population of the United States in 1860, 8th Census*.

22. Campbell, *Southern Community in Crisis*, 10.

23. US Department of the Interior, *Population of the United States in 1860, 8th Census*.

24. Howell, *James Webb Throckmorton*, 44.

25. US Department of the Interior, *Statistics of the Population of the United States, 9th Census*.

26. US Department of the Interior, *Statistics of the Population of the United States, 9th Census*. The county included 1,206 born in Alabama, 611 from Mississippi, 989 from Georgia, and 606 from Louisiana, compared to 726 from Tennessee.

27. Howell, *James Webb Throckmorton*, 74, 76.

28. Randolph B. Campbell, *Grass-Roots Reconstruction in Texas: 1865–1880* (Baton Rouge: Louisiana State University Press, 1997), 65.

29. *Dallas Herald*, January 16, 1866.

30. Campbell, *Grass-Roots Reconstruction*, 65.

31. *Texas Republican*, February 2, 1861.

32. Howell, *James Webb Throckmorton*, 78.

33. *McKinney Messenger*, June 28, 1861.

34. Harry Eckstein, "A Culturalist Theory of Political Change," *American Political Science Review* 82, no. 3 (September 1988): 793.

35. Richard B. McCaslin, "Wheat Growers in the Cotton Confederacy: The Suppression of Dissent in Collin County, Texas, during the Civil War," *Southwestern Historical Quarterly* 96, no. 4 (April 1993): 528.

36. Stambaugh and Stambaugh, *History of Collin County*, 66.

37. Claude Elliot, "Union Sentiment in Texas: 1861–1865," *Southwestern Historical Quarterly* 50, no. 4 (April 1947): 454.

38. Howell, *James Webb Throckmorton*, 84.

39. *Houston Tri-Weekly Telegraph*, October 27, 1862. The actual extent of the Peace Party influence is unknown. The *Tri-Weekly Telegraph* referred to the movement as an "abolition organization" with roots in the North and possibly including members of the Union Army. This is likely an exaggeration, as there is no reason to doubt the efficacy of homegrown Union sympathy in a region that had so strongly opposed secession to begin with.

40. McCaslin, "Wheat Growers in the Cotton Confederacy," 533.

41. Stambaugh and Stambaugh, *History of Collin County*, 64; McCaslin, "Wheat Growers in the Cotton Confederacy," 535.

42. David Paul Smith, *Frontier Defense in the Civil War: Texas'
    Rangers and Rebels* (College Station: Texas A&M University
    Press, 1992), 171.
43. Smith, *Frontier Defense*, 170.
44. *Texas Republican*, April 28, 1865.
45. *Texas Republican*, April 28, 1865.

Chapter 3

1. Moneyhon, *Republicanism in Reconstruction Texas*, 26.
2. Howell, *James Webb Throckmorton*, 101.
3. Emory M. Thomas, "Rebel Nationalism: E. H. Cushing and the
   Confederate Experience," *Southwestern Historical Quarterly*
   73, no. 3 (January 1970): 344.
4. *Houston Tri-Weekly Telegraph*, July 24, 1865.
5. *Texas Republican*, June 30, 1865.
6. Ramsdell, *Reconstruction in Texas*, 92.
7. Moneyhon, *Edmund J. Davis*, 79.
8. *Journal of the Secession Convention of Texas 1861*, 62.
9. *Texas Republican*, June 16, 1865.
10. *Texas Republican*, July 24, 1865.
11. Barry Crouch, *The Freedmen's Bureau and Black Texans* (Austin:
    University of Texas Press, 1992), 9.
12. William L. Richter, *Overreached on All Sides: The Freedmen's
    Bureau Administrators in Texas, 1865–1868* (College Station:
    Texas A&M University Press, 1991), 4.
13. Gregory's official title was assistant commissioner for Texas
    of the Bureau of Refugees, Freedmen, and Abandoned Lands.
    See Richter, *Overreached on All Sides*, 3.
14. *Texas Republican*, August 4, 1865.
15. Crouch, *Freedmen's Bureau*, 14.
16. *Texas Republican*, July 21, 1865.
17. After Gregory and Kiddoo, Charles Griffin and then Joseph
    Reynolds would take on the dual roles of bureau chief and
    military commander. They are discussed further below.
18. Crouch, *Freedmen's Bureau*, 25.

19. *Weekly State Gazette*, September 8, 1866.
20. Moneyhon, *Edmund J. Davis*, 76.
21. *Texas Republican*, January 19, 1866.
22. Moneyhon, *Republicanism in Reconstruction Texas*, 31.
23. *Texas Republican*, January 19, 1866.
24. *Texas Republican*, January 19, 1866.
25. Howell, *James Webb Throckmorton*, 101.
26. *The Liberator*, September 4, 1863. For a published version of Hamilton's lengthy letter, see "Letter of Gen. A. J. Hamilton, of Texas, to the President of the United States" (New York: Loyal Publication Society, 1863), available through the Internet Archive at https://archive.org/details/letterofgenajham01hami/mode/2up.
27. Howell, *James Webb Throckmorton*, 103.
28. *McKinney Messenger*, February 2, 1866.
29. *Texas Republican*, January 5, 1866.
30. The status of Confederate war debt would remain a legislative quagmire throughout the Reconstruction era.
31. Max S. Lale, "Burke, John (1830–1871)," *Handbook of Texas Online*, accessed Mar. 3, 2021, https://tshaonline.org/handbook/entries/burke-john.
32. *Texas Republican*, December 29, 1865.
33. *Journal of the Texas State Convention, Assembled at Austin, Feb. 7, 1866. Adjourned April 2, 1866*, 5, 37.
34. *Journal of the Texas State Convention, Assembled at Austin, Feb. 7, 1866*, 7.
35. *Journal of the Texas State Convention, Assembled at Austin, Feb. 7, 1866*, 24.
36. Johnson's approach to amnesty was more in line with Lincoln's Ten Percent Plan for readmission, a plan detested by Radical Republicans in Congress as well as Texas Unionists.
37. Andrew Johnson, "May 29, 1865: Proclaiming Pardoning Persons who Participated in the Rebellion," Presidential Speeches: Andrew Johnson Presidency, Miller Center, University of Virginia, accessed June 30, 2021, https://millercenter.org/the-presidency/presidential-speeches/may-29-1865-proclamation-pardoning-persons-who-participated.

38. Moneyhon, *Republicanism in Reconstruction Texas*, 23.
39. Moneyhon, *Edmund J. Davis*, 81.
40. *Journal of the Texas State Convention, Assembled at Austin, Feb. 7, 1866*, 66.
41. *Southern Intelligencer*, March 1, 1866.
42. Howell, *James Webb Throckmorton*, 13.
43. US Department of War, *Annual Report of the Secretary of War, 1866*, 39th Cong, 2d sess., House Executive Document 1 (Washington, DC: 1866), 48.
44. Robert Wooster, *The Military and United States Indian Policy, 1865–1903* (New Haven: Yale University Press, 1988), 116.
45. Moneyhon, *Republicanism in Reconstruction Texas*, 36.
46. Howell, *James Webb Throckmorton*, 109.
47. Texas Constitution of 1866, art. III, sec. 1 (superseded 1876).
48. Texas Constitution of 1866, art. VIII, sec. 2 (superseded 1876).
49. Moneyhon, *Edmund J. Davis*, 85.
50. *Texas Republican*, May 12, 1866.
51. Howell, *James Webb Throckmorton*, 113.
52. *Texas Republican*, June 9, 1866.
53. *Texas Republican*, June 16, 1866.
54. Howell, *James Webb Throckmorton*, 113.
55. Elizabeth Whitlow, *Identified with Texas: The Lives of Governor Elisha Marshall Pease and Lucadia Niles Pease* (Denton: University of North Texas Press, 2021), 176.
56. *Dallas Herald*, May 5, 1866.
57. *Dallas Herald*, May 5, 1866.
58. Moneyhon, *Edmund J. Davis*, 89.
59. *Southern Intelligencer*, May 31, 1866.
60. Howell, *James Webb Throckmorton*, 113.
61. *Texas Republican*, July 14, 1866.
62. *Journal of the House of Representatives. Eleventh Legislature, State of Texas* (Austin: Printed at the Office of the *State Gazette*, 1866).
63. *Journal of the House of Representatives. Eleventh Legislature*, 22.
64. *Journal of the House of Representatives. Eleventh Legislature*, 22.

65. Aragorn Storm Miller, "Richardson, Samuel J. (1826–1876)," *Handbook of Texas Online*, accessed March 3, 2021, https://tshaonline.org/handbook/entries/richardson-samuel-j.

66. Moneyhon, *Texas after the Civil War*, 53.

67. Howell, *James Webb Throckmorton*, 116.

68. Barry Crouch, "'All the Vile Passions': The Texas Black Code of 1866," *Southwestern Historical Quarterly* 97, no. 1 (July 1993): 15.

69. Campbell, *Southern Community in Crisis*, 265.

70. *Journal of the Senate of Texas. Eleventh Legislature, State of Texas* (Austin: Printed at the Office of the *State Gazette*, 1866), 527.

71. Howell, *James Webb Throckmorton*, 115.

72. *Flake's Weekly Galveston Bulletin*, August 29, 1866.

73. Campbell, *Grass-Roots Reconstruction*, 11.

74. Originally devised during the war, the Ironclad Oath was meant to remove ex-Confederate political influence during Reconstruction and was widely detested in the Southern states due to its broad nature. In addition to eliminating former Confederate soldiers and officers from public service, it also prohibited civilians whose work had in any way aided the rebellion.

75. Barry A. Crouch and Donaly E. Brice, *The Governor's Hounds: The Texas State Police, 1870–1873* (Austin: University of Texas Press, 2011), 14.

76. *Texas Republican*, February 2, 1867.

77. Moneyhon, *Edmund J. Davis*, 102.

78. Ramsdell, *Reconstruction in Texas*, 149.

79. Ramsdell, *Reconstruction in Texas*, 148.

80. Robert Wooster, *The United States Army and the Making of America: From Confederation to Empire, 1775–1903* (Lawrence: University of Kansas Press, 2021), 204–6, 211–12.

81. Moneyhon, *Texas after the Civil War*, 69.

82. *Texas Republican*, March 23, 1867.

83. *Texas Republican*, March 23, 1867.

84. Howell, *James Webb Throckmorton*, 154; "Reconstruction in Texas," July 31, 1867, *New York Times*.

85. Ramsdell, *Reconstruction in Texas*, 163.
86. Gregory P. Downs, *After Appomattox: Military Occupation and the Ends of War* (Cambridge, MA: Harvard University Press, 2015), 2.
87. *Texas Republican*, May 11, 1867.
88. Barry A. Crouch, "'Unmanacling' Texas Reconstruction: A Twenty-Year Perspective," *Southwestern Historical Quarterly* 93, no. 3 (January 1990): 278.
89. Cantrell, "Racial Violence and Reconstruction Politics," 349.
90. Ramsdell, *Reconstruction in Texas*, 172.
91. Moneyhon, *Republicanism in Reconstruction Texas*, 69.
92. *Texas Republican*, August 3, 1867.
93. Campbell, *Grass-Roots Reconstruction*, 116.
94. Hancock, of course, would become the Democratic Party's nominee for president in the election of 1880.
95. Carl Moneyhon, "Reconstruction," *Handbook of Texas Online*, accessed May 20, 2021, https://www.tshaonline.org/handbook/entries/reconstruction.
96. Stambaugh and Stambaugh, *History of Collin County*, 72.
97. Moneyhon, *Republicanism in Reconstruction Texas*, 71.
98. *Texas Republican*, January 18, 1868.
99. "Capt. John H. Bingham," Collin County History, accessed May 26, 2021, www.collincountyhistory.com/bingham1.html.
100. *McKinney Messenger*, February 28, 1868.
101. Moneyhon, *Republicanism in Reconstruction Texas*, 83, 85.
102. *Journal of the Reconstruction Convention: Which Met at Austin, Texas. Texas Constitutional Convention (1868–1869)*, (Austin: Tracy, Siemering & Co., 1870), 534.
103. *Texas Republican*, February 22, 1868.
104. *McKinney Messenger*, February 28, 1868.
105. Whitlow, *Identified With Texas*, 244.
106. Cantrell, "Racial Violence and Reconstruction Politics," 350.
107. Robert M. Utley, *Frontier Regulars: The United States Army and the Indians, 1866–1891* (New York: Macmillan, 1973), 168.
108. US Department of War, *Annual Report of the Secretary of War, 1868*, 40th Cong., 3d sess., House Executive Document 1 (Washington, DC: 1868), XVI.

109. Wooster, *Military and United States Indian Policy*, 116; see also Robert Wooster, *The American Military Frontiers: The United States Army in the West, 1783–1900* (Albuquerque: University of New Mexico Press, 2009).
110. *Journal of the Reconstruction Convention*, 3.
111. *Journal of the Reconstruction Convention*, 14.
112. *Journal of the Reconstruction Convention*, 30.
113. *Journal of the Reconstruction Convention*, 195.
114. *Journal of the Reconstruction Convention*, 213.
115. Moneyhon, *Edmund J. Davis*, 125.
116. Ramsdell, *Reconstruction in Texas*, 208, 212.
117. *The Constitution, as Amended, and Ordinances of the Convention of 1866, Together with the Proclamation of Governor Declaring the Ratification of the Amendments to the Constitution, and the General Laws of the Regular Session of the Eleventh Legislature of the State of Texas* (Austin: Printed at the *Gazette* Office, by Jo. Walker, state printer, 1866), 3.
118. Texas Constitution of 1866, 3 (superseded 1876).
119. *McKinney Messenger*, November 13, 1868.
120. Claude Elliott, "Constitutional Convention of 1868–69," *Handbook of Texas Online*, accessed June 14, 2022, https://www.tshaonline.org/handbook/entries/constitutional-convention-of-1868-69.
121. *Texas Republican*, December 25, 1868.
122. *Texas Republican*, April 2, 1869.
123. Moneyhon, *Edmund J. Davis*, 138.
124. Whitlow, *Identified with Texas*, 265.
125. *McKinney Messenger*, June 19, 1869.
126. Lale, "Robert W. Loughery," 4.

Chapter 4

1. Moneyhon, *Republicanism in Reconstruction Texas*, 116. For Reynolds's letter to Grant of September 4, 1869, see John Y. Simon, *The Papers of Ulysses S. Grant* (Carbondale: Southern Illinois University Press, 1995) 19n216–18.
2. *Houston Tri-Weekly Telegraph*, October 7, 1869.
3. Whitlow, *Identified with Texas*, 265.

4. Moneyhon, *Republicanism in Reconstruction Texas*, 116.

5. *Houston Tri-Weekly Telegraph*, September 30, 1869.

6. Moneyhon, *Edmund J. Davis*, 145. Davis, for his part, attempted during the convention to create a compromise solution to the issue.

7. *Houston Tri-Weekly Telegraph*, October 7, 1869.

8. Moneyhon, *Edmund J. Davis*, 147.

9. *Tri-Weekly State Gazette*, October 18, 1869.

10. *Tri-Weekly State Gazette*, October 18, 1869.

11. Moneyhon, *Republicanism in Reconstruction Texas*, 119.

12. Moneyhon, *Edmund J. Davis*, 151.

13. Campbell, *Grass-Roots Reconstruction*, 122.

14. *Dallas Herald*, December 11, 1869.

15. *McKinney Messenger*, July 16, 1870.

16. *Houston Tri-Weekly Telegraph*, December 16, 1869.

17. *House Journal of the Twelfth Legislature, State of Texas. First Session* (Austin: Tracy, Siemering & Co., State Journal Office, 1870), 14.

18. *House Journal of the Twelfth Legislature*, 15.

19. *House Journal of the Twelfth Legislature*, 15.

20. *House Journal of the Twelfth Legislature*, 18.

21. *House Journal of the Twelfth Legislature*, 19.

22. *Tri-Weekly State Gazette*, May 7, 1870.

23. *Evening Telegraph*, May 9, 1870.

24. *Belton Weekly Journal*, May 14, 1870.

25. *McKinney Messenger*, June 18, 1870.

26. Moneyhon, *Texas after the Civil War*, 135.

27. Moneyhon, *Texas after the Civil War*, 132.

28. *Houston Tri-Weekly Telegraph*, June 9, 1870.

29. A past career in law was undoubtedly an asset for Davis. See Texas Constitution of 1869, art. X (superseded 1876).

30. *House Journal of the Twelfth Legislature*, 23.

31. *House Journal of the Twelfth Legislature*, 22.

32. Moneyhon, *Texas after the Civil War*, 134.

33. Yes, you read that right.

34. Crouch and Brice, *Governor's Hounds*, 28.

35. *The Representative*, July 15, 1871.
36. Carl Moneyhon, "Public Education and Texas Reconstruction Politics, 1871–1874," *Southwestern Historical Quarterly* 92, no. 3 (January 1989): 394.
37. *McKinney Messenger*, April 30, 1870.
38. *McKinney Messenger*, June 18, 1870.
39. Moneyhon, *Texas after the Civil War*, 140.
40. Ramsdell, *Reconstruction in Texas*, 303.
41. Moneyhon, *Texas after the Civil War*, 133.
42. Crouch and Brice, *Governor's Hounds*, 69.
43. *Tri-Weekly State Gazette*, January 20, 1871.
44. *Houston Tri-Weekly Telegraph*, August 17, 1871.
45. Donaly Brice, "Finding a Solution to Reconstruction Violence: The Texas State Police," in *Still the Arena of Civil War: Violence and Turmoil in Reconstruction Texas 1865–1874*, ed. Kenneth H. Howell (Denton: University of North Texas Press, 2012), 189.
46. Moneyhon, *Texas after the Civil War*, 171.
47. *Weekly Democratic Statesman*, August 31, 1871.
48. Moneyhon, *Texas after the Civil War*, 181.
49. *McKinney Messenger*, September 16, 1871.
50. *McKinney Messenger*, September 16, 1871.
51. *Weekly Democratic Statesman*, September 14, 1871.
52. *Weekly Democratic Statesman*, August 24, 1871.
53. Moneyhon, *Texas after the Civil War*, 184.
54. *Journal of the House of Representatives of the State of Texas: Being the Session of the Thirteenth Legislature begun and held at the city of Austin, January 14, 1873* (Austin: John Cardwell, State Printer, 1873), 12.
55. Moneyhon, *Texas after the Civil War*, 187.
56. Campbell, *Southern Community in Crisis*, 308.
57. Moneyhon, *Republicanism in Reconstruction Texas*, 182.
58. Moneyhon, *Texas after the Civil War*, 186.
59. *Houston Tri-Weekly Telegraph*, November 14, 1872.
60. Ramsdell, *Reconstruction in Texas*, 313.
61. Brice, "Finding a Solution to Reconstruction Violence," 203.
62. *McKinney Messenger*, September 11, 1873.

63. Moneyhon, *Edmund J. Davis*, 221.

64. Campbell, *Southern Community in Crisis*, 310.

65. *Dallas Weekly Herald*, December 6, 1873.

66. *McKinney Messenger*, September 11, 1873.

67. Carl Moneyhon, "Ex parte Rodriguez," *Handbook of Texas Online*, accessed July 2, 2021, https://tshaonline.org/handbook/entries/ex-parte-rodriguez. Art. III, Sec. 6, of the 1869 Texas Constitution declares, "All elections for State, district and county officers shall be held at the county seats of the several counties, until otherwise provided by law; and the polls shall be opened for four days, from 8 o'clock, A.M., until 4 o'clock, P.M., of each day."

68. Claudia Hazlewood, "Wheeler, Thomas Benton (1840–1913)," *Handbook of Texas Online*, accessed July 1, 2021, https://tshaonline.org/handbook/entries/wheeler-thomas-benton.

69. T. B. Wheeler, "Reminiscences of Reconstruction in Texas," *Quarterly of the Texas State Historical Association* 11, no. 1 (July 1907): 56–65.

70. Moneyhon, *Texas after the Civil War*, 198.

71. *McKinney Messenger*, February 12, 1874.

72. Moneyhon, *Edmund J. Davis*, 223.

73. *McKinney Messenger*, February 12, 1874.

74. *Weekly Democratic Statesman*, January 15, 1874.

Chapter 5

1. *Journal of the House of Representatives: Thirteenth Legislature*, 723.

2. Moneyhon, *Republicanism in Reconstruction Texas*, 184.

3. Seth Shepard McKay, "Making the Texas Constitution of 1876" (PhD diss., University of Pennsylvania, 1925), 48.

4. *Journal of the Senate of the State of Texas: Being the Session of the Thirteenth Legislature begun and held at the city of Austin, January 14, 1873* (Austin: John Cardwell, State Printer, 1873), 628.

5. *Journal of the House of Representatives of the State of Texas: Being the Session of the Fourteenth Legislature Begun and*

Held at the City of Austin, January 13, 1874 (Austin: Cardwell and Walker, 1874), 40.

6. McKay, "Making the Texas Constitution of 1876," 46.
7. John Walker Mauer, "Southern State Constitutions in the 1870s: A Case Study of Texas," (PhD diss., Rice University, 1983), 108, https://scholarship.rice.edu/handle/1911/19046.
8. *Journal of the House of Representatives: Fourteenth Legislature*, 40.
9. John Walker Mauer, "State Constitutions in a Time of Crisis: The Case of the Texas Constitution of 1876," *Texas Law Review* 68, no. 7 (June 1990): 1630.
10. *McKinney Messenger*, February 12, 1874.
11. *McKinney Messenger*, February 19, 1874.
12. *Times-Picayune*, December 31, 1874.
13. *Journal of the Senate of Texas. Fourteenth Legislature – Second Session* (Austin: Caldwell & Walker, Printers, 1875), 15.
14. *Journal of the Senate of Texas. Fourteenth Legislature*, 100. Culberson would later resign to serve in US Congress from 1875 to 1897. See Anne W. Hooker, "Culberson, David Browning (1830–1900)," *Handbook of Texas Online*, accessed July 3, 2021, https://www.tshaonline.org/handbook/entries/culberson-david-browning.
15. *Dallas Daily Herald*, August 4, 1875.
16. *Galveston Daily News*, August 4, 1875.
17. *Tri-Weekly Herald*, April 20, 1875.
18. Joe E. Ericson and Ernest Wallace, "Constitution of 1876," *Handbook of Texas Online*, accessed July 3, 2021, https://www.tshaonline.org/handbook/entries/constitution-of-1876.
19. A cost-cutting measure meant to deprofessionalize the Texas government. For the elected heads of the executive branch, this was not extended to four years until the passage of a constitutional amendment nearly a century later.
20. *Tri-Weekly State Gazette*, August 28, 1875.
21. Technically, the tradition of the plural executive in Texas was already in place following an 1850 amendment to the 1845 Constitution. It is emphasized here to highlight the effort to

break apart what was perceived as Davis's autocracy. See Texas Constitution of 1845 (superseded 1876).

22. McKay, "Making the Texas Constitution of 1876," 75.

23. J. E. Ericson, "The Delegates to the Convention of 1875: A Reappraisal," *Southwestern Historical Quarterly* 67, no. 1 (July 1963): 22.

24. Patrick G. Williams, "Of Rutabagas and Redeemers: Rethinking the Texas Constitution of 1876," *Southwestern Historical Quarterly* 106, no. 2 (October 2002): 231.

25. *The Democrat* (McKinney), August 10, 1899.

26. Barbara H. Fisher, "Edward Bradford Pickett (1823–1882)," *Handbook of Texas Online*, accessed July 30, 2021, https://tshaonline.org/handbook/entries/pickett-edward-bradford.

27. *Journal of the Constitutional Convention of the State of Texas: Begun and Held at the City of Austin Texas. Constitutional Convention (1875)*, (Galveston: Printed for the Convention at the "News" Office, 1875), 13.

28. *Tri-Weekly Herald*, September 7, 1875.

29. Brett J. Derbes, "Weaver, William Thomas Green (1832–1876)," *Handbook of Texas Online*, accessed July 30, 2021, https://www.tshaonline.org/handbook/entries/weaver-william-thomas-green.

30. *Debates in the Texas Constitutional Convention of 1875 Texas. Constitutional Convention (1875)* (Austin: Published by the University of Texas, 1930), 11.

31. *Debates in the Texas Constitutional Convention of 1875*, 9.

32. *Dallas Daily Herald*, September 28, 1875.

33. Citizens Conference on State Legislatures, *The Impact of the Texas Constitution on the Legislature* (Houston: University of Houston, Institute for Urban Studies, 1973), 35.

34. "2020 Legislator Compensation," National Conference of State Legislators, modified June 17, 2020, https://www.ncsl.org/research/about-state-legislatures/2020-legislator-compensation.aspx.

35. Peverill Squire, "Measuring State Legislative Professionalism: The Squire Index Revisited," *State Politics and Policy Quarterly* 7, no. 2 (Summer 2007): 211.

36. It should be noted that without the generous pension offered to legislators after twelve years of service, their pay would

rank among the lowest in the nation and Texas would drop dramatically in its professionalization ranking. See Squire, "Measuring State Legislative Professionalism," 220.

37. Sec. 24 was amended on November 4, 1930, November 2, 1954, November 8, 1960, April 22, 1975, and November 5, 1991. See Texas Constitution of 1875 (superseded 1876).

38. "To make all Laws which shall be necessary and proper for carrying into Execution the foregoing Powers, and all other Powers vested by this Constitution in the Government of the United States, or in any Department or Officer thereof." See US Constitution, art. I, sec. 8, cl. 18.

39. *Journal of the House of Representatives: Fourteenth Legislature*, 196.

40. *Journal of the Constitutional Convention (1875)*, 26.

41. *Debates in the Texas Constitutional Convention of 1875*, 140.

42. McKay, "Making the Texas Constitution of 1876," 82.

43. Texas Constitution of 1876, art. I, sec. 2.

44. Texas Constitution of 1876, art. IV, sec. 2.

45. Texas Constitution of 1867, art. IV, sec. 1 (superseded 1876).

46. Texas Constitution of 1867, art. IV, sec. 1 (superseded 1876).

47. Charles Shannon West of Travis County had already proposed the same losing measure on October 4, the twenty-fifth day of the convention. See *Debates in the Texas Constitutional Convention of 1875*, 152, 257.

48. McKay, "Making the Texas Constitution of 1876," 85.

49. Texas Constitution of 1866, art. V, sec. 4 (superseded 1876).

50. Texas Constitution of 1876, art. IV, sec. 4.

51. Proposed by Jonathan Russell of Wood County, the measure failed by only two votes. See *Debates in the Texas Constitutional Convention of 1875*, 152.

52. *Debates in the Texas Constitutional Convention of 1875*, 153.

53. Measuringworth.com, an interesting resource for economic historians, notes that traditional adjustments for inflation do not tell a complete story about the value of money in the past. For example, George Washington's presidential pay of $25,000 annually would equate to $720,000 in 2020 when using the consumer price index. As a measure against GDP per capita, his pay was well over $15 million, an unsurprising amount

given the vast number of unskilled workers in the United States at the time. And as a share of the overall GDP, his pay equated to $2.8 billion. In the case of the Texas governor, multiplying $4,000 by the percent increase in the consumer price index since 1876 would yield a result of $99,600, significantly less than the $153,750 paid to Governor Greg Abbott in 2020. Considering the necessary expenditures implicit in the office of Texas governor, the amount designated by the 1876 constitution was not paltry but was not particularly good either.

54. *Tri-Weekly Herald*, September 7, 1875.
55. *Book of the States, 2020 Edition, Volume 52* (Lexington, KY: National Council on State Governments, 2020), 113.
56. McKay, "Making the Texas Constitution of 1876," 84.
57. Fred Gantt Jr., *The Impact of the Texas Constitution on the Executive* (Houston: University of Houston, Institute for Urban Studies, 1973), 17.
58. Gantt, *Impact of the Texas Constitution on the Executive*, 18.
59. Nelson C. Demetrius, "Measuring Gubernatorial Power," *Journal of Politics* 41, no. 2 (May 1979): 590.
60. Thad Beyle, "The Governor's Formal Powers: A View from the Governor's Chair," *Public Administration Review* 28, no. 6 (November 1968): 543.
61. Yanna Krupnikov and Charles Shipan, "Measuring Gubernatorial Budgetary Power: A New Approach," *State Politics and Policy Quarterly* 12, no. 4 (December 2012): 439.
62. Gantt, *Impact of the Texas Constitution on the Executive*, 7.
63. James R. Norville, "The Railroad Commission of Texas: Its Origin and Its History," *Southwestern Historical Quarterly* 68, no. 4 (April 1965): 469.
64. *The Democrat* (McKinney), April 24, 1884.
65. David Minor, "Brown, Thomas Jefferson: 1836–1915," *Handbook of Texas Online*, accessed August 8, 2022, https://www.tshaonline.org/handbook/entries/brown-thomas-jefferson.
66. *The Democrat* (McKinney), February 27, 1890.
67. Citizens Conference on State Legislatures, *Impact of the Texas Constitution on the Legislature*, 4.

68. Texas Constitution of 1876, art. III, sec. 49.

69. According to art. VII, sec. 33, of the constitution of 1845 (superseded 1876), "The aggregate amount of debts hereafter contracted by the legislature shall never exceed the sum of one hundred thousand dollars, except in case of war, to repel invasions, or suppress insurrections; and in no case shall any amount be borrowed except by a vote of two-thirds of both houses of the legislature." See also *Debates in the Texas Constitutional Convention of 1875*, 114.

70. *Debates in the Texas Constitutional Convention of 1875*, 114.

71. *Debates in the Texas Constitutional Convention of 1875*, 115.

72. The possible exception coming from Tim Boyd, former mayor of Colorado City, who, in the grips of the January 2021 deep freeze that enveloped Texas and led to massive blackouts and the deaths of at least 246 people, told his constituents via social media, "No one owes you [or] your family anything . . . . I'm sick and tired of people looking for a damn handout!" He resigned shortly after. See Antonia Noori Farzan, "Texas Mayor Tells Residents to Fend for Themselves during Power Outage: 'Only the Strong Will Survive,'" *Washington Post*, February 17, 2021, https://www.washingtonpost.com/nation/2021/02/17/texas-mayor-power-outages-colorado/.

73. For a more detailed examination of the Patrons of Husbandry, or the Grange, see chap. 6.

74. *Weekly Democratic Statesman*, October 21, 1875.

75. *Weekly Democratic Statesman*, October 21, 1875.

76. *Tri-Weekly Herald*, October 16, 1875.

77. *Tri-Weekly Herald*, August 12, 1875.

78. Mauer, "State Constitutions in a Time of Crisis," 1620.

79. Mauer, "State Constitutions in a Time of Crisis," 1626.

80. Alexander Hamilton, John Jay, and James Madison, *The Federalist Papers* (Salt Lake City: Project Gutenberg Literary Archive, 2006), 253.

81. State of Texas Judicial Branch, *Texas Courts: A Descriptive Summary*, 2014, 2, accessed November 6, 2021, https://www.txcourts.gov/media/994672/court-overview.pdf.

82. Allen E. Smith, *The Impact of the Texas Constitution on the Judiciary* (Houston: University of Houston, Institute for Urban Studies, 1973), 29.

83. Michael Ariens, *Lone Star Law: A Legal History of Texas* (Lubbock: Texas Tech University Press, 2011), 48.

84. *Tri-Weekly Herald*, September 7, 1875.

85. James L. Haley, *The Texas Supreme Court: A Narrative History, 1836–1986* (Austin: University of Texas Press, 2013), 92.

86. Texas Constitution of 1876, art. V, secs. 2 and 5. Also see Texas Constitution of 1867, art. V, secs. 2, 6, 10, 11, and 14 (superseded 1876).

87. *Weekly Democratic Statesman*, September 23, 1875.

88. Texas Constitution of 1876, art. V.

89. Lyle C. Brown et al., *Practicing Texas Politics, 2017–2018 Edition* (Boston: Cengage Learning, 2018), 374.

90. The same general will that had on the eve of secession led James Throckmorton to remark, "When the rabble hiss, well may patriots tremble!"

91. Wallace Jefferson, "Reform from Within: Positive Solutions for Elected Judiciaries," *Seattle University Law Review* 33, no. 3 (March 2010): 631.

92. *Debates in the Texas Constitutional Convention of 1875*, 429.

93. Texas Constitution of 1876, art. V, secs. 2 and 5. Also see Texas Constitution of 1867, art. V, sec. 13 (superseded 1876).

94. *Tri-Weekly Herald*, December 4, 1875.

95. Kevin B. Smith, Alan Greenblatt, and Michele Mariani Vaughn, *Governing States and Localities*, 3rd ed. (Washington, DC: CQ Press, 2011), 89.

96. Texas Constitution of 1876, art. III, sec. 5.

97. *Model State Constitution*, 6th ed (New York: National Municipal League, 1968), sec. 4.08.

98. Citizens Conference on State Legislatures, *Impact of the Texas Constitution on the Legislature*, 21.

99. *Model State Constitution*, sec. 2.01.

100. *Dallas Morning News*, October 7, 1972.

101. Texas Legislative Council, *Analysis of Proposed Constitutional Amendments: November 6, 2001, Election*, (September 2001), 3, https://www.tlc.texas.gov/docs/amendments/analyses01.pdf.

Chapter 6

1. There were subsequently additional claims to the title of Last Surviving Confederate Widow. See Associated Press, "Alberta Martin, 97, Confederate Widow, Dies," *New York Times*, June 1, 2004, https://www.nytimes.com/2004/06/01/us/alberta-martin-97-confederate-widow-dies.html.

2. Texas Legislative Council, *Amendments to the Texas Constitution since 1876* (July 2022), 37–38, https://tlc.texas.gov/docs/amendments/Constamend1876.pdf.

3. Texas Legislative Council, *Amendments to the Texas Constitution since 1876*, 19.

4. Patrick Williams, *Beyond Redemption: Texas Democrats after Reconstruction* (College Station: Texas A&M University Press, 2007), 16.

5. *Weekly Democratic Statesman*, August 7, 1873.

6. Ralph A. Smith, "The Grange Movement in Texas: 1873–1900," *Southwestern Historical Quarterly* 42, no. 4 (April 1939): 310. Also See McKay, *Making the Texas Constitution of 1876*, 69; Boardman Buckley Paddock, *History of Texas: Fort Worth and the Texas Northwest*, vol. 2 (London: Forgotten Books, 2018), 144. Edgar P. Sneed's 1969 historiography includes the revelations of Joe Ericson in 1963 (discussed below) regarding Grange control at the convention and therefore serves as a valuable resource to bridge the gap between Dunning School historians and the revisionists: Edgard P. Sneed, "A Historiography of Reconstruction in Texas: Some Myths and Problems," *Southwestern Historical Quarterly* 72, no. 4 (April 1969): 442.

7. This hasn't happened. Texas has thrived in spite of its constitution. See Williams, "Of Rutabagas and Redeemers," 232.

8. *Journal of the House of Representatives: Fourteenth Legislature*, 43.

9. Democratic Party of Texas, *Minutes of the Democratic State Convention of the State of Texas: Held at the City of Austin, September 3rd, 4th, and 5th, 1873* (Austin: Statesman Book and Job Office, 1873), 29, 30.

10. Oliver Hudson Kelley, *Origins and Progress of the Order of the Patrons of Husbandry in the United States: A History from 1866 to 1873* (Philadelphia: J. A. Wagenseller, 1875), 13.

11. Kelley, *Origins and Progress of the Order of the Patrons of Husbandry*, 70.

12. Roscoe C. Martin, "The Grange as a Political Factor in Texas," *Southwestern Political and Social Science Quarterly* 6, no. 4 (March 1926): 368.

13. *Weekly Democratic Statesman*, September 12, 1872.

14. Specifically, an ad valorem tax on real and personal property of .5 percent on each one hundred dollars of assessed value, along with a one dollar poll tax and a 1 percent tax on railroad and telegraph companies. County governments took this even further. See Moneyhon, *Texas after the Civil War*, 152–53.

15. *House Journal of the Twelfth Legislature*, 29.

16. It would appear, ironically, that some of E. J. Davis's preferences did survive the purge of Republicanism. This position is basically identical to Davis's position as laid out in his opening address to the Twelfth Legislature upon taking office. See *House Journal of the Twelfth Legislature*, 22. Also see Williams, "Of Rutabagas and Redeemers," 240.

17. Democratic Party of Texas, *Minutes of the Democratic State Convention*, section IX.

18. *Weekly Democratic Statesman*, November 25, 1875.

19. Mauer, "State Constitutions in a Time of Crisis," 1623.

20. Mauer effectively proves a case for the restrictive nature of the 1876 Constitution (as opposed to the liberal nature of all previous constitutions) by categorizing all Texas constitutions according to legislative pay and length of sessions; gubernatorial pay and term of office; supreme court size, term of office, and salary; and state support for education. See Mauer, "State Constitutions in a Time of Crisis," 1624, 1626.

21. Tax rates under Coke remained as high as they had under Davis and the Republicans, deficit spending remained high, and spending continued to outpace revenue. The indication here is that Democratic fiscal practices had done little to curb the very excesses of Radicalism that they had so vocally condemned. Members of the Grange were understandably frustrated. See Mauer, "State Constitutions in a Time of Crisis," 1638.

22. Moneyhon, *Texas after the Civil War*, 200.

23. McKay, "Making the Texas Constitution of 1876," 178.

24. The poll tax mentioned in art. VII, sec. 3, as well as the legislature's power to implement a poll tax according to art. VIII, sec. 1, did not expressly state that a poll tax was a requirement for voting. As Dick Smith noted, the majority report from the Committee on Suffrage at the convention recommended payment of the poll tax as a requirement for voting, only to be disregarded by the delegates in the name of passage of the constitution. See Dick Smith, "Texas and the Poll Tax," *Southwestern Social Science Quarterly* 45, no. 2 (September 1964): 167.

25. *Debates in the Texas Constitutional Convention of 1875*, 191.

26. *Debates in the Texas Constitutional Convention of 1875*, 203.

27. *Debates in the Texas Constitutional Convention of 1875*, 203.

28. Williams, "Of Rutabagas and Redeemers," 235.

29. Ericson, "Delegates to the Convention of 1875," 24.

30. McKay, "Making the Texas Constitution of 1876," 74.

31. Ericson, "Delegates to the Convention of 1875," 24.

32. *Weekly Democratic Statesman*, September 25, 1873.

33. *Weekly Democratic Statesman*, November 13, 1873.

34. Postel, *Equality*, 21.

35. Postel, *Equality*, 19.

36. James S. Ferguson, "The Grange and Farmer Education in Mississippi," *Journal of Southern History* 8, no. 4 (November 1942): 500.

37. Postel, *Equality*, 74.

38. *Debates in the Texas Constitutional Convention of 1875*, 151.

39. *Debates in the Texas Constitutional Convention of 1875*, 103.

40. *Galveston Daily News*, January 14, 1876.

41. *Weekly Democratic Statesman*, January 20, 1876.

42. *Panola Watchman*, January 26, 1876.

43. *New York Times*, January 20, 1876. Readers may notice that the *Telegraph's* prediction, reprinted in the *Watchman*, was not printed until nearly a week after the actual platform was printed in the *New York Times*. Such was the state of information flow in Texas in 1876.

44. *Weekly Democratic Statesman*, November 4, 1875.

45. Campbell, *Southern Community in Crisis*, 313.

46. *Tri-Weekly Herald*, January 29, 1876.

47. *Debates in the Texas Constitutional Convention of 1875*, 459.

48. *Galveston Daily News*, February 22, 1876.

49. Collin County's affirmation of the Democratic constitution (95 percent for, 5 percent against) went well beyond that of Dallas County, which reported 15 percent against—a stark contrast from the prewar relative positions of the two adjoining counties.

50. Janice C. May, *The Texas Constitutional Revision Experience in the 70s* (Austin: Sterling Swift, 1975), 25.

51. May, *Texas Constitutional Revision Experience*, 148.

52. Joel Lieske, "Regional Subcultures of the United States," *Journal of Politics* 55, no. 4 (November 1993): 889.

53. Richard Ellis and Aaron Wildavsky, "A Cultural Analysis of the Role of Abolitionists in the Coming of the Civil War," *Comparative Studies in Society and History* 32, no. 1 (1990): 92.

54. Ellis and Wildavsky, "Cultural Analysis of the Role of Abolitionists," 116.

55. Moneyhon, *Texas after the Civil War*, 202.

56. Alan Abramovitz and Jennifer McCoy, "United States: Racial Resentment, Negative Partisanship, and Polarization in Trump's America," *Annals of the American Academy of Political Science* 681, no. 1 (January 2019): 147.

57. The final wording of the section was, "There shall be set apart annually not more than one-fourth of general revenue of the State, and a poll tax of one dollar on all male inhabitants in this State between the ages of twenty-one and sixty years, for the

benefit of the public free schools." See Texas Constitution of 1876, art. VII, sec. 3.

58. Thomas W. Cutrer, "Flournoy, George M. (1832–1889)," *Handbook of Texas Online*, accessed October 26, 2021, https://www.tshaonline.org/handbook/entries/flournoy-george-m.

59. *Debates in the Texas Constitutional Convention of 1875*, 225.

60. Moneyhon, *Texas after the Civil War*, 202.

61. Moneyhon, *Texas after the Civil War*, 203.

62. Cecil Harper Jr. and E. Dale Odom, "Farm Tenancy," *Handbook of Texas Online*, accessed November 11, 2021, https://www.tshaonline.org/handbook/entries/farm-tenancy.

63. Campbell, *Grass-Roots Reconstruction*, 141.

64. Campbell, *Southern Community in Crisis*, 340.

65. US Department of the Interior, Census Office, *Report on Cotton Production in the United States* (Washington, DC: Bureau of the Census, 1884), 4.

66. *Dallas Herald*, November 23, 1872.

67. Stambaugh and Stambaugh, *History of Collin County, Texas*, 74.

68. John L. Waller, *Colossal Hamilton of Texas: A Biography of Andrew Jackson Hamilton, Militant Unionist and Reconstruction Governor* (El Paso: Texas Western Press, 1968), 130.

69. Waller, *Colossal Hamilton*, 137.

70. *Weekly Democratic Statesman*, April 15, 1875.

71. Howell, *James Webb Throckmorton*, 192.

72. While not excusing Throckmorton's white supremacy, Kenneth Howell does point out Throckmorton's unquestionable loyalty to his constituents and devotion to Texas economic development. See Howell, *James Webb Throckmorton*, 16.

73. L. W. Kemp, "Throckmorton, William Edward (1795–1843)," *Handbook of Texas Online*, accessed October 30, 2021, https://www.tshaonline.org/handbook/entries/throckmorton-william-edward.

74. Moneyhon, *Edmund J. Davis*, 227.

75. Roger Allen Griffin, "Connecticut Yankee in Texas: A Biography of Elisha Marshall Pease" (PhD diss., University of Texas at Austin, 1973), 266.

76. Griffin, *Connecticut Yankee in Texas*, 270.

77. Moneyhon, *Edmund J. Davis*, 225.
78. *New York Times*, October 15, 1874.
79. *Weekly Democratic Statesman*, February 15, 1883.
80. *Weekly Democratic Statesman*, December 2, 1875.
81. *The Democrat* (McKinney), August 10, 1899.
82. Lale, "Robert W. Loughery," 4.
83. Lale, "Robert W. Loughery," 7.
84. *McKinney Courier*, November 9, 1906.
85. *McKinney Enquirer*, May 29, 1871.
86. *Weekly Democratic Statesman*, August 28, 1873.
87. *McKinney Courier*, November 9, 1906.

Epilogue

1. Inglehart, "Renaissance of Political Culture," 1204.
2. Jerry Thompson, "When General Albert Sidney Johnston Came Home to Texas: Reconstruction Politics and the Reburial of a Hero," *Southwestern Historical Quarterly* 104, no. 4 (April 2000): 467.
3. Buenger, "Texas and the South," 324.
4. Savannah Jordan, "Remove the McKinney, TX Confederate Statues!" Change.Org, accessed July 4, 2021, www.change.org/p/remove-the-mckinney-tx-confederate-statue.
5. Frank Heinz and Demetrius Harper, "McKinney Tables Decision to Remove Confederate James Throckmorton Statue from City Square," NBC DFW, updated March 19, 2021, www.nbcdfw.com/news/local/mckinney-tables-decision-to-move-james-throckmorton-statue-from-city-square/2540935/.

Bibliography

Archives

Lawrence T. Jones III Texas Photographs Collection. DeGolyer Library, Southern Methodist University, Dallas, TX.

Texas State Library and Archives Commission, Austin, TX.

Primary Sources

Citizens Conference on State Legislatures. *The Impact of the Texas Constitution on the Legislature*. Houston: University of Houston, Institute for Urban Studies, 1973.

Debates in the Texas Constitutional Convention of 1875 Texas. Constitutional Convention (1875). Austin: Published by the University of Texas, 1930.

Democratic Party of Texas. *Minutes of the Democratic State Convention of the State of Texas: Held at the City of Austin, September 3rd, 4th, and 5th, 1873*. Austin: Statesman Book and Job Office, 1873.

Greer, J. L. *Reminiscences of the Boys in Gray: 1861–1865*. Edited by Mamie Yeary. Dallas: Smith and Lamar, 1912.

Hamilton, Alexander, John Jay, and James Madison, *The Federalist Papers* (Salt Lake City: Project Gutenberg Literary Archive, 2006), 253.

House Journal of the Twelfth Legislature, State of Texas. First Session. Austin: Tracy, Siemering and Co., State Journal Office, 1870.

Johnson, Andrew. "May 29, 1865: Proclaiming Pardoning Persons who Participated in the Rebellion." Presidential Speeches: Andrew Johnson Presidency, Miller Center, University of Virginia. Accessed June 30, 2021. https://millercenter.org/the-presidency/presidential-speeches/may-29-1865-proclamation-pardoning-persons-who-participated.

Journal of the Constitutional Convention of the State of Texas: Begun and Held at the City of Austin Texas. Constitutional Convention (1875). Galveston: Printed for the Convention at the *News* Office, 1875.

Journal of the House of Representatives. Eleventh Legislature, State of Texas. Austin: Printed at the Office of the *State Gazette*, 1866.

Journal of the House of Representatives. Provisional Session of 1870. Austin: Tracy, Siemering and Co., State Journal Office, 1870.

Journal of the House of Representatives of the State of Texas: Being the Session of the Fourteenth Legislature Begun and Held at the City of Austin, January 13, 1874. Austin: Cardwell and Walker, 1874.

Journal of the House of Representatives of the State of Texas: Being the Session of the Thirteenth Legislature Begun and Held at the City of Austin, January 14, 1873. Austin: John Cardwell, State Printer, 1873.

Journal of the House of Representatives of the Twelfth Legislature. Adjourned Session. Austin: J. G. Tracy, State Printer, 1871.

Journal of the House of Representatives of the Twelfth Legislature. Part First. Austin: J. G. Tracy, State Printer, 1870.

Journal of the Reconstruction Convention: Which Met at Austin, Texas. Texas Constitutional Convention (1868–1869). Austin: Tracy, Siemering & Co., 1870.

Journal of the Secession Convention of Texas, 1861. Edited from the original in the Department of State by Ernest William Winkler. Austin: Austin Print Co., 1912.

Journal of the Senate. Eleventh Legislature, State of Texas. Austin: Printed at the Office of the *State Gazette*, 1866.

Journal of the Senate of the State of Texas: Being the Session of the Thirteenth Legislature Begun and Held at the City of Austin, January 14, 1873. Austin: John Cardwell, State Printer, 1873.

Journal of the Senate of the State of Texas. Provisional Session of 1870. Austin: Tracy, Siemering and Co., State Journal Office, 1870.

Journal of the Senate of Texas. Fourteenth Legislature – Second Session. Austin: Caldwell & Walker, Printers, 1875.

Journal of the Senate of the Twelfth Legislature. Austin: J. G. Tracy, State Printer, 1871.

Journal of the Senate of the Twelfth Legislature. Adjourned Session. Austin: J. G. Tracy, State Printer, 1871.

Journal of the Texas State Convention: Assembled at Austin, Feb. 7, 1866. Adjourned April 2, 1866. Austin: Printed at the *Southern Intelligencer* Office, 1866.

Kelley, Oliver Hudson. *Origins and Progress of the Order of the Patrons of Husbandry in the United States: A History from 1866 to 1873.* Philadelphia: J. A. Wagenseller, 1875.

Population of the United States in 1860; Compiled from the Original Returns of The Eighth Census. Washington, DC: Government Printing Office, 1864.

Senate Journal of the Twelfth Legislature, State of Texas. First Session. Austin: Tracy, Siemering and Co., State Journal Office, 1870.

State of Texas Judicial Branch. *Texas Courts: A Descriptive Summary.* 2014. Accessed November 6, 2021. https://www.txcourts.gov/media/994672/court-overview.pdf.

The Statistics of the Population of the United States, Compiled from the Original Returns of the Ninth Census. Washington, DC: Government Printing Office, 1872.

Texas Legislative Council. *Amendments to the Texas Constitution since 1876.* July 2022. https://tlc.texas.gov/docs/amendments/Constamend1876.pdf.

Texas Legislative Council. *Analysis of Proposed Constitutional Amendments: November 6, 2001, Election.* September 2001. https://www.tlc.texas.gov/docs/amendments/analyses01.pdf.

US Department of the Interior. *Population of the United States in 1860, 8th Census.* Washington, DC: Bureau of the Census, 1864.

US Department of the Interior. *The Statistics of the Population of the United States, 9th Census.* Washington, DC: Bureau of the Census, 1872.

US Department of the Interior, Census Office. *Report on Cotton Production in the United States.* Washington, DC: Bureau of the Census, 1884.

US Department of War. *Annual Report of the Secretary of War, 1866.* 39th Cong., 2d sess., House Executive Document 1. Washington, DC: 1866.

US Department of War. *Annual Report of the Secretary of War, 1868.* 40th Cong., 3d sess., House Executive Document 1. Washington, DC: 1868.

Winkler, Ernest William, ed. *Journal of the Secession Convention of Texas 1861*. Edited from the original in the Department of State. Austin: Texas Library and Historical Commission, 1912.

Secondary Sources

Abramovitz, Alan, and Jennifer McCoy. "United States: Racial Resentment, Negative Partisanship, and Polarization in Trump's America." *Annals of the American Academy of Political Science* 681, no. 1 (January 2019): 137–56.

Almond, Gabriel A. *The Politics of the Developing Areas*. Princeton, NJ: Princeton University Press, 1960.

Almond, Gabriel Abraham, and Sidney Verba. *The Civic Culture: Political Attitudes and Democracy in Five Nations*. 1963; repr., Princeton, NJ: Princeton University Press, 2015.

Ariens, Michael. *Lone Star Law: A Legal History of Texas*. Lubbock: Texas Tech University Press, 2011.

Baggett, James Alex. "Origins of Early Texas Republican Party Leadership." *Journal of Southern History* 40, no. 3 (August 1974): 441–54.

Beyle, Thad. "The Governor's Formal Powers: A View from the Governor's Chair." *Public Administration Review* 28, no. 6 (November 1968): 540–45.

Book of the States, 2020 Edition, Volume 52. Lexington, KY: National Council on State Governments, 2020.

Braden, George D. *The Constitution of the State of Texas: An Annotated and Comparative Analysis*. Austin: Texas Advisory Commission on Intergovernmental Relations, 1977.

Brice, Donaly. "Finding a Solution to Reconstruction Violence: The Texas State Police." In Howell, *Still the Arena of Civil War*, 187–213.

Brown, Lyle C., Joyce A. Langenegger, Sonia R. Garcia, Robert E. Biles, Ryan Rynbrandt, Veronica Vega Reyna, and Juan Carlos Huerta. *Practicing Texas Politics, 2017–2018 Edition*. Boston: Cengage Learning, 2018.

Buenger, Walter L. *Secession and the Union in Texas*. Austin: University of Texas Press, 1984.

Buenger, Walter L. "Texas and the South." *Southwestern Historical Quarterly* 103, no. 3 (2000): 308–24.

Campbell, Randolph B. "Carpetbagger Rule in Reconstruction Texas: An Enduring Myth." *Southwestern Historical Quarterly* 97, no. 4 (April 1994): 587–97.

Campbell, Randolph B. *Grass-Roots Reconstruction in Texas: 1865–1880*. Baton Rouge: Louisiana State University Press, 1997.

Campbell, Randolph B. "Harrison County." *Handbook of Texas Online*. Accessed June 22, 2022. https://tshaonline.org/handbook/entries/harrison-county.

Campbell, Randolph B. *A Southern Community in Crisis: Harrison County, Texas 1850–1880*. 2nd ed. Austin: Texas State Historical Association, 2016.

Cantrell, Gregg. "Racial Violence and Reconstruction Politics in Texas: 1867–1868." *Southwestern Historical Quarterly* 93, no. 3 (January 1990): 333–55.

Collin County History. "Capt. John H. Bingham." Accessed May 26, 2021. www.collincountyhistory.com/bingham1.html.

Crouch, Barry A. "'All the Vile Passions': The Texas Black Code of 1866." *Southwestern Historical Quarterly* 97, no. 1 (July 1993): 12–34.

Crouch, Barry A. *The Freedmen's Bureau and Black Texans*. Austin: University of Texas Press, 1992.

Crouch, Barry A. "'Unmanacling' Texas Reconstruction: A Twenty-Year Perspective." *Southwestern Historical Quarterly* 93, no. 3 (January 1990): 275–302.

Crouch, Barry A., and Donaly E. Brice. *The Governor's Hounds: The Texas State Police, 1870–1873*. Austin: University of Texas Press, 2011.

Cutrer, Thomas W. "Flournoy, George M. (1832–1889)." *Handbook of Texas Online*. Accessed October 26, 2021. https://www.tshaonline.org/handbook/entries/flournoy-george-m.

de la Teja, Jesús, ed. *Lone Star Unionism, Dissent, and Resistance: Other Sides of Civil War Texas*. Norman: University of Oklahoma Press, 2016.

Demetrius, Nelson C. "Measuring Gubernatorial Power." *Journal of Politics* 41, no. 2 (May 1979): 589–610.

Derbes, Brett J. "Weaver, William Thomas Green (1832–1876)." *Handbook of Texas Online*. Accessed July 30, 2021. https://tshaonline.org/handbook/entries/weaver-william-thomas-green.

Downs, Gregory P. *After Appomattox: Military Occupation and the Ends of War*. Cambridge, MA: Harvard University Press, 2015.

Eckstein, Harry. "A Culturalist Theory of Political Change." *American Political Science Review* 82, no. 3 (September 1988): 789–804.

Elazar, Daniel J. *American Federalism: A View from the States*. 2nd ed. New York: Harper and Row, 1972.

Elazar, Daniel J. "Political Culture on the Plains." *Western Historical Quarterly* 11, no. 3 (July 1980): 261–83.

Elliott, Claude. "Constitutional Convention of 1868–69." *Handbook of Texas Online*. Accessed June 14, 2022. https://www.tshaonline.org/handbook/entries/constitutional-convention-of-1868-69.

Elliot, Claude. "Union Sentiment in Texas: 1861–1865." *Southwestern Historical Quarterly* 50, no. 4 (April 1947): 449–77.

Ellis, Richard, and Aaron Wildavsky. "A Cultural Analysis of the Role of Abolitionists in the Coming of the Civil War." *Comparative Studies in Society and History* 32, no. 1 (January 1990): 89–116.

Ericson, J. E. "The Delegates to the Convention of 1875: A Reappraisal." *Southwestern Historical Quarterly* 67, no. 1 (July 1963): 22–27.

Ericson, Joe E., and Ernest Wallace, "Constitution of 1876." *Handbook of Texas Online*. Accessed July 3, 2021. https://www.tshaonline.org/handbook/entries/constitution-of-1876.

Farzan, Antonia Noori. "Texas Mayor Tells Residents to Fend for Themselves during Power Outage: 'Only the Strong Will Survive.'" *Washington Post*, February 17, 2021. https://www.washingtonpost.com/nation/2021/02/17/texas-mayor-power-outages-colorado/.

Ferguson, James S. "The Grange and Farmer Education in Mississippi." *Journal of Southern History* 8, no. 4 (November 1942): 497–512.

Fisher, Barbara H. "Edward Bradford Pickett (1823–1882)." *Handbook of Texas Online*. Accessed July 30, 2021. https://tshaonline.org/handbook/entries/pickett-edward-bradford.

Formisano, Ronald P. "The Concept of Political Culture." *Journal of Interdisciplinary History* 31, no. 3 (Winter 2001): 393–426.

Gantt, Fred Jr. *The Impact of the Texas Constitution on the Executive.* Houston: University of Houston, Institute for Urban Studies, 1973.

Griffin, Roger Allen. "Connecticut Yankee in Texas: A Biography of Elisha Marshall Pease." PhD diss., University of Texas at Austin, 1973.

Haley, James L. *The Texas Supreme Court: A Narrative History, 1836–1986.* Austin: University of Texas Press, 2013.

Harper, Cecil Jr., and E. Dale Odom. "Farm Tenancy." *Handbook of Texas Online.* Accessed November 11, 2021. https://www.tshaonline.org/handbook/entries/farm-tenancy.

Hazlewood, Claudia. "Wheeler, Thomas Benton (1840–1913)." *Handbook of Texas Online.* Accessed July 1, 2021. https://tshaonline.org/handbook/entries/wheeler-thomas-benton.

Heinz, Frank, and Demetrius Harper. "McKinney Tables Decision to Remove Confederate James Throckmorton Statue from City Square." NBC DFW. Updated March 19, 2021. www.nbcdfw.com/news/local/mckinney-tables-decision-to-move-james-throckmorton-statue-from-city-square/2540935/.

Hooker, Anne W. "Culberson, David Browning (1830–1900)." *Handbook of Texas Online.* Accessed July 3, 2021. https://www.tshaonline.org/handbook/entries/culberson-david-browning.

Howell, Kenneth Wayne, ed. *Still the Arena of Civil War: Violence and Turmoil in Reconstruction Texas, 1865–1874.* Denton: University of North Texas Press, 2012.

Howell, Kenneth Wayne. *Texas Confederate, Reconstruction Governor: James Webb Throckmorton.* College Station: Texas A&M University Press, 2008.

Inglehart, Ronald. *Modernization and Postmodernization.* Princeton, NJ: Princeton University Press, 1997.

Inglehart, Ronald. "The Renaissance of Political Culture." *American Political Science Review* 82, no. 4 (1988): 1203–30.

Jefferson, Wallace. "Reform from Within: Positive Solutions for Elected Judiciaries." *Seattle University Law Review* 33, no. 3 (March 2010): 625–32.

Johnson, Charles A. "Political Culture in the American States: Elazar's Formulation Examined." *American Journal of Political Science* 20, no. 3 (August 1976): 491–509.

Jordan, Savannah. "Remove the McKinney, TX Confederate Statue!" Change.Org. Accessed July 4, 2021. www.change.org/p/remove-the-mckinney-tx-confederate-statue.

Jordan, Terry G. *German Seed in Texas Soil: Immigrant Farmers in Nineteenth-Century Texas.* Austin: University of Texas Press, 1966.

Kamphoefner, Walter D. "New Americans or New Southerners? Unionist German Texans." In de la Teja, *Lone Star Unionism*, 101–22.

Kemp, L. W. "Throckmorton, William Edward (1795–1843)." *Handbook of Texas Online.* Accessed October 30, 2021. https://www.tshaonline.org/handbook/entries/throckmorton-william-edward.

Krupnikov, Yanna, and Charles Shipan. "Measuring Gubernatorial Budgetary Power: A New Approach." *State Politics and Policy Quarterly* 12, no. 4 (December 2012): 438–55.

Lale, Max S. "Burke, John (1830–1871)." *Handbook of Texas Online.* Accessed March 3, 2021. https://tshaonline.org/handbook/entries/burke-john.

Lale, Max. "Robert W. Loughery: Rebel Editor." *East Texas Historical Journal* 21, no. 2 (1983): 3–15.

Lieske, Joel. "American State Cultures: Testing a New Measure and Theory." *Publius* 42, no. 1 (Winter 2012): 108–33.

Lieske, Joel. "The Changing Regional Subcultures of the American States and the Utility of a New Cultural Measure." *Political Research Quarterly* 63, no. 3 (2010): 538–52.

Lieske, Joel. "Regional Subcultures of the United States." *Journal of Politics* 55, no. 4 (November 1993): 888–913.

Marten, James. *Texas Divided: Loyalty and Dissent in the Lone Star State, 1856–1874.* Lexington: University Press of Kentucky, 1990.

Martin, Roscoe C. "The Grange as a Political Factor in Texas." *Southwestern Political and Social Science Quarterly* 6, no. 4 (March 1926): 363–83.

Mauer, John Walker. "Southern State Constitutions in the 1870s: A Case Study of Texas." PhD diss., Rice University, 1983. https://scholarship.rice.edu/handle/1911/19046.

Mauer, John Walker. "State Constitutions in a Time of Crisis: The Case of the Texas Constitution of 1876." *Texas Law Review* 68, no. 7 (June 1990): 1615–48.

May, Janice C. *The Texas Constitutional Revision Experience in the 70s*. Austin: Sterling Swift, 1975.

McCaslin, Richard B. "Wheat Growers in the Cotton Confederacy: The Suppression of Dissent in Collin County, Texas, during the Civil War." *Southwestern Historical Quarterly* 96, no. 4 (April 1993): 526–39.

McGowen, Stanley S. "Battle or Massacre? The Incident on the Nueces, August 10, 1862." *Southwestern Historical Quarterly* 104, no. 1 (July 2000): 64–86.

McKay, Seth Shepard. "Making the Texas Constitution of 1876." PhD diss., University of Pennsylvania, 1924.

Miller, Aragorn Storm. "Richardson, Samuel J. (1826–1876)." *Handbook of Texas Online*. Accessed March 3, 2021. https://tshaonline. org/handbook/entries/richardson-samuel-j.

Minor, David. "Brown, Thomas Jefferson: 1836–1915." *Handbook of Texas Online*. Accessed August 8, 2022. https://www.tshaonline. org/handbook/entries/brown-thomas-jefferson.

Model State Constitution. 6th ed. New York: National Municipal League, 1968.

Mondak, Jeffrey J., and Damarys Canache. "Personality and Political Culture in the American States." *Political Research Quarterly* 67, no. 1 (March 2014): 26–41.

Moneyhon, Carl. *Edmund J. Davis: Civil War General, Republican Leader, Reconstruction Governor*. Fort Worth: Texas Christian University Press, 2010.

Moneyhon, Carl. "Edmund J. Davis: Unlikely Radical." In de la Teja, *Lone Star Unionism*, 226–52.

Moneyhon, Carl. "Ex parte Rodriguez." *Handbook of Texas Online*. Accessed July 2, 2021. https://tshaonline.org/handbook/entries/ ex-parte-rodriguez.

Moneyhon, Carl. "Public Education and Texas Reconstruction Politics, 1871–1874." *Southwestern Historical Quarterly* 92, no. 3 (January 1989): 393–416.

Moneyhon, Carl. "Reconstruction." *Handbook of Texas Online.* Accessed May 20, 2021. https://www.tshaonline.org/handbook/ entries/reconstruction.

Moneyhon, Carl. *Republicanism in Reconstruction Texas.* Austin: University of Texas Press, 1980.

Moneyhon, Carl. *Texas after the Civil War.* College Station: Texas A&M University Press, 2004.

Norville, James R. "The Railroad Commission of Texas: Its Origin and Its History." *Southwestern Historical Quarterly* 68, no. 4 (April 1965): 465–80.

Paddock, Boardman Buckley. *History of Texas: Fort Worth and the Texas Northwest.* Vol. 2. London: Forgotten Books, 2018.

Postel, Charles. *Equality: An American Dilemma, 1866–1896.* New York: Farrar, Straus, and Giroux, 2019.

Putnam, Robert. *Bowling Alone: The Collapse and Revival of the American Community.* New York: Simon and Schuster, 2000.

Ramsdell, Charles. *Reconstruction in Texas.* Austin: University of Texas Press, 1910.

Richter, William L. *Overreached on All Sides: The Freedmen's Bureau Administrators in Texas, 1865–1868.* College Station: Texas A&M University Press, 1991.

Shelley, George E. "The Semicolon Court of Texas." *Southwestern Historical Quarterly* 48, no. 4 (April 1945): 449–68.

Simon, John Y. *The Papers of Ulysses S. Grant.* Carbondale: Southern Illinois University Press, 1995.

Smith, Allen E. *The Impact of the Texas Constitution on the Judiciary.* Houston: University of Houston, Institute for Urban Studies, 1973.

Smith, David Paul. *Frontier Defense in the Civil War: Texas' Rangers and Rebels.* College Station: Texas A&M University Press, 1992.

Smith, Dick. "Texas and the Poll Tax." *Southwestern Social Science Quarterly* 45, no. 2 (September 1964): 167–73.

Smith, Kevin B., Alan Greenblatt, and Michele Mariani Vaughn. *Governing States and Localities.* 3rd ed. Washington, DC: CQ Press, 2011.

Smith, Ralph A. "The Grange Movement in Texas: 1873–1900." *Southwestern Historical Quarterly* 42, no. 4 (April 1939): 297–315.

Smyrl, Frank H. "Texans in the Union Army, 1861–1865." In Wooster and Wooster, *Lone Star Blue and Gray*, 243–58.

Sneed, Edgar P. "A Historiography of Reconstruction in Texas: Some Myths and Problems." *Southwestern Historical Quarterly* 72, no. 4 (April 1969): 435–48.

Squire, Peverill. "Measuring State Legislative Professionalism: The Squire Index Revisited." *State Politics and Policy Quarterly* 7, no. 2 (Summer 2007): 211–27.

Stambaugh, J. Lee, and Lillian J. Stambaugh. *A History of Collin County, Texas*. Austin: Texas State Historical Association, 1958.

Thomas, Emory M. "Rebel Nationalism: E. H. Cushing and the Confederate Experience." *Southwestern Historical Quarterly* 73, no. 3 (January 1970): 343–55.

Thompson, Jerry. "When General Albert Sidney Johnston Came Home to Texas: Reconstruction Politics and the Reburial of a Hero." *Southwestern Historical Quarterly* 104, no. 4 (April 2000): 452–78.

"2020 Legislator Compensation." National Conference of State Legislators. Modified June 17, 2020. https://www.ncsl.org/research/about-state-legislatures/2020-legislator-compensation.aspx.

Utley, Robert M. *Frontier Regulars: The United States Army and the Indians, 1866–1891*. New York: Macmillan, 1973.

Waller, John L. *Colossal Hamilton of Texas: A Biography of Andrew Jackson Hamilton, Militant Unionist and Reconstruction Governor*. El Paso: Texas Western Press, 1968.

Weber, David J. *The Mexican Frontier, 1821–1846*. Albuquerque: University of New Mexico Press, 1982.

Wheeler, T. B. "Reminiscences of Reconstruction in Texas." *Quarterly of the Texas State Historical Association* 11, no. 1 (July 1907): 56–65.

Whitlow, Elizabeth. *Identified with Texas: The Lives of Governor Elisha Marshall Pease and Lucadia Niles Pease*. Denton: University of North Texas Press, 2021.

Wildavsky, Aaron. "Choosing Preferences by Constructing Institutions: A Cultural Theory of Preference Formation." *American Political Science Review* 81, no. 1 (March 1987): 3–22.

Williams, Patrick G. *Beyond Redemption: Texas Democrats after Reconstruction*. College Station: Texas A&M University Press, 2007.

Williams, Patrick G. "Of Rutabagas and Redeemers: Rethinking the Texas Constitution of 1876." *Southwestern Historical Quarterly* 106, no. 2 (October 2002): 230–53.

Woodard, Colin. *American Nations: A History of the Eleven Rival Regional Cultures of North America*. New York: Penguin Books, 2011.

Wooster, Ralph A. *The Secession Conventions of the South*. Princeton, NJ: Princeton University Press, 1962.

Wooster, Ralph A., and Robert Wooster. *Lone Star Blue and Gray: Essays on Texas and the Civil War*. 2nd ed. Denton: Texas State Historical Association, 2015.

Wooster, Robert. *The American Military Frontiers: The United States Army in the West, 1783–1900*. Albuquerque: University of New Mexico Press, 2009.

Wooster, Robert. *The Military and United States Indian Policy, 1865–1903*. New Haven: Yale University Press, 1988.

Wooster, Robert. *The United States Army and the Making of America: From Confederation to Empire, 1775–1903*. Lawrence: University of Kansas Press, 2021.

Zelinsky, Wilbur. *The Cultural Geography of the United States*. Rev. ed. Upper Saddle River, NJ: Prentice-Hall, 1992.

Newspapers

Belton Weekly Journal
Dallas (Daily) Herald
Dallas Morning News
Democrat (Fort Worth)
Democrat (McKinney)
Evening Telegraph
Flake's Weekly Galveston Bulletin
Galveston Daily News
Houston Tri-Weekly Telegraph
Liberator

McKinney Courier
McKinney Enquirer
McKinney Messenger
New York Times
Panola Watchman
Representative
Rusk Observer
Southern Intelligencer
Texas Republican
Times-Picayune
Tri-Weekly Herald
Tri-Weekly State Gazette
Weekly Democratic Statesman

Index